The War has Begun

Charles E. Frye

FIRST EDITION

Copyright © 2017 Charles E. Frye

ISBN: 1543073743
ISBN-13: 978-1543073744

DEDICATION

To Isaac and Elizabeth's descendants; there are nearly two thousand of us now.

To U.S. military veterans, soldiers, and their families.

CONTENTS

ACKNOWLEDGMENTS

My wife, Amanda, suggested researching Isaac Frye's story, and once it was obvious there was more to it than I could have imagined, she recommended I start writing a book. She has persevered through what must have seemed like endless details about Isaac Frye's life. I am grateful for her encouragement and support.

Over the years, I have cold-called many of my Frye relatives to pick their brains about genealogy, traits and mannerisms common to the Frye lines, and so on. In particular, my uncles David and Bill, who spent their childhood roaming all over Wilton, and our cousin Gary who today owns much of the original land from Isaac's farm, have provided insights gleaned from past generations of Fryes.

To the Sons of the American Revolution whose membership boasts many authors, historians, and genealogists who for generations have produced inspiring works portraying all aspects of the American Revolution. Chiefly, the Sons of the American Revolution has a mission to educate present and future generations about how the United States of America became a country. As I began learning about Isaac Frye, I realized his story was so much more than just family history. I especially wish to thank the members of the Redlands Chapter, of which I am a member, who have encouraged me throughout the years of research and writing.

Libraries and Librarians: without the help of these institutions and their staff, this work would not have been possible. I am particularly grateful for those libraries with map collections. I was lucky enough to visit the Library of Congress, Boston Public Library, the New Hampshire Historical Society, the New Hampshire State Archives, the library at The Huntington in San Marino, California, the Wilton Public and Gregg Free Library (thank you, Jane). I visited numerous university libraries, including The Pennsylvania State University, the University of Colorado at Boulder, the University of California at Riverside and Irvine, Cal Poly Pomona, and the University of Redlands.

To Mary DeSantis, exactly the kind of editor I needed: passionate about verbiage and full of ideas and patience. Thank you for helping me turn Isaac's story into a novel.

To Scott Mason, who discovered the pair of letters Isaac and his wife, Elizabeth, had written to each other in 1775 and 1776. Those letters provided fundamental inspiration for *The War has Begun*.

To the Written By Veterans writers group at California State University, San Bernardino, Veterans Success Center: Andreas, Greg, Suzy, Augie, Jorge, Richard, John, Jeff, Alfonso, Ruben, Carol, and Marci. In such company, there was no way to fail.

PREFACE

The War Has Begun is the first of four books in the *Duty in the Cause of Liberty* series. The books trace the path of my great-great-great-great-grandfather, Isaac Frye, through the American Revolutionary War. For over a dozen years, I have researched Isaac Frye's service in the Continental Army and his life in Wilton, New Hampshire in the 1770s and 1780s and I still find it amazing I can account for his location most days, sometimes down to the hour and minute.

My family's oral history was sparse on Isaac; we knew he fought at the Battle of Breed's Hill and held the rank of major. The road called, "Major Isaac Frye Highway" running by my grandparents' house was a big clue for me as a child visiting every other year. They told me about him being in the battle. We also passed down through the generations his words upon receiving the alarm given by Paul Revere and William Dawes when it reached Wilton early on the morning of April 19, 1775, "The war has begun, I must be going." That was the extent of our knowledge of his history. Later, I learned the road was not always named after Isaac Frye. In 1922, the town of Wilton renamed it to commemorate the Revolutionary War services of Major Isaac Frye.

Researching my family tree during the summer of 2003 kindled my interest in Isaac. That fall my wife suggested my oldest son and I learn what Isaac did during the Battle of Breed's Hill. It was to help with my son's fifth grade history project. It seemed like a reasonable idea. Our first surprise was that no published history of the battle mentioned him, even though he was a major. Within a few days, we came across records of him being a second lieutenant and quartermaster for his regiment at the time of the battle. We narrowed Isaac's location during the battle to two possibilities in the weeks my son had to complete his project. It took nearly three more years to prove one of them was correct.

My son drew a great map of the battlefield and wrote a few paragraphs about Isaac's participation. All that made me curious, because one of the sources I found indicated that Isaac had served and fought in other battles.

We were also surprised to find that Isaac's name was not on the plaques around the Bunker Hill Memorial in Boston. I began to worry, but eventually found sources in the New Hampshire State Papers, though not a part of the Revolutionary War Rolls used by those planning the monument. Within those rolls was a muster roll for Isaac's regiment called the Third New Hampshire regiment, but the regiment's Quartermaster, Isaac, and Adjutant, Stephen Peabody were not counted. That despite the high likelihood that Isaac Frye and Stephen Peabody authored this muster roll. Such rolls were their job to produce and check before submitting to the commanding officers for signatures.

The proof of Isaac being in the battle was in the New Hampshire State Papers, volume VII, which is not part of the Revolutionary War Rolls. A transcription of a document listing the men who had lost clothing or equipment during the battle listed Isaac as having lost his coat and hat.

Isaac being an officer in the Continental Army meant there are quite a few documents in the National Archives that show where he was, what regiment he was in, etc.

Early on, as I got into the research, I started wondering what caused Isaac to not only become a minuteman, but also serve for the entire war. He left his pregnant wife and family at home. How did that work? That he continued in the Continental Army after 1776 dumbfounded me given what happened to his family and the disastrous circumstances endured by the army. What could evoke such a response and the will to sustain it for nearly nine years? In writing this book, I had to answer and present what motivated Isaac and so many others to undertake the duty, and bear the sacrifices, for liberty and then independence at what seemed to me the same level as defending their own homes and families.

To organize what turned out to be hundreds of documents and references, I applied the skills of my day jobs: cartographer, geographic information systems analyst, software product engineer, and information scientist to map the parts of North America where Isaac traveled during the war. My goal turned into tracing Isaac's path through the war, and I have now spent over a dozen years researching his story.

Throughout the book, military ranks are often used when introducing soldiers, particularly officers. After introducing officers, I chose to continue using their ranks when referring to superior officers, or those whose office was above Isaac's. For those officers of equivalent or lesser rank, I used their rank when Isaac may not have known them well, as a means of reinforcing the formality.

This book is fictional; however, all the names of people, the events, and the dates and times they occurred are factual. The dialog, with a very few exceptions, is fictional; a product of my imagination. The dialog is styled to favor an 18th century way of speaking, with a few 18th century words added for flavor. I had no intention of mimicking the speech and idioms used by the people at that time. My purpose is to tell Isaac Frye's story to a contemporary audience, allowing them to appreciate what duty, sacrifice, and American ideas about liberty might have meant to him, his family, and people he knew.

The War Has Begun

MAPS

Map of the Part of Wilton Isaac Frye Lived

I compiled this map using Wilton's lot and range map and Abiel Abbot Livermore's History of the Town of Wilton, Hillsborough County, New Hampshire with a Genealogical Register. In the genealogical register, Livermore included the locations of many of the inhabitants' farms, the names of the original proprietors, and the names of those who lived there during the Revolution. This made it possible to roughly locate Isaac's neighbors. Isaac's farm is highlighted and indicates the lots as described on the land records.

The roads are my best conservative estimate based on an 1805 survey by Daniel Searle, an 1858 railroad map of Wilton, which included family names, and the USGS 1:62,500 scale 1900 Peterborough quadrangle and 1906 Milford quadrangle topographic maps. I suspect the path that is today Gage Road was likely present before Isaac bought the property, and may have been laid by Henry Parker as early as 1760 when he built the bridge over the Souhegan River.

The grid on this map represents the proprietors' lot and range system used to first describe the land in Wilton. Range numbers run north and south, i.e., range 4 is a north-south column; and lots are numbered from 20 in the north, to 1 in the south.

Map of the Last Part of the Battle of Breed's Hill

This is an adaptation of a manuscript map I published in 2004 depicting the first two phases of the Battle of Breed's Hill (LCCN Permalink: https://lccn.loc.gov/2005628234). Using the landscape portrayed in that map, I showed the probable location of Wyman's command. The location of Crosby's line and Peabody's squad, described in Chapter 5, are my inventions. I have yet to locate any material to support specific locations for any units during the retreat. What drove the account in Chapter 5 is that only two men in Reed's regiment were specifically mentioned for their valor during the battle: Sergeant William Adrian Hawkins of Wilton (cited in Chapter 7's sources), and Stephen Peabody (cited in Chapter 5's sources). What I portrayed in Chapter 5 could plausibly have happened. That Colonel James Frye sustained a wound is well documented, and that Crosby's company was in the vicinity covering the retreat is very likely. The question of where would a regiment's adjutant be on the battlefield is more difficult to answer. Thus, Stephen Peabody could have been with Colonel Reed on the rail fence, though I felt because his list of missing articles during the battle was in the same report as Isaac's, it tipped the likelihood in favor of what I portray herein.

Regional Maps of Colonial America

I compiled these maps working from primary-source manuscript map documents or high-resolution scans of these maps. No map newer than a publishing date of 1785 was used. I had the good fortune to visit numerous libraries in the United States and explore their map collections. In my spare time, over several years, I used over one hundred maps to compile a 1:500,000 scale map of northeastern North America extending from the southern boundary of Virginia in the south, to Quebec in the north, and west into Ohio.

I chose to depict only the towns, roads, landmarks, etc., appearing on the colonial maps, using the spellings shown on those maps. I used modern geographic information systems (GIS) data for terrain and bodies of water, though this required removing dams and replacing corresponding lakes with the original stream courses. The coastline around Boston was also adjusted to reflect my approximation of the 1775 coastline.

These maps are all excerpted from one GIS database I created using ArcGIS software beginning in 2003, with the bulk of the work being done by 2008, though minor edits have been ongoing. Initially I intended to use this map as a research aid, helping to organize the locations and events in which there are records of Isaac Frye's participation. Early on, it became evident that I could use the GIS map as a basis to trace Isaac Frye's path through the Revolutionary War, both geographically and through time. I hope these excerpts work to help you do the same.

The GIS map also acted as a proving ground for the various histories, journals, and records I was reading, at times disproving statements born of poor memories, license, and perhaps revisionism.

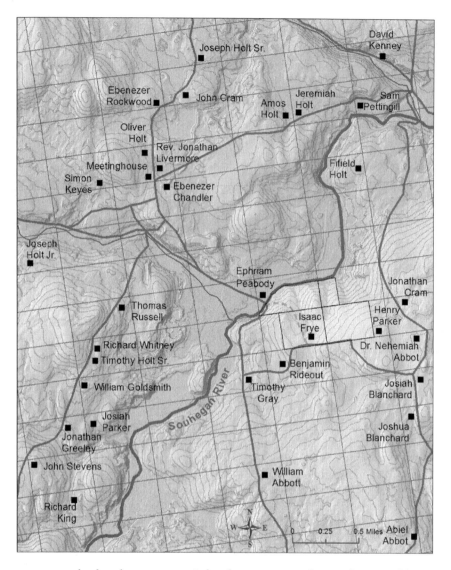

Map 1. The locale Isaac Frye's land occupies within Wilton, and his neighbors in 1775.

Note: Sources exist to locate only about one third of Wilton's inhabitants. Most who have not been located lived to the north and west of Isaac Frye's Farm. The empty lots to the south of Isaac's farm were not built on until later.

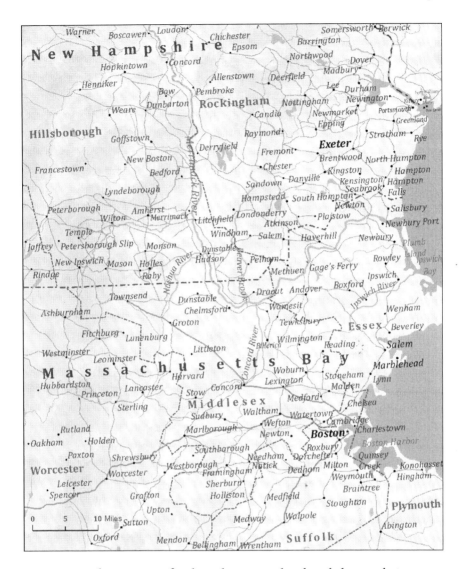

Map 2. Shows part of Colonial New England and the roads into Concord, Lexington, and Medford from the many southern New Hampshire towns that minutemen came from on April 19, 1775.

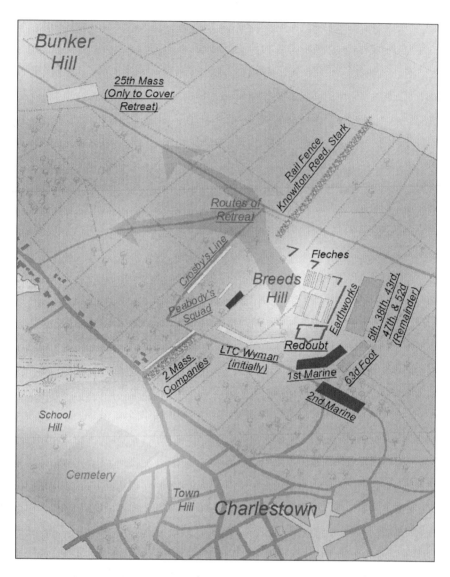

Map 3. Shows the approximate deployment of American and British forces during the last part of the Battle of Breed's Hill.

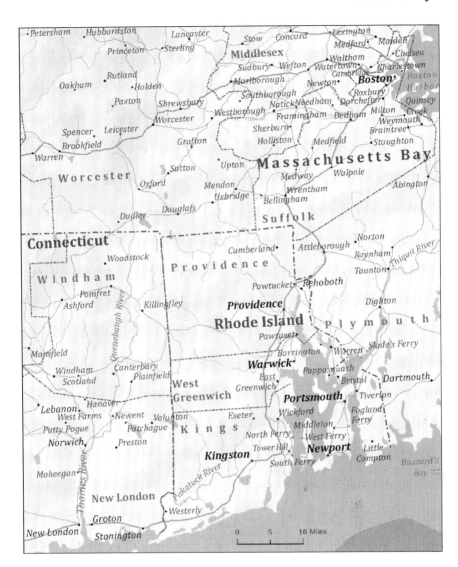

Map 4. Showing the part of Colonial New England from Boston to New London, Connecticut where Sullivan's Brigade marched in early April 1776. Note: At the time, Rhode Island had five capitals

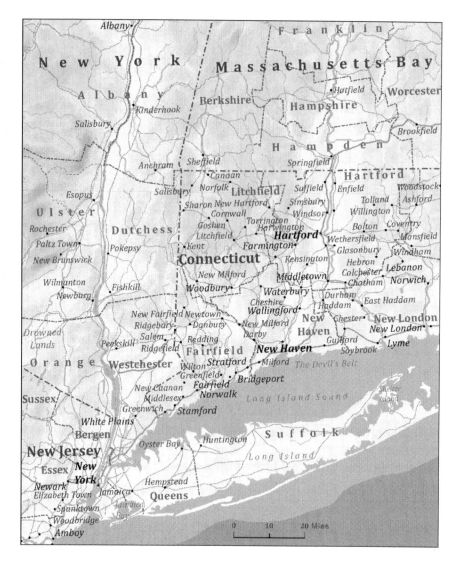

Map 5. Showing the part of Colonial New England from New London, Connecticut to New York and along the Hudson River to Albany.

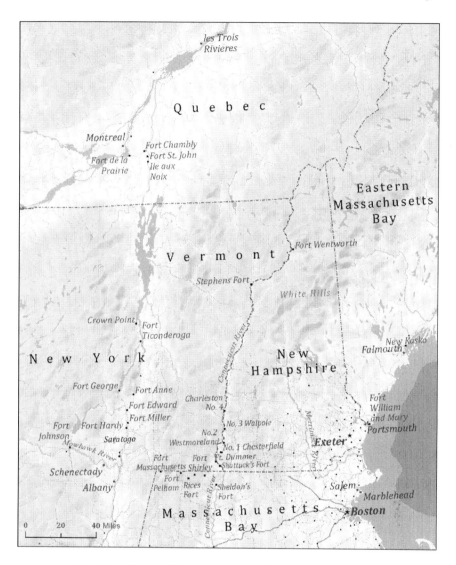

Map 6. Showing the northern portion of Colonial New England and Quebec where Sullivan's Brigade traveled and encamped during the summer of 1776.

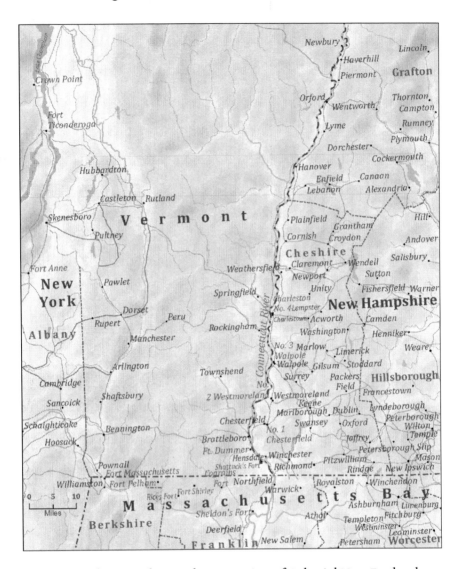

Map 7. Showing the northern portion of Colonial New England
between Wilton and Fort Ticonderoga.

1 THE ALARM

"Voted, to raise as minute men 25 privates, two commissioned officers, two sergeants, twenty nine in all. Voted, 6 dollars a month to each officer and soldier after they are called to an expedition, till they have proper time to return after they are dismissed."

From the minutes of the town of Wilton,
New Hampshire, April 4, 1775

Early morning, fifteen days after the town meeting, Isaac Frye is laboring behind an ox team plowing the lower part of a field in Wilton. Steam rises from the oxen in the brisk morning air as they pull the plow through the ground, turning up the dark soil. Isaac's farm sits on the shoulder of a large hill on the south side of the Souhegan River. The field ends at a steep, wooded slope that drops two hundred feet to the river and defines the southern edge of the valley.

In the woods to the east, the trees have yet to produce leaves, though some have a few green buds. There are chestnuts, sugar maples, elms, and a few poplars, oaks, hemlocks, and beeches. Small patches of snow remain on the hillside further back in the trees. At the edges of the field, where sunlight is more plentiful, clumps of mountain laurel provide a pleasing break in the otherwise chilly brown and gray landscape.

Split-rail fences zigzag around the farmhouse, barn, and garden, and run along a road separating Isaac's land from his neighbor, Benjamin Rideout, to the south. A recently planted apple orchard blankets the hillside to the west of the field Isaac is plowing. The orchard extends westward to Timothy Gray's land. To the east of the field, a wooded, slope rises up to an even larger orchard owned by Isaac, and to the east of that is Henry Parker's farm. Jonathan Cram and Nehemiah Abbott have farms on the hilltop to the south and east of Henry Parker's land.

Isaac Frye, in his late twenties, is tall with broad shoulders and a wiry build. He has blue eyes, is clean-shaven, and his unruly, brown-blond hair is mostly tied back. His face flushes red, like it is now, when he is working hard. His brown coat is patched in a few places, as are his linen trousers. His dark-brown boots are well worn and muddy from several passes around a few wet patches in the lower part of the field.

Six years earlier, Isaac moved from Andover, Massachusetts to Wilton, which is a collection of farms spread over a township in the southern New Hampshire hills. The Souhegan River runs through its midst on the way east to the Merrimack River. Evergreens predominate in the valleys, and the slopes and hilltops have a patchwork of cleared fields, old-growth deciduous forest, and recently logged open lots. A new meetinghouse, sited halfway up a rise on the north side of the river, near the center of the township, is the tallest building. Its bell tower rises three stories above the main entrance. Just over six hundred people live in Wilton, most on seventy-acre farm lots. Some families own two or three lots, with grown children and their families living on the additional lots.

After climbing to near the high point of the field, Isaac stops the oxen so they can all catch their breath. A moment later, the meetinghouse bell begins ringing. The first peal bursts across the valley, ending—mid-thought—all tranquility and expectations for the next minute, day, and month. From Isaac's neck down to his knees, a jolt of shock straightens his body, causing his gaze to jerk from the backs of the oxen up to the sky and then sharply west towards the sound of the bell.

Isaac takes a deep breath as he sets his jaw. In the time it takes to let his breath out, the list of what he must do next runs through his mind. He raises the plow, then urges the oxen toward a path between the field and apple orchard, leading toward his farmhouse. As he moves, he looks every few seconds toward the sound of the bell. Just before reaching the path, he catches sight of Will Burton, a sandy-haired boy of twelve years, riding up the path from the river.

Isaac signals to Will, who sees him and rides to meet him. Will's face is red and he pauses to catch his breath. The excitement in Will's voice is unmistakable. "The alarm from Boston just came. I am out to call the militia to muster at the meetinghouse."

Isaac nods as he listens, and before Will finishes, Isaac begins motioning for him to continue with his ride. "I'm on my way. Keep going! We need everyone there as quickly as possible."

Will starts his horse to a walk, and looks back and calls to Isaac, "On my way up to Cram's place next."

Will kicks the horse to a gallop and covers the ground to Isaac's house, while Isaac leads the oxen onto the path. Isaac's house has a coat of yellow paint, and is bright spot on the early spring hillside. As he walks, he can see Will on the road, passing behind the farmhouse, and then as the road starts uphill, disappearing into the woods. In a little over a minute Isaac arrives in the farmyard and ties the ox team to the fence. Behind his house, a horse, already saddled, waits.

Isaac enters through the back door long enough to take off his coat, exchanging it for a coat from a peg on the other side of the door. The coat is blue, of a military style, with green facings and brass buttons. A Brown Bess firelock and powder horn lean against the wall in the corner by the door as well. Isaac steps out towards the horse.

"Is that you, husband?" Elizabeth, Isaac's wife, opens the back door to have a look. Her straight, dark-brown hair disappears as she pins it up in back and settles her bonnet into place. Her features are sharp but warm, and her dark eyes take command of everything she sees. She is five months pregnant.

Isaac stops, turns, and looks at Elizabeth with a thousand thoughts and no words to express them. His hurry and sense of purpose return a moment later. "The war has begun. I must be going."

3

"I heard the bell." She looks determined, and then fixes Isaac with a look of disbelief. She breaks off, shaking her head before turning back to the house and calling, "Boys! Come see your father off." Turning to Isaac she adds, "I cannot believe it." Her eyes begin to show worry. "It's so soon."

They both turn when two boys, ages five and three, bound out of the house, jumping over the two steps below the back door. Isaac Jr. is older and has a tight grip on his father's haversack, while Abiel—named after Isaac's father and oldest brother—carries Isaac's tricorn hat. Elizabeth moves past them into the house and returns a moment later with a third son, Timothy, who is about a year old, in her arms.

Isaac kneels in front of the two older boys. "You boys help your mother. Do everything she says."

Both boys nod in affirmation. "Yessir."

Isaac takes his haversack and hat. Then fixing his look at Isaac Jr., charges him to "Keep a sharp eye out for trouble and help Mother and your aunts and your grandparents." Turning to Abiel, he commands, "Help Brother and Mother." Abiel nods, returning Isaac's serious look.

Isaac rises and walks to Elizabeth, clasping her arms. His eyes show he does not know what to say. Her expression is tight, nearly frozen with tension; she inhales slowly and holds her breath for a few seconds, then firmly urges him, "Go."

He takes in her firm look, her eyes. Despite his expression showing resoluteness, his thoughts are close to panic as he wonders how she will know how much he loves her and that for the sake of honor and liberty he must go now. After what feels like a long moment he pulls back and holds her at arm's length, and nods to acknowledge his commitment to return as soon as possible, then he lets go and turns purposefully toward his horse.

He mounts and rides off on the path toward the river. Approaching the last point from which he can look back and see the farm, he relaxes and pulls one rein to turn his horse. For a few long seconds, he takes in the view, even memorizing how the smoke drifts lazily upward from the chimney. At the end of a deep breath, he nudges his horse and they turn, heading down the steep path into the woods. As Isaac rides across the bridge over the Souhegan River and onto the familiar road to the meetinghouse, he realizes that just three days ago he would not have bet on the alarm coming so soon; it was a Sunday afternoon and Isaac, Elizabeth, and their sons had been visiting Elizabeth's parents who also live in Wilton about a thirty-minute walk from the farm.

During their visit, Elizabeth's seventeen-year-old sister Sarah was outside watching the older boys play. Inside, Isaac sat with Elizabeth's parents at their trestle table, while Elizabeth rested comfortably in a rocking chair, holding a sleepy Timothy. Everyone was dressed in their best clothes. An oil lamp added light to the room where two small windows could not reach. The room served as a sitting room, dining room, kitchen, and pantry. Everything in its place. A fire was lit in the fireplace, as the evenings and nights were still cold.

Elizabeth's father, Timothy Sr., looking only a few years past his prime, gray streaking though his dark hair, turned to Isaac with a look that said, 'Give me the unvarnished version,' and asked, "Well, how did the militia look?"

Isaac gave a slow nod as he thought for a moment. "As expected for their first muster. They learned some of marching as a unit well enough. We covered the basics of loading and firing on command, and inspected their muskets, most of which will serve. They know what to carry with them, should the alarm come this week."

Timothy Sr. leaned back, nodding with approval. "How often will you drill?"

"Once a week. Paul Sargent asked the officers to meet one or two additional evenings in Amherst to plan our response for an alarm. The men from Wilton will be in a company under Captain Josiah Crosby from Amherst. I will muster with them at the meetinghouse first."

The older man, now shaking his head, commented, "Doesn't seem enough, given these troubles. Times aren't like they were when I was young. The men all brought their arms to the meetinghouse every Sunday to drill so we would not lose our martial skills."

Isaac nodded. "I think they will do well, but you're right, it isn't enough."

Mother Holt, a thin woman with her nearly-black hair pulled back tightly into a severe-looking bun, gave her husband an incredulous look. Tension made her shoulders rise. "Has it really come to this? So many men will be away from their farms. Isaac, thirty men will be gone from Wilton. That's too many."

Isaac considered before responding. "At least that many. All the men at the town meeting the week before last spoke for doing this. None spoke against. No one called to table the discussion. I heard the same was true a few days later in Amherst for the County Congress. Everyone will have to help. We will need food and supplies." Isaac stood and his voice became a little louder. "We all learned how little it matters what we produce on our farms." Isaac began pacing beside the table. "The king and Parliament ended our hope of making a decent living when they closed Boston's port."

Isaac stopped at the window and glanced out. "I cannot fathom how the king and Parliament think cutting off our livelihood will make us better subjects. This militia call-up is only about one thing: the king's troops will be coming for the cannon and powder taken from Boston last fall and from William and Mary in December. We mean to turn them back." Isaac's tone took on a note of strong frustration. "Enough is enough!" Isaac pounded his fist into his other hand, grinding it against his palm, and repeating the motion. "We cannot make a living. We have no say in Parliament. We will have our say."

Timothy Sr. slumped a little and shook his head. "I wish it were not so. All the young men talk about is war. War, war, war, nothing less."

Isaac continued in a calmer voice. "We all know the cause of such talk. The king and Parliament act as though they have us on strings. Yanking us about, taking our liberties, taking our means for defending ourselves, and taxing us more each year. We have less again this year. Every yank of those infernal strings makes us more servants and puppets than men!" Walking back to the table, but not taking his seat, Isaac summed up his frustration. "It serves no logical purpose."

Mother Holt commiserated. "We know, Isaac. Our situation is no better."

Isaac took a deep breath, shook his head slowly, and then looked at his hands and feet for a moment. "I bought my lots, two of the best in Wilton. I figured two would amount to more. Even if prices were bad, we would still do well. I have already had to sell fifteen acres to pay debts to my sisters' husbands. I still cannot believe they sued me. What was I to do? All of us have a pile of debt and credit papers. There is so little hard money these days." He sighed. "But I hold no grudge, because I know it's hard for them, too."

Nobody said anything for a few moments. Mother Holt decided to change the subject. "It sounds as though the alarm could come any day." Then she rose and looked out the window. "The boys are out in the field and look to be in fine spirits." She paused a moment. "We are proud of you, Isaac. Your commission as quartermaster for the militia... you have an excellent mind for figures and money, so that makes perfect sense. Paul Sargent chose a good man in you." She moved from the window and opened the door to the bedroom. "We've got something for you; it's to show our faith in you."

She disappeared into the other room for a moment and returned with a military coat folded over her arms. It was dark blue with green facings. As she came back into the main room she explained, "We had the fabric for some time now, and Elizabeth had the idea to make you a coat, and sewed it together on visits over the past months."

Isaac's mouth opened with surprise, and then he smiled and looked quickly back and forth between his wife and her mother. His voice turned warm. "I... I'm surprised. I mean thank you. Thank you all. I am fortunate to be part of such a family."

Elizabeth and her mother grinned and chimed in together, "You're welcome!" Then Mother Holt said eagerly, "Try it on. We've been anxious to see how it fits."

Isaac unfolded the coat and held it up, admiring the buttons and cut. "This is truly a handsome coat. I will wear it with pride."

Timothy rose to help him into it. "An officer needs to look like an officer."

Timothy Sr. looked Isaac up and down. "The coat looks good."

Elizabeth rose and handed Timothy to her mother, then walked completely around Isaac, inspecting the seams. "It does seem a good fit. Move your arms about. We had to guess a bit." She smiled. "I think we got it right, Mother."

Isaac moved his shoulders and arms, testing the range of motion. "The fit is excellent. It's wonderful." Isaac continued to move about and then stopped and looked to Elizabeth. "I am a lucky man to have a wife of so many talents."

Elizabeth beamed. "Thank you. I'm so glad Mother had the cloth."

Isaac turned to the others. "There is something I hadn't mentioned about Paul Sargent. He was suing me, too."

Timothy Sr. recovered first. "What? I didn't hear of this."

Isaac motioned everyone to sit again. After they took their seats, Isaac explained, "I owed him for the materials to repair the barn the summer before last. If I hadn't been hurt when the meetinghouse collapsed that fall," Isaac shook his head slowly, "I likely would have paid what I owed him. Now, there are times when I cannot help thinking I would have gotten a higher rank. I—"

Timothy Sr. cut in with a hint of impatience in his voice. "There's no point lamenting the past. The arrangement you've got as quartermaster is a good one." Timothy Sr. paused and looked Isaac in the eye with gentle reproach and held up a hand to forestall a reaction on Isaac's part. "I'm not so certain about that higher rank. We Holts, and those of us that came from Andover, know your family's contributions. Your father was a militia captain and your uncle a colonel. Wilton is not Andover, where all that is well-known history. The men here have lived nearer to the wilderness and the threat of the Abenaki. They have earned their rank, and we should respect them."

Mother Holt moved behind Timothy Sr., resting her hands on his shoulders. "We will help if an alarm does come," she said for Isaac's benefit. "Elizabeth and the boys will be fine."

Elizabeth noticed her mother's lead. "I'll do what I can for crops, and care for the new apple trees. Surely an alarm will not keep you away long."

Mother Holt continued, "If it lasts more than a week or two—"

Isaac interrupted. "If the alarm comes, it could last months. To the end of the year, or longer, if we succeed in forcing the king to act. We don't want a battle, only to guard against the ministerial troops taking what is ours."

Elizabeth, leaning forward in the rocker, protested. "Surely they will let you return to the farms in the interim. There will be so much to do."

Isaac took a slow breath before responding. "That would be something to hope for, but I do not count on it. I fear there are too many hotheads to hold back and it could get quite bad. If blood is spilled, it may take until the end of the year to sort out. Even longer if it isn't to our liking."

The door opened and young Sarah came in. Her eyes were bright and animated, and she looked to her parents. "I can stay with Elizabeth to help with the boys. For as long as she needs."

Timothy Sr. and his wife exchanged a glance, realizing their youngest daughter heard much of the conversation while sitting outside the door.

Before either can say anything, Elizabeth came to her sister's aid. "I will rely on you to do that, Sarah. How are the boys?"

Sarah, looking excited, reported, "They're fine. I took them down to the creek to look for tadpoles. The days are cold yet, but they still had fun looking. They're outside, waiting."

Elizabeth nodded. "Thank you for going with them. They like having you lead their expeditions. I know sister Hannah and brother Richard will help us, too."

Isaac added, "Richard's a good man. Last year would've been much harder if all of you hadn't moved to Wilton after he and Hannah were married."

Timothy Sr., sounding resolute, placed his hand on the table as if to swear an oath, and declared, "We will help. We will prepare for the worst, but hope for the best."

Isaac moved to the door. "Everyone I've spoken with feels the same. The Congress hasn't convened since setting the boycotts in September. We've held to the boycotts and all the rest of it. Congress gave Parliament and the king a year to act. They even threatened to stop trade altogether. If the king won't budge, we will have war, and then I fear it won't be over quickly."

9

Elizabeth, sounding like she wanted to end this sort of talk, said, "If we want to get home with some sunlight left, we should get going."

Timothy Sr. took the hint. "True, and we've got plenty to get done before dark, as well. Come, Isaac. Let's get those boys of yours ready."

Isaac opened the door and stepped out. Timothy Sr. rose and followed Isaac outside.

Mother Holt retrieved a small, covered basket from the pantry. "Here, Elizabeth. I've prepared some jam and rolls. The boys can carry it on the way home."

Elizabeth accepted the basket and thanked her mother, then joined Isaac and the boys outside for the walk home.

Half an hour later, Isaac and his family were nearly home, and crossing a bridge over the Souhegan. The river, about twenty feet wide, flowing rapidly with early spring melt. Instead of continuing on the road which turns to the right and rises gently, wrapping around the hill before straightening and heading north by Isaac's house half a mile later, the family turned left, through a gate in the rail fence, onto a well-worn track heading up the steep hill and directly home.

The path rose, and as it crested the steep slope, it came out of the trees into the lower end of an unplowed field where Isaac would be at work in a few days. The family emerged, with Isaac carrying Timothy, who was now awake. The older boys ran ahead on the familiar path.

Elizabeth, looking worried, asked, "Do you really think it will come to war? You said 'months' if the alarm comes, but if blood is shed, a lot longer. Do you honestly believe it will come to war?"

Isaac's tone was solemn. "I'm not optimistic. I don't know what will happen if blood is shed. So many things have happened in the past weeks. We chose the side of liberty from the beginning. If it comes to war, I won't likely be back until next year—there's no avoiding that. Mayhaps cooler heads will prevail and Parliament or the king will see sense by summer or fall, when the year given to them by the Congress is out."

Elizabeth shook her head and her eyes narrowed, showing tension. "It's not the king I worry about. General Gage sent a pair of regulars, officers I heard, dressed as farmers into the countryside. Trying to find the route to Worcester, I heard. He may cause a war before the king or—"

Isaac's words came in a measured, almost too-calm tone. "You have family here to watch over you and the boys. As for that pair of spies, for that's what they were, they barely found Worcester, and everyone from Lexington to Springfield knew what they were about. We can hope General Gage learned a lesson that he is badly outnumbered and lacks knowledge of the land."

"Husband, I know you could be gone a long time, and I find such to be an unwanted notion."

"Aye. True. We may have to carry a heavy burden, so that this one—" He nods to Timothy. "—and his brothers have a future on this land."

They crested the hill, walking in silence, their farmhouse less than a hundred paces away. Elizabeth peered into the trees on their right and exclaimed, "Oh look, some mayflowers are up. I didn't see them this morning. Boys, let's have a closer look." Isaac and Abiel came jogging back, excited at the prospect of a hunt for spring flowers.

They spent a few minutes finding what turned out to be several dozen mayflowers on the side of the hill. Elizabeth sets the boys running on toward the farmhouse as she returned to Isaac on the path. "Our world here is calm," she said. "I know the wider world has its troubles, but those are far from here."

They reached the rail fence around the farmyard and Isaac's gaze traveled around the farm. "May trouble never find this place. I would not leave if I thought you and the boys unsafe. The last years of hardships have made Wilton strong." Isaac looked around at the small house and barn. "I need to take care of everything before it gets dark." He handed Timothy to Elizabeth and strode toward the barn.

The War Has Begun

2 ROAD TO BOSTON

"Whereas it is necessary for the Defense of any People that they perfect themselves in the Military Art... we Earnestly recommend to this County to form themselves into Companys and make choice of such men as they shall think Best Qualified for Teaching the Military Art, to meet once a week at least..."

From the proceedings of the Hillsborough County Congress, April 1775 at the Court House, Amherst, April 5, 1775

Isaac's thoughts come back to the present as he takes in the scene around Wilton's meetinghouse. He slows his horse to a trot as they approach. The two-story building with large, mullioned windows commands a gently sloping field to the south, and a level area to the north where the militia have begun gathering.

Isaac counts ten others who have already arrived and three more approaching from the opposite direction. The men are wearing hunting clothes and tricorn hats, and carrying firelocks, haversacks, canteens, and rolled blankets. Some have powder horns and cartridge boxes.

Isaac rides toward the steps below the bell tower entrance, where two other men— Lieutenants James Brown and Sam Pettingill—are converging on horseback. Both men are built like Isaac: fit, wiry, and a little taller than average, though Brown is perhaps twenty years older than the other two. They all dismount and tie their horses' reins to the posts beside the steps. Isaac is the only one there wearing a military-style coat.

Isaac approaches the pair of lieutenants and shakes their hands. "Lieutenant Brown. Lieutenant Pettingill. Have you any news as to the nature of the alarm?"

Brown nods to both, his demeanor showing high alert. "Quartermaster. Lieutenant Pettingill," he greets, then looks quickly at the road in both directions before continuing. "I've only heard that General Gage sent troops to arrest Adams and Hancock, and to confiscate the powder and fieldpieces which they believe to be in Concord."

Isaac's shoulders sag a little, and then he recovers and scratches the back of his neck. "I was hoping they wouldn't try that." He shakes his head. "A lot like sticking a torch into a powder keg so you can see where the fuse has gotten to."

Brown turns and spits. "And for what? To take the powder and arms we've always held for our defense?" He shakes his head with a strong look of disgust.

Pettingill laughs a little. "General Gage fancies himself as quick and wise. Perhaps he will learn differently today." He looks around and scratches his unshaven jaw. "Have you any new words on our plans, Quartermaster? Do we still intend to march towards Dunstable and meet Captain Crosby at the road to Monson?"

Isaac nods. "Still the plan. We will all march on foot. Will Burton and some of the other boys will take our horses home. We met yesterday in Amherst with Colonel Sargent, and he confirmed the plan for the march is the same as he described when we last mustered. I'll leave an account of any of the public stores we take today, though it looks as though the men are well prepared. We will be short of tents, but we knew that already." Isaac looks around to see two more men arriving. His expression remains grim. "We needed more time. I'll be in the meetinghouse. Send any men who need items or powder from the public stores to me." Brown and Pettingill nod to

Isaac, who turns on his heel and heads inside.

•••

A little over an hour later, the Wilton militia are marching east. The road runs along the north side of the Souhegan River. There are twenty-five men marching two abreast, and the three lieutenants in a file to the left of the men. The valley is broad and clear of trees, making the two columns of men seem small by comparison.

Pettingill and Brown, who had been marching behind Isaac, come up on either side. Pettingill asks, "So, Quartermaster, how do our ranks work? I mean who do you believe is in charge?"

Isaac looks at Pettingill and then Brown and clears his throat. "I know you both are first lieutenants according to the town meeting, and I am a second lieutenant. Though because I am also a staff officer, if I give an order it's because I am passing along the order from our commanding officer."

Pettingill nods. "I see."

Brown gets a speculative look on his face. "So if we was to be attacked by a company of regulars while we march today, and there ain't no commander about, what then?"

Isaac thinks a moment. "Each of you would have charge of the squad of men you've been leading in drills, and being outnumbered you would likely shift for yourselves as best you could, move to where we expect the Amherst men to meet us, and keep an eye out for more regulars.

Jeremiah Holt, one of the younger privates who is marching in the middle of the squad closest to the lieutenants, has been listening. "You don't think the regulars have got this far already, do you?"

Brown laughs. "No. Even on horseback they would be at least an hour or two away."

Isaac turns toward Holt. "The regulars haven't got the slightest reason to be on this road, or any that we will travel today. We will all know more tonight."

Pettingill waits for a minute before continuing the earlier discussion. "So, is Paul Sargent to be our colonel?"

Isaac thinks a moment. "I can't say I know the answer to that. I think he expects to be a colonel. My understanding is he and John Stark were chosen at a meeting in January to command, whereby Stark would muster the northern towns and Sargent the southern towns. I don't know under whose authority that was done. Under normal circumstances the province's House of Representatives would be the proper body to commission colonels of the militia."

Brown smirks. "Last I checked, they hadn't met in almost a year, and they're led by a Tory—I mean our esteemed Governor Wentworth."

Isaac chuckles. "Aye, true. I s'pose we will sort things out as we go."

They march for another half hour, turning a little to the south as the road leads into wooded lots and up out of the valley. Ahead, their road ends, intersecting the road north to Amherst and south to Dunstable. A moment later, a rider enters the intersection from the north. He catches sight of the men from Wilton and waves them to come forward, and waits for them to close the distance.

Isaac recognizes the rider as Nahum Baldwin, Amherst's blacksmith, and a deacon of the Congregational Church in Amherst. Lieutenant Brown calls the column to a halt about fifty feet short of the intersection.

Baldwin urges his horse forward. He is in his early fifties and still fit and strong from his work. "Good. You men made good time. Well done."

Isaac steps forward. "Aye, we were mustered and marching in less than hour. Do you have news of those who mustered at Amherst?"

"Captain Crosby says to wait here. I expect he and the rest that mustered at Amherst will be along within a quarter hour. It looks as though you are short a few men."

Brown steps up beside Isaac. "Yes, four. They are loading supply wagons and we expect they will follow two or three hours behind us."

Baldwin nods with satisfaction. "Well enough. Colonel Sargent with Cap'ns Crosby, Towne, and Spaulding are marching now from Amherst. With the Wilton men, there will be well over a hundred." Baldwin turns away from the lieutenants and looks over the rest of the Wilton men. "It's good to see the Blanchards, Browns, and Greeles all well represented." He turns to the youngest in the group from Wilton, David Kenney, who is not even fifteen. His older brother Archelaus, who is seventeen, stands behind him. "Tis good to see the sons of a fellow blacksmith in this column of men." He turns to Archelaus. "You keep your brother with you, and look after him."

"Yes, sir." Archelaus nods firmly. "David is in place of our older brother Daniel. Daniel's got the ague. When he's better he will come and David will go home. David's a good shot, and you can see he's already bigger than some men."

Baldwin claps the older brother on the shoulder. "Just the same, keep him with you."

Lieutenant Brown tells the men to rest while they wait for the column from Amherst to arrive. Only a few of the men sit; the rest are keyed up with nervous energy, and mill around, frequently glancing south as though able to see what lies ahead through miles of trees and hills.

Brown comes over to speak with Isaac, who is standing with Pettingill and Baldwin. "Deacon, have you got any news about the Alarm?"

Baldwin shakes his head with a look that says he sorely wished he did know more. "None, though I've got a bad feeling. This has been escalating since August or September and if Gage has sent the regulars out of Boston into the countryside, there's some who, I am sure, will take a shot or two."

Brown clears his throat and spits off to the side of the road. "That would suit me just fine. I've had enough of loyalist curs settin' the rules."

Baldwin with his hands on his hips, augmenting the physical advantages of being a blacksmith, nods and cocks an eyebrow at Brown. "I'm with you, James, but I think if blood is shed, it will cost us a lot more than petty satisfaction. You prepared to pay?"

"Pay what?" Brown fixes Baldwin with a challenging look.

"Eight months or a year, maybe more away from your farm? There's worse if it comes to a battle."

"I wouldn't be here if feared any of that. I hope it comes to a battle. Between New Hampshire and Massachusetts, the militias outnumber the regulars five to one. I like those odds. I expect Connecticut and Rhode Island will add more for our side."

Pettingill, with a look that says he already chewed this bone, adds, "The king will send more troops, but it won't matter. We'll burn their ships to the water a'fore they can land."

Baldwin raises an eyebrow, but says nothing.

Isaac takes a swig of water from his canteen. "Seems inevitable. It's seemed so for a long time. I expect we'll have to see whatever's happened this morning through to the end."

None of the men look as though they approve of their fate being beyond their control, and they lapse into silence. Baldwin leaves the group to go check the road to the north for signs of the Amherst men. Ten minutes go by before the sounds of drum and fife begin to drift in from the north. A column of nearly a hundred men comes into view.

The Amherst militia halts at the intersection. Several men are mounted, all wearing military coats, though none matching in color. Captain Paul Dudley Sargent has command of the men from the southern part of Hillsborough County. He rides a spirited horse towards the group from Wilton.

Isaac, Brown, and Pettingill approach Sargent and offer a military salute. Isaac speaks first. "Sir, Lieutenants Brown and Pettingill here are to have charge of the Wilton men, and await your orders."

Sargent sits his horse proudly and with easy command. This role of commander favors him, and the tone of his voice shows he knows it. "Excellent. You're under Captain Crosby." Sargent motions for Captain Josiah Crosby, one of the other mounted men, to join him.

Brown responds quickly, "Yessir."

Sargent resumes, "I've also got Captains Spaulding and Towne, with parts of their companies, in this column. Crosby's company is at the rear."

Captain Crosby rides forward. He has the manner of a veteran who has learned to watch and listen before acting. He scans the men from Wilton as he rides forward, angling toward Brown. "Lieutenant Brown, is all in order?"

"Yessir. We left four men arranging wagons of supplies to be brought to Concord, and the rest of the men are present and fit for duty."

Captain Crosby looks over the minutemen from Wilton again before nodding. "Good. Amherst will be sending supplies as well. Colonel Shepard is overseeing that."

"Excellent," adds Captain Sargent. "You will fall in at the end of the formation. We will march for Concord today." He turns to Isaac. "Quartermaster Frye, see the Adjutant, Lieutenant Peabody." He points to another mounted man near the rear of the column. Turning back to Isaac, he orders, "Get a count, by company, of the men, types of arms, their condition, and ammunition. Also, a count of tents and blankets."

Isaac responds quickly, "Yessir, I will."

Isaac moves off in the direction Captain Sargent indicated. Lieutenant Peabody is a few years older than Isaac, has a clean-cut appearance, and moves with an athletic, efficient manner. He is tall, like Isaac, with brown hair and green eyes that dart about, taking in details. As he sees Isaac coming towards him, he greets him familiarly, "Isaac..." then catches himself, "I mean Quartermaster Frye. I'm glad to see you. I presume Captain Sargent set you to the task of taking an inventory?"

"He did. Good to see you, too, Stephen. I mean Adjutant Peabody."

"Ha! I'm not the only one unaccustomed to military forms of address."

Isaac shakes his head and grins. "No, you're not. It's going to take some getting used to. I believe Captain Sargent expects me to get this done while marching, so I better get started."

"Yes, check in with me when we next stop."

The captains give the orders to continue marching, and the column begins to move south. Isaac jogs to the front of the column and begins the task of interviewing the sergeants and men.

•••

An hour and a half later, the column led by Captain Sargent emerges from the woods to arrive in a broad clearing in the center of the township of Hollis. There are three separate groups of militia waiting on the commons, and other men are busy loading wagons.

Like Wilton, Hollis is mostly a farming township, but with a larger population. Just over a dozen houses cluster near the meetinghouse and commons.

Captain Sargent calls for his column to halt, as Captains Crosby, Towne and Spaulding, and Lieutenant Peabody approach. Sargent takes in the three waiting groups of militia at a glance. Turning to the captains he orders, "Tell your men to eat their noon meal in place. In the meantime, I will see if the men from other towns are all here." He dismounts and walks purposefully toward the first group of militia.

The officers for the other groups of militia wear a motley collection of blue, brown, and green coats. Some carry pistols and others have muskets strapped on their shoulders. All the militia carry themselves with the pride and vigor of efficient men with business to complete.

A few minutes later, Isaac is sitting on the ground among the men from Wilton, finishing his meal of nuts, bread, butter, and jam. The captains return to the Amherst militia to meet with Captain Sargent. Lieutenant Peabody breaks off and motions for Isaac to approach. Isaac rises and hurries to the front of the column. Peabody motions toward the first of the waiting groups of militia, explaining, "Quartermaster Frye, those men are from New Ipswich." He points to the other groups as being from Mason and Temple. "Get counts of what they've brought with them as quickly as you can, then release them to join the column. It's almost noon, and Captain Sargent wishes to commence marching to Groton as soon as you're finished. I am to ride ahead and will rejoin the column at Groton."

Within a few minutes the column heads out, with many of the men still finishing their meal while marching. They march at a quick pace for about two and half hours. As they come into Massachusetts, the farms and hilly woodlands give way to a low, miles-wide, swampy area surrounding the Nashua River. The road rises onto dry ground close to Groton, which is similar to Hollis, though with a more settled feel to it due to a higher portion of the fields being cleared of trees.

As they arrive in the town's center, Isaac is with a group of officers at the front of the column. Captain Crosby points and the others turn to see a horseman approaching from the west. Lieutenant Peabody rides in at a gallop, coming to a stop not far away. His horse is winded. He dismounts and approaches the group.

"Captain Sargent, the men from Peterborough will arrive within three quarters of an hour."

Captain Sargent takes in the news. "Thank you, Lieutenant Peabody. Get some food if you haven't eaten yet. Captain Crosby, have one of your men make sure his horse gets water."

Crosby turns to Sam Pettingill. "Lieutenant..."

"I'll see to it," says Pettingill, already walking toward Peabody, who offers him the reins.

"Thank you, Lieutenant." Before leaving the group, Peabody nods to the group with a respectful, "Gentlemen."

Captain Sargent speaks to the remaining officers. "We will give the Peterborough men a short rest when they arrive, then we march to Concord as quickly as possible."

Captain Ezra Towne joins the group. "I've checked, and nobody here has any particular news of the alarm or what has occurred since."

"I fear it will be full dark when we arrive in Concord," responds Sargent, looking to Spaulding. "Nobody here has news of what took place today. Captain Spaulding, ride ahead and see what you can learn. Find us a place to encamp tonight as well."

Captain Spaulding nods in affirmation. "Yessir," he says, and heads for his horse.

•••

As dusk settles over the northern part of Concord, Massachusetts, the New Hampshire militia is hastily encamping in an unplowed field. The three hundred men in Capt. Sargent's column are setting up their tents and lighting small campfires. Isaac stands in an open area with Lieutenants Peabody, Brown, and Pettingill, and Captains Sargent, Town, and Crosby.

Sargent addresses the group generally. "Quartermaster Frye and

Adjutant Peabody, get a count of tents tonight and tell me how well it matches your earlier count, but most importantly, confirm how many men are without tents." He turns as he catches sight of Captain Spaulding crossing the field at a brisk pace. "Captain Spaulding, you did well in securing the location for our encampment. What news do you have?"

"Thank you, sir." Spaulding takes a few swallows from his canteen. "I went as far as Lexington where I learned what's happened. Bad news. There was a running battle, starting at one of the farms here in Concord, and it seems the militia pushed the regulars back, perhaps all the way to Boston. They may yet be engaged. A great deal of blood was spilt this day."

Captain Spaulding pauses, seeing the shock register on the faces of the other officers. "It started when two regiments of redcoats came out looking for the fieldpieces taken from Boston and the powder and other items the militias secured. That was, in part, the cause of the alarm. It began at Lexington, where the redcoats came upon the militia while looking for Hancock and Adams, who were gone by then. The moment got the better of someone, because a shot was fired. The redcoats fired volleys into the militia. The militia retreated irregularly and some returned fire. Everyone I spoke with says the redcoats fired first. The worst part is several men from the Lexington militia were killed."

Captain Sargent shakes his head incredulously. "Two entire regiments fired on the Lexington militia?"

Captain Spaulding holds his hand up, acknowledging his haste had caused the message to become confused. "No, most of the king's troops were already moving on to this place, and yet another smaller part was searching elsewhere in Lexington. The regiment of redcoats that came here was likewise split up. They did a search and found a little of what they were looking for, but while they were searching, our brethren from Massachusetts arrived in numbers. Our militia had the redcoats well outnumbered, so they attacked them warmly. I think maybe they had news of the clash with the Lexington militia, and decided not to let the redcoats regroup, and undertook to drive them back to Lexington."

Looking bemused and not a little astonished, Captain Sargent takes a deep breath and lets it out slowly. Then his expression turns serious. "Do you have a sense for how many more were killed and wounded?"

Captain Spaulding shakes his head. "Hard to say. Likely dozens for both sides, I guess." He holds up a hand to pause any more questions before continuing. "That's only the half of it. There was a larger battle back near Lexington. At least another regiment of redcoats with some fieldpieces reinforced the first two regiments that we had in retreat. By then, I heard, our militia outnumbered the three regiments of redcoats by more than two to one, and drove them off the field even though the redcoats tried to make a stand. From what I could learn, the redcoats was in an organized retreat, or a bit worse, from there back to Boston. I thought about our numbers on the way back here, and it seems to me there was four or five thousand militia turned out to give that warm reception and then send them back to Boston in such a state."

Captain Sargent takes another deep breath, analyzing the news. "This will tear things for sure. Dozens, maybe a hundred ministerial troops dead and likely double that wounded. There will be chaos tomorrow if we cannot keep the redcoats in Boston."

Isaac looks around the group. The men's faces register a mix of shock and fierce determination. The wide-eyed looks show none of them had expected such news. Lieutenant Peabody whispers to Isaac, "It seems the war really has begun."

Isaac turns slightly to respond. "I know. But somehow, I thought I would be there to see it. In the ranks, fighting for our liberties."

Captain Sargent continues, his voice shifting from grimness to pride. "I s'pose Parliament will dream up a tax for those deaths." His expression and tone becomes purposeful. "Captains, make sure your men know what's happened. We will march early for Cambridge or Medford, depending on what we learn tomorrow." Turning to Isaac and Lieutenant Peabody, he adds, "Thank you, gentlemen. You are dismissed."

Isaac and Peabody nod. "Yessir," they reply in unison, and break off to rejoin their company. As soon as they are out of earshot of the officers, Peabody admits to Isaac, "This is worse than I ever imagined. No skirmish of hotheads to be buried in paperwork. Lexington was turned into a battlefield, with thousands of men engaged."

Isaac nods and sighs. "A lot of blood spilled today. The king will want heads, not silver. I'll have to write Elizabeth; she was hopeful this would be done in a matter of days. I tried to explain that it could be this bad, but today's battles couldn't be imagined a week ago."

Peabody sighs too. "I fear you're right; we will be at this for weeks and months, at the least." He pauses for a few strides. "We need to take our minds off what we cannot know. Let us get about our counts. We will have little enough sleep tonight with the anticipation of what's to come tomorrow." tomorrow."

3 A SIEGE

*"...being informed that General Gage has proposed a Treaty with the
inhabitants of the Town of Boston, wherein he stipulates that the women
and children, with all their effects, shall have safe conduct without the
Garrison, and their men also, upon condition that the male inhabitants
within the Town shall, on their part, solemnly engage that they will not
take up arms against the King's Troops within the Town..."*

From the Massachusetts Committee of Safety to the
Inhabitants of Boston, April 22, 1775

Medford, Massachusetts is another town like Wilton—a township
of farms with a river running through it—though a larger portion of
the land is north of the Mystic River and far more of the land is level
enough for farming. On the south side of the Mystic River, the
western part is hilly and mostly wooded, while the east next to
Charlestown is cleared. From the high places above the north side of
the Mystic River the ocean can be easily seen past Boston Harbor.

By early afternoon on April 20, Isaac and most of Captain
Sargent's men have crossed on the ferry to the south side of the
Mystic. They have been ordered to encamp on Winter Hill, which
overlooks the smaller Plowed Hill to the east. A little further east is

Bunker Hill, the tallest, affording the best views in all directions. It is situated on the Charlestown Peninsula, which thrusts into the bay at the meeting of the Charles and the Mystic Rivers. South of Winter Hill is a broad plain leading to Cambridge, where General Artemas Ward, who commands the Massachusetts militia, has set up command.

From above, more than a thousand tents can be seen cutting Boston off from the rest of New England. The greatest concentrations are in the north, on Winter Hill, around to Cambridge and then south to Roxbury. The entirety of New Hampshire's militia has begun encamping on and behind Winter Hill. The road out of Medford leads north to Exeter, the seat of New Hampshire's provincial congress, which has called an emergency session to meet on April 21 to discuss what New Hampshire will do in support of Massachusetts.

On Winter Hill, Isaac and Stephen Peabody walk up on a small gathering of officers. Captain John Stark is addressing them. Stark, who is in his late forties, has the build of a lean, athletic man half his age. He has a prominent, aquiline nose, graying hair, and hawk-like eyes. He carries himself in a military fashion and is obviously accustomed to being in charge of men and officers. Stark's voice carries well over the assembled group that includes Captains Crosby, Spaulding, Towne, and several other officers Isaac does not know. "Gentleman, given what I've learned of yesterday's events, we outnumbered four regiments of the ministerial troops by two to one. Too many killed on both sides, and there remains much anger to spare."

Stark pauses to gauge the sentiment his words effect, then continues, "Two hours ago, Captain Sargent, who is Amherst's representative, was summoned to Exeter, to the provincial Congress. He left instantly, expecting to be in Exeter late today. An emergency session will meet tomorrow. In the meantime, we need to organize our companies into regiments and set officers to gain some sense of order."

Next to Stark is another captain, James Reed of Fitzwilliam. Reed, a little older than Stark, is a solid figure with a strong jawline. His posture is not military, but nonetheless of one who is accustomed to being listened to, though more for his wisdom than his commands.

Reed is studying Stark intently while listening to him. As Stark finishes, Reed adds with his own strong voice, "If John Wentworth still presides," his tone derisive, "that body may be rendered useless for weeks. Thus, I agree, the sooner we organize, the better."

Captains Spaulding and Crosby call out their agreement. Most of the men appear to be of the same mind. Reed scans their faces and the way they are standing. Seeing no scowls or folded arms, he continues, "If we assemble the men, I expect we can set officers by acclamation. Should we wait for Captain Sargent to return?"

Stark considers the idea a moment. "Let's give him three days. We may want to know any immediate decisions made, but we will have trouble holding the men here longer if we do not organize soon."

Reed gives Stark a calculating look. "I will arrange the assembly of the men and preside over the meeting, presuming it will be yourself and Colonel Sargent being set as regiment commanders. Are there others?"

"Perhaps yourself," Stark says thoughtfully, "if there are enough men for three regiments."

Reed nods. "Let's start with two. I will meet with the other captains today and put the idea to them. We shall expect no surprises in three days, and a smooth transition to organizing the regiments will increase confidence and morale."

Stark is nodding while Reed speaks. "I completely agree. Let's assemble all the captains now. The sooner their men know of these plans, the better. The knowledge will work to steady the men for the next three days." Stark's look turns calculating for a few moments. "Let us reconvene in two hours' time on this same ground."

Crosby turns to Isaac, Peabody, and Pettingill. "Lieutenants, summon the captains to the upcoming council."

The three lieutenants answer with their affirmatives and leave the group, motioning their intended directions and heading off in those separate ways.

•••

Late the next morning, the men within the New Hampshire part of the encampment are in various states of duty, from companies drilling in formation to squads carrying out various tasks to establish defensive works, such as creating bundles of four- to six-foot-long wood branches, and stacking them into V-shaped walls called fascines. Several small groups of troops are finishing meals or standing before sergeants or corporals who are giving orders for their next jobs.

A man in his early fifties, wearing the military-style coat of an officer, rides in on the road from Cambridge. Isaac with Stephen are walking through camp at the same time and initially take little notice. Once the unfamiliar officer is well within the camp, he stops and stands tall in his stirrups and announces in a loud, authoritative voice, "Gentlemen of New Hampshire! I have just come from General Ward's council of war, where he has declared the men of New Hampshire are no longer needed. He thanks us for our service and bids us God speed returning to our homes and farms. Pray, I need a few volunteers to help me carry the word to the rest of our men." The effect of the message is instantaneous. Men change direction and others start moving toward their tents.

Isaac turns to Stephen as the man rides on. "What do you make of that Stephen?"

Stephen's features harden. "It makes no sense. I've only heard Massachusetts welcoming us, and the men from Connecticut for that matter. I can't say as I recognize the man, do you?"

"No. Too many groups of men arriving in camp in the past day. Half don't even look familiar."

About fifty yards further, they hear the man repeating his speech. Isaac sees more men stopping their work and moving towards their tents. Realizing they need to act quickly, he decides, "I'll go to Cambridge to confirm what he is saying. Captains Stark and Reed need to know about this as soon as possible, too."

Stephen, already turning away, confirms, "You're right. I will find them and meet you here on your return."

Nearly forty-five minutes later, Captains Stark, Reed, Towne, and several lieutenants are waiting with Stephen as Isaac runs, with arms and legs pumping at full speed, into the encampment. The lanes between the tents are much quieter, quite a few tents have already been struck, and all the work on the defenses has ceased. Even the sergeants have left the work sites. Isaac pulls to a stop in front of the assembled officers. He is a little short of breath as he starts. "The man was lying. General Ward made no such declaration. He sends his assurances the New Hampshire militia are very much needed."

"Goddammit!" Captain Stark turns to the others with a foul, reddening visage. "Spread the word. We are to stay! Quickly! Men have been leaving for the past thirty minutes. Get me the name of that lying rascal of a Tory who brought this false news into camp."

The officers break out of the group, moving rapidly in several directions, and within seconds can be heard renouncing the lie, ordering the men to stay, and reiterating that General Ward has just sent word of the great need for the New Hampshire Militia.

•••

In the morning, two days later, the New Hampshire militia assembles at the base of Winter Hill. They gather in groups according to the towns they come from. Stark stands with a few other officers behind Captain Reed, who is addressing the men.

"Gentlemen! As we yet have no news from Exeter, and by the urging of General Ward, we are here to elect colonels for two regiments, which we expect to fill with the men present. By show of hands, who is for John Stark as commander of the First Regiment of New Hampshire Militia?"

A large majority raise their hands. Captain Reed turns to Isaac and Stephen. "Lieutenants, is that a clear majority?"

Stephen responds in a strong voice that projects to reach everyone present. "Yessir. Captain John Stark is duly and properly elected colonel of the First Regiment by a clear majority."

Reed nods, then turns to the assembled compatriots. "Gentlemen! By show of hands, who is for Paul Sargent as commander of a second regiment of New Hampshire Militia?" Nearly as many men raise their hands as before.

Reed turns again to Isaac and Stephen. "Is there a clear

majority?"

Isaac responds, "Yessir! Paul Sargent is also duly and properly elected as colonel of the Second Regiment."

Captain Reed now proclaims, "Colonel Stark has chosen Isaac Wyman as lieutenant colonel and Andrew McClary as major. Captains Baldwin, Woodbury, Richards, Moore, Abbot, Hutchins, Dearborn, Kinsman, and George Reid will report to Colonel Stark henceforth. All other captains will report to Colonel Sargent when he returns from Exeter." He pauses a moment, turns to Colonel Stark and cocks and eyebrow to ask whether he is ready. Stark nods once. "Colonel Stark has some additional news from General Ward's headquarters."

Stark moves to the fore. "General Ward had news from the Massachusetts Committee of Safety, who have made a treaty with General Gage on behalf of the inhabitants of Boston and Charlestown. The treaty grants safe passage, for any who wish it, out of those towns, through the lines of the king's troops and through our lines. They will be coming through today, and we are not to impede their route. I expect that only Tories will remain with the ministerial troops in Boston. All companies will post guards about their areas of the encampment to prevent any of those persons from straying from the road through our encampment."

The newly appointed colonel looks to his officers. "Have I missed anything?" All shake their heads. Stark turns back to the men. "Captains in the First Regiment should attend me immediately. Have your subalterns assign your guards. Dismissed!"

Isaac sees Crosby waving him over. Crosby looks to be in a good mood.

"Quartermaster, good news. I've just got word that Colonel Shepard is here from Amherst with several wagons of food and supplies. Take a squad of men to unload the wagons, and set up a distribution point within our encampment. It looks like dinner tonight will be pork, beans, and bread."

Isaac breaks into a smile. "Yessir. That's excellent news."

•••

In the tent that serves as headquarters for Colonel Sargent's regiment, Stephen and Isaac are the only officers present. Both sit at field desks writing tables of numbers. Stephen's show the count of men by town in each company, and Isaac's tally the number of flints and cartridges reported for each company. There are four more such desks in the tent. The floor is made of thick, loose, wide planks. Several oil lamps provide light now that the sun has set.

Isaac straightens up from his work. "I'm surprised. In only three days, it looks as though all of Charlestown left their homes. Did you expect that?"

Stephen finishes the line he is writing before responding, "It does seem as though not a soul remains. I saw no lights late last night. It makes the place seem like a graveyard—at least at night. I've heard not so many patriots left Boston as expected. I'm not sure what that will mean, though I wager it is keeping General Gage busy wondering who to trust."

"Graveyard. That's it. I couldn't think of the word for how it felt. I find it bothersome; it portends nothing good. I was thinking of something else, too. It's an awkward thing, Massachusetts offering commissions to our colonels and enlisting our men. What do you think?"

Stephen pushes back from his desk. "I think they're trying to hurry our Congress in Exeter into some decisions. The Massachusetts Congress worries more men would leave if they weren't properly enlisted soon. I disagree with the hurry. Our Congress took the prudent course and chose to send a committee to see the situation here. The committee can meet with the Massachusetts Congress to assure them New Hampshire is fully committed to the cause."

Isaac nods. "At least we have enough men back in camp for three regiments now. But it looks as though it will be over a week before our Congress can make any decision, because the committee will have to return to Exeter, have a meeting, and then convey whatever they decide back here."

Stephen looks thoughtful. "True." Then he his tone turns optimistic. "Oh, they did make one other good decision, which was to supply us with food. I take your sentiment though. It is a peculiar balance with this new arrangement of Colonel Stark now having fourteen companies and Colonels Reed and Sargent having only four each.

Isaac's expression becomes worried. "That has me concerned. With Colonel Sargent being gone much of the time, he hasn't been seen or heard from by most of the men. Colonel Stark seems to have the knack of being wherever he's needed, so no wonder most of the captains have gone into his regiment. I was glad to learn our Congress recognized he's got a commission and a command now. They requested another from Amherst to take his place as the town's representative in Exeter."

"I agree, it will be better for him to be in camp." Finished with the regiment's rolls, Stephen opens a satchel of correspondence for the regiment and begins scanning each of the dozen or so letters. "Well here is something. Samuel Dudley. You know that name?"

"No, only heard the family name, and infrequently at that."

"Well, it seems he was the captain a few days back who invited our men back to their farms. It seems he is, in fact, a militia captain—from New Hampshire, I'm sad to say. He is known to be a Tory as well. Peculiar he chose that moment to suffer a crisis of loyalties. It says here he went home per his announcement. Though I am certain he is soon to be confined, as his name and actions are now know to our Congress."

Isaac sighs and leans forward, resting his head in his hands. "Well I hope he's made to pay for his mischief."

Stephen stretches his arms. "I suppose he taught us some valuable lessons. Movement in and out of the encampment needs to be controlled, and—sadly—so many men see the comforts of home as weighing more than our liberty."

"I suppose that's true," says Isaac as an evil grin forms, "but I'd like to see him wearing some hot, sticky, goose feathers next time he comes through this camp."

Stephen chuckles and then yawns. "Well, I am done for the night. You have the guard tonight?"

Isaac gets up and bounces on his toes, then stretches his arms. "I do, and I need to get my blood moving." He bounces a few more times.

"Would you mind sending the sergeant in on your way out?"

Stephen rises and quickly organizes his stacks of reports. "I will. Good night." With his reports in hand, Stephen heads for the tent's exit.

"Good night, I'll see you a bit later than usual tomorrow." Isaac settles back into his chair and awaits the guard sergeant.

•••

By the last week of May at the New Hampshire camp on Winter Hill, the scene is changed. A large redoubt tops Winter Hill, replacing the rows of tents in fields on either side of muddy roads. The walls extend south nearly to the road to Cambridge, and north to the road along the Mystic River. Neat rows of soldier's tents extend down the backside of Winter Hill, protected by the new fortifications. The walls follow the contour of the terrain, enhancing the natural steepness to cut off any prospect of a stranger simply walking through the patriots' lines. Immediately behind walls, a headquarters building is partially complete and in several places batteries for mortars are laid out. The roads have extra barriers to allow the guards to block the way, and sentries are now posted at all hours.

After leaving their tents, Isaac and Stephen walk toward the main fortification. Stephen notices a company of men starting new construction, and piles of wood planks ready for use. "Where did we get all the wood planks for those barracks?"

"They're on loan from the Massachusetts public stores. My understanding is many citizens contributed them, and so we are to return them when we are done here." Isaac grimaces. "It took an entire month for our Congress to finally approve monies for our military supplies. What could have taken them so long? Then, as if those delays were sensible, they've appointed a colonel for a regiment not yet raised, before affirming the appointments of Colonels Stark and Sargent, who marched with us on the day of the alarm." Isaac exhales strongly, as if trying to blow his frustration with the provincial congress out in one breath.

"I agree, it took much too long, and it's fortunate General Gage in

Boston has not seen fit to test us. At least a budget is approved."

Isaac lets out a little snort. "Approved, but with only five hundred pounds in credit issued. I've already spent nearly three hundred pounds to get us shovels, axes, pails, and the like, all on credit from the Massachusetts stores. At least what's left will be enough to arm those who didn't have muskets. But, more important, my understanding is General Ward has no firm idea of how much ammunition and powder is available. As much as I hate to admit it, I believe that is the real reason for the lack of decisions."

Stephen tips his tricorn hat back and scratches his head. The days are warming and both men are sweating as they walk through the encampment. "I s'pose there was quite a hot debate owing to just a committee of three from our Congress coming here to see this situation. I suppose not seeing any firm plan to end this standoff is causing worry. That, and former Governor Wentworth's loyalty to the king, which precipitated his hasty departure—or illness, as some say— kept anyone from thinking about organizing the militias beyond the level of towns. Not everyone was like Colonel Sargent, who understood there would likely be a battle or possibly a war. Though this stand-off we now enjoy was certainly not on anyone's minds two months ago."

"True. It's just that once a man believes he knows something, it becomes easier to make decisions with confidence. Those who have been here since the alarm believe we know what we need. Those in Exeter seem to credit lengthy discussions as the equivalent of being encamped here for over a month."

"Well, what we know may not be all our Congress in Exeter knows. They're wise men, Isaac." Stephen pauses to wipe his brow. "I've been saying to you for weeks now: have a little patience."

"Your idea of a little patience is quite a sum for me. I have high expectations, a pregnant wife, and a farm neglected for over six weeks."

"Well, I cannot do much for your farm or your wife," Stephen grins, "but I will say your impatience to get on with things is good for the cause. I'm lucky my oldest, Tom, is able to help with the farm. Though you must know impatience runs against the grain of many of those doing the planning for this army of ours. You're part of that, and I like to think even the lowest-ranking officer has a voice."

"I am the lowest-ranking officer," Isaac sighs. "This situation vexes me, and I'm afraid that shows more than my appreciation for you hearing my impatient voice." Isaac is quiet for a few moments. "To change the subject, our Congress has yet to commission Colonels Sargent, Stark, or perhaps Reed. Yet, did I see correctly—Enoch Poor was made colonel of the non-existent regiment they're calling the Second Regiment?"

"You did. As I read it, they authorized three regiments, but only named one of the commanders."

Isaac pauses to shake a clod of mud loose from the heel of his boot. "I think this Colonel Poor is kin to my Aunt Mehitable. Married to my Uncle Joseph. They are good people, the Poors. I'm just at a loss for their putting the cart well ahead of this horse."

After a moment, Stephen looks Isaac in the eye, already tired of the topic. "I've heard some talk that Colonel Stark is already considered the commander of the First Regiment, and there will only be three regiments. That second regiment, and I have no idea what logic was employed to call it the Second New Hampshire Regiment, is to be a reserve corps, and won't be here anytime soon."

"Well, that puts our Colonel Sargent in a peculiarly uncomfortable seat."

"It does. It most certainly does. His being an outspoken Massachusetts man since he came to Amherst may be troubling our Congress. They may see him as too often in contact with the Massachusetts leadership."

•••

Isaac and Stephen enter Colonel Sargent's tent a few days later and find him sitting at a field desk piled with letters, ledgers, and a satchel.

"Lieutenants," he begins. "Today I learned you will be assigned to Colonel Reed. Yesterday, he was commissioned colonel of New Hampshire's Third Regiment of militia. Please prepare a proper roll of his regiment, which will consist of these companies." He picks up a half sheet of paper and offers it to Stephen. "I have already informed the captains, so you may proceed immediately."

"Yessir." Taking the paper, Stephen pauses. "If I may ask a question?"

Sargent, who had already taken up his quill, sets it down and fixes Stephen with a tired gaze. The lieutenants now see his eyes are bloodshot from too little sleep and his shoulders are bunched with the strain of more letters to write this evening. Nonetheless, Sargent consents. "Yes."

"What of you, sir? The men, principally those from and near Amherst, will wish to know of your next assignment. What would you have them know?"

"I expect to be offered a commission to command a regiment from Massachusetts. More men have been coming in, so there is opportunity for me. I may be able to keep one company from New Hampshire with me, as well."

Isaac nods slowly, realizing he needs to say more, given that Colonel Sargent personally established him as the regiment's quartermaster. "Sir... Thank you. For—"

"Say no more, Lieutenant Frye. I have faith you'll serve Colonel Reed equally well as you have me." Then he addresses both lieutenants. "I've got quite a lot to do tonight. You are dismissed."

•••

Nearly forty lieutenants and captains, now assigned to Colonel Reed, gather at eight the next morning, June 3, outside a farmhouse the colonel has chosen as his headquarters. Reed faces them atop the stone steps leading into the house. Beside him is Major General Nathaniel Folsom, who commands the New Hampshire Militia. Folsom, not quite as tall as Reed, still appears active and soldierly, despite his nearly fifty years and shocks of gray at his temples.

All the staff officers are wearing military-style coats, although the combinations of colors, facings, and buttons vary.

General Folsom briefs the assembled officers. He is reading from a sheaf of papers in his right hand. "Gentlemen, I present to you Colonel James Reed, commander of the Third New Hampshire Regiment—your regimental commander!"

The officers heartily respond with, "Huzzah! Huzzah! Huzzah!"

"Gentlemen," the general continues, "it is also my honor to announce the appointments of Lieutenant Colonel Israel Gilman and Major Nathan Hale."

At the bottom of the steps, the newly appointed staff officers face the assembly. Lieutenant Colonel Gilman is in his mid-forties, of average height, with dark hair, a light complexion, and quick to smile. Major Hale is tall, fit, and in his early thirties. Both men tip their hats to the assembled officers.

Folsom turns to Reed, who promptly takes over. "Thank you, General Folsom. Gentlemen, it would be my honor to address the regiment two hours hence, at ten o'clock. I would confirm the roll provided by Lieutenant Peabody. The men should be equipped as though marching to battle, and I would like to confirm the number and readiness of our men's arms." Glancing toward Isaac, he finishes with, "Quartermaster Frye, you will note the condition and needs. Dismissed."

The officers disperse. Reed, Gilman, Hale, and Folsom file into the farmhouse.

•••

Each of the following days prove more monotonous and unremarkable than the previous. General Folsom sends Colonel Reed to the western part of New Hampshire to bring in additional men. The armies in and around Boston seem outwardly content to do nothing, while inwardly the men wonder how their leaders fail to produce orders to take even a little more ground than they currently hold.

Early in the morning of June 9, Lieutenant Colonel Gilman enters the farmhouse, which is furnished with small field desks and chairs for Colonel Reed and his regiment's staff officers.

"Gentlemen," Gilman greets them.

Hale asks, "How was breakfast with General Folsom?"

Gilman rubs his hands together, massaging the joints. "Excellent. He had news that we all are to take an oath of loyalty. He gave me orders for the regiment to assemble by ten o'clock this morning, when he will personally administer our oaths." Looking to Isaac and Stephen he commands, "See to it that all men in the regiment are assembled. No exceptions."

Isaac and Stephen rise immediately and salute, "Yessir."

At ten o'clock General Folsom stands before Reed's assembled regiment. There are nine companies, each with about sixty men; counting the officers, about six hundred men in all. In a booming voice, General Folsom calls out, "Men of the Third New Hampshire Regiment, you are hereby required to say an oath of allegiance to our cause. Your officers will now come to stand in front of their respective companies to observe that all present give the oath our Congress has provided." The captains and lieutenants position themselves in front of their companies.

General Folsom reads, pausing at intervals for the men to repeat the words—

> *"I, state your name,*
> *Swear, I will truly & faithfully serve in the New Hampshire Troops*
> *to which I belong for the defense and security*
> *of the Estates, Lives, and Liberties*
> *of the good People of this and the sister Colonies in America,*
> *in opposition to ministerial Tyranny by which they are or may be*
> *oppressed,*
> *and to all other enemies and opposers whatsoever,*
> *and that I will adhere to the Rules and Regulations of said army,*
> *and observe and obey the General and other officers set over me,*
> *and disclose and make known to said officers*
> *all Fractious Conspiracies, attempts and designs whatsoever,*
> *which I shall know to be made against said army,*
> *or any of the English Colonies. So Help Me God."*

Afterward, Isaac and Stephen are walking back to Reed's headquarters when Isaac gives a short laugh. "I suppose we really are in the army now."

Stephen grins. "Yes, I was wondering when we would be required to take such an oath. I heard the Massachusetts men took a similar one over a month ago."

•••

Two days later, on June 11, in the main room of Colonel Reed's headquarters, each of the staff officers is seated and writing either ledgers or letters. They are all a little surprised to hear a knock on the door. Lieutenant Colonel Gilman sets his quill down and calls out, "Enter."

A lieutenant by the last name of Hardy, whom they recognize as being from New Hampshire, enters and scans the room. Not seeing Reed, he looks about the room for help.

Gilman motions him to his desk. "I am Colonel Gilman. What do you require?"

Hardy approaches and hands Gilman a satchel. "Sir, these dispatches arrived for Colonel Reed from Exeter this morning. They were mixed in with those for General Folsom, who ordered me to deliver them as soon as possible."

"Colonel Reed is expected any day now. He was sent by General Folsom to march more men here. Does the general require a response?"

Hardy shakes his head. "No, sir." He salutes and leaves the farmhouse.

Gilman opens the satchel, takes out maybe a dozen sheets, and sifts through them. After the first few, he exclaims happily, "Well now, this is a surprise. At last!" He grins at Isaac. "Quartermaster Frye, you will be happy to know we finally have proper funds. Thirty-five hundred pounds, to be exact! You are authorized five hundred this week to secure additional tents, firewood, tools, and the rest of what we need to properly fortify this place."

"Yessir! That is a relief. I will set out immediately to secure contracts for the supplies we have been wanting."

Gilman catches himself, and his expression turns serious. "I am certain Colonel Reed would agree with my saying this: Have care in the prices you agree to. The members of our Congress have personally signed as bondsmen for this sum. Also, take no commission for yourself. I've heard some of the Massachusetts quartermasters have been profiting on their regiments' contracts. We cannot have that. Once you've seen to the tents and basic tools, draw up a plan for the other items we need. Present it to me once it is completed. I also require your thoughts on which towns in New Hampshire you could arrange those later contracts with. Our towns need as much business as we can send them."

Isaac stands and salutes. "Yessir. I will make the inquiries needed. Do the dispatches say when the notes of credit will arrive?"

Gilman smiles. "They are with General Folsom now, and will be drafted based on the contracts. I will extend the initial five hundred in credit for you right now." He takes a new sheet paper and drafts the note, waving a few times to dry it before offering it to Isaac.

While Gilman is writing, Isaac gets his hat and coat on. "Thank you, sir. I will get Sergeant Stone and a squad of men to go with me to the public stores in Watertown."

"That sounds like a good start. I think our men will appreciate belonging to even a modestly supplied army."

•••

When Isaac returns that evening, he finds only Stephen still working in the main room. He hears the other officers in the next room, drinking and conversing convivially. The air is muggy and Isaac is sweating.

Stephen cocks an eyebrow along with a good-natured smirk as he takes in Isaac's half-soaked coat and damp hair. "Looks like you made productive use of the day once you had a little money to spend."

"I did. Though I still cannot believe it took over fifty days to fund the militia we ostensibly have been organizing for years. Getting the men armed last week was a help. Maybe if our Congress had to sleep in camp they would act with less patience."

Stephen laughs. "Yes, I think they would. Though I think if it were only about the conditions they would lose heart after only a few hours and vote we all go home."

Isaac's eyes go wide with mock alarm, and then he smiles. "Aye. True enough. It does feel good to finally be doing the job I thought I would be doing six weeks ago."

Stephen glances at his paperwork. His expression turns sour and irritated. He looks around the room, stretches, then yawns. "Well, we'd better get rest. The days are getting long, and tomorrow morning will be here soon."

Isaac wipes his brow with a handkerchief. "The sea breeze is finally picking up tonight, and it definitely feels better outside." Stephen rises and quenches the extra oil lamps, and they exit the farmhouse together.

The War Has Begun

4 NEW ORDERS

"Charlestown, June 16, 1775.

GENTLEMEN:

I take this opportunity to inform you of the state of Colonel Read' s Regiment now at Charlestown. The Regiment is full officered; the soldiery will appear by the return; there is good harmony in said Regiment. A chaplain, surgeon, and armourer very much wanting in said Regiment.

Gentlemen, I am, with respect, your most obedient, &c˙,
ISRAEL GILMAN.

To the Honourable Committee of Safety.

P'S It is still times with the Regular Troops at present; we expect they will make a push for Bunker' s Hill or Dorchester Neck very soon."

Colonel Reed paces headquarters in agitation. It is the afternoon of Monday, June 12. On his second lap of the room he pauses in front of Isaac's desk. "Colonel Gilman's instructions to you regarding prices and commissions were very well put, and would have been my orders, so consider them my orders as of now. Forgive me, I know I am interrupting your work to finish the supply plan, but I would know the state of our ammunition stores."

"Sir, we have sixteen hundred cartridges, so roughly three per man, and we have two hundred and twenty extra flints."

They all turn as a crisp set of knocks sound on the door. Colonel Reed calls out, "Enter."

A man enters, neatly dressed in a military uniform. "Gentle sirs, I am Major Samuel Osgood, aide-de-camp to General Ward. I am looking for Colonel Reed."

"Major Osgood, I am Colonel Reed, how may I be of service?"

"Colonel Reed, I have orders from General Ward. Would you be so kind as to review them and provide him with assurances they will be immediately acted upon?" Osgood offers Reed a sealed packet.

Reed breaks the seal, unfolds the packet, and begins reading. After a few moments, he responds. "I understand what is expected, and you may convey to General Ward that my regiment will immediately remove to the location he has indicated and will set guards as he designed. Has General Folsom been apprised of these orders?"

"Excellent, and yes, General Folsom approved of this plan, and Colonel Stark has also been informed."

"Very good then. Is that all, Major?"

"Yes, sir, and good day, sir." Major Osgood turns on his heel and leaves.

Isaac, Stephen, and Gilman quickly finish writing and turn to face their commander.

"Gentlemen, we have received the following, which I will read verbatim:

"General Orders--That Colonel Reed quarter his Regiment in the Houses near Charlestown neck and keep all necessary Guards between his Barracks and the Ferry on Bunkers Hill. Signed J. Ward Sectary."

Reed scans the room for reactions from his staff officers. "Besides land being scarce near Winter Hill, do any of you have information as to why we've been ordered to repair to Charlestown Neck and guard it?"

Isaac looks around to see if anyone else wants to respond, before voicing his own opinion. "The rumor in camp this morning is some of the redcoat officers were in their cups last night and got to bragging about the beating they would soon be giving us. Granted, sir, that's third-hand news, at best."

"Well, I suppose such is plausible. Colonel Gilman, would you please verify this with Colonel Stark's staff? Lieutenants, get to General Ward's headquarters as quickly as you can and see about borrowing wagons and teams to effect moving our camp. Quartermaster, do your utmost to secure additional powder and bullets for the guards. I think it best not to confuse the needs of guarding the Neck with our general readiness for battle. Return here in two hours' time and we will reconnoiter that ground to determine the best placement of barracks and guard stations. I will be visiting General Folsom during those two hours."

•••

The Third Regiment parades the following morning on the road south of the Mystic River, between Ploughed Hill and Winter Hill. Colonel Reed, Lieutenant Colonel Gilman, and Stephen are on horses, and Isaac is standing a short distance behind them as Stephen reads orders to the regiment.

"Upon arriving on the eastern side of Ploughed Hill," Stephen motions to the rise to their east, "Captain Mann's company is assigned to guard the Neck leading to Charlestown. Shifts of eight hours will be observed. During the day, prior to nine of the clock at night, none shall pass without showing proper passes, and after that time until dawn, none shall pass without giving the countersign. Each captain of a company will see Colonel Gilman to be given the location of their encampment on Ploughed Hill." He turns to Reed and asks, "Sir, is there anything else before we prepare to march?"

"No, Adjutant. Have the captains prepare their companies and let us be on our way."

While Stephen is giving the captains the order to prepare their companies to march, Reed turns his horse and rides back to Isaac. "Quartermaster, did we receive powder and balls for the use of the guards?"

"Yessir. A hundred and fifty weight of powder and three hundred weight of balls. Sargent Stone had ten men work until late last night to roll fifteen hundred cartridges."

"Excellent, report to Captain Mann, when he arrives, to distribute twenty cartridges per man on guard duty. With each changing of the guard, you or your sergeant will verify that none has gone missing. Keep the rest separately with the cartridges the regiment received two weeks past."

Isaac salutes. "Yessir."

•••

Late that same evening, Isaac and Stephen are at work in the regiment's new headquarters, a home abandoned in the days after the battles at Lexington and Concord. This one is rustic compared to their previous headquarters. Several oil lamps provide light, though the windows have layers of heavy cloth over them to hide the light from those outside, particularly the enemy's scouts. Besides the field desks and chairs, the only other feature in the room is a fireplace.

Isaac pushes his chair back from his field desk and leans forward, elbows on his knees, as he rubs his tired eyes and neck. "Tomorrow we will receive five hundred and eighty-two flints and nearly twenty-one hundred cartridges. That puts us at ten cartridges per man. It seems whatever we are getting ready for is more than rumors, and that being the case, we should have twenty to twenty-five per man"

Stephen sets his quill aside and stands up, shaking out his cramped hands and wrists. "Whether it's the redcoats sowing false rumors, or a not-so-secret plan that we've become privy to, we need to be prepared. I've been thinking about this for the past day, and realize that until now we were not so well prepared to defend, though our works looked impressive." Stephen sighs. "Then to add another concern, I heard a rumor that Roxbury is just as likely to be General Gage's target."

Isaac stands and stretches. "Then I would expect General Ward has another regiment guarding the Boston Neck as well. Yet, I think this must be more than just an assignment to guard the Neck. You're right; on the surface our preparation appears good, and fully arming the guards on the Charlestown and Boston Necks is an improvement, but if the enemy beat the drums to attack this instant, I know not what our next step would be. One company of guards could not hold them for more than a few minutes." Isaac shakes his head to clear out thoughts of being overrun. "What are you working at tonight?"

"I'm finishing the forms for the companies to use for their rolls tomorrow. What about you? Hear any news today?"

"Captain Towne's company has the guard tomorrow. The men from Wilton got split up amongst three companies. Captains Mann and Crosby each with a quarter, while Captain Walker has half. Seems strange to split the men of a town, don't you think?"

"Yes, although Colonel Reed ordered the companies to be balanced with respect to the number of men assigned to each. When Captain Crosby arrived, he had over a hundred and twenty, which is over two full companies, according to this new arrangement. They had to be split somehow. Captain Crosby already has good men in Wilkins and Maxwell for lieutenants. Walker and Mann had none. I don't think it will be a problem, do you?"

"No, I suppose not. There's an officer they know and respect in every company." Isaac takes his seat again, picks up his quill, and tries to focus on tallying the figures for how much food the regiment consumed over the previous week. After several seconds he gives into what is really bothering him. "If it comes to a battle, do you think we... I mean you and I... will get to fight?"

"Oh yes. We are assigned under Captain Crosby."

Isaac's shoulders relax and his sigh of relief is louder and longer than he expected. "Good, it would be wrong to be left behind." He goes back to work, his quill scratching furiously for several minutes before a new thought strikes him. "I think both sides are tired of sitting on their hands. My feeling is we will try to fortify this side of Bunker Hill soon. That's the closest and highest point on the other side of the Neck, plus none of His Majesty's ships or gun boats have bothered to come up the Mystic. Bunker Hill would be an ideal location for our fieldpieces to cover us while taking more of the peninsula."

Stephen, intrigued by the idea, gets up and begins pacing. "I think Admiral Gage would have something to say about that. It seems a warship could be brought to bear on that position, and even our current location. So why not? I agree with you; things have gotten to the point that any provocation will lead to a battle. Arming our regiment—and I heard Stark's as well—is effectively building a large supply of dry tinder. I'm worried all this preparation will make it easy for us to take the first shot."

Isaac snorts a short laugh. "I know a lot of men who would volunteer to be the one to discharge that first load into a company of redcoats venturing too close."

Stephen laughs. "I have to admit I'm curious. If there's another battle, I don't imagine a peaceful reconciliation will be possible. With our boys turning the redcoats back at Grape Island three weeks ago, and again at Chelsea two weeks ago, I think the redcoat officers are feeling their royal pride has been pricked. They cannot stand to lose, and their honor and reputations are at stake. But their men; well, they're only in it for the coin. Our men are in it for everything."

"Aye, that's true. The redcoats do suffer from false pride. Our officers and many of the men were in the last war and have as much or more experience in battle." Isaac tallies two more days of rations, then takes up where he left off. "This notion of liberty we've had these past few years has become something else entirely. I cannot fully explain it, but I have a strong sense of hope for the future. Do you?"

"I hadn't thought of it that way. That's a good notion. Do you think it's worth fighting for?"

"Absolutely."

Stephen rubs his forehead. "Well, let's finish up. We muster at seven in the morning."

"Sergeant Stone and I have a busy day tomorrow. We've got kettles, wood, and ammunition arriving."

Stephen's look changes, as though an interesting idea has struck him. "Your sergeant, he seems a dependable sort?"

"Yes. Good with wagons, teams, and figures. Why do you ask?"

"It's good to know who we can rely on when it comes to ascertaining the men's state of mind."

Isaac thinks a moment. "Add Sergeant William Adrian Hawkins to that list. Unflappable, and a keen mind. I know him well, as he's from Wilton."

Stephen cleans his nib, places it carefully inside a small box where he keeps several spares, and rises. "Good to know. You about done?"

"Yes." Isaac cleans and dries the nib of his quill pen. "Let's be about putting these lamps out. Captain Hinds has the guard tonight. I'll let him know we're finished, and to keep anyone out until morning."

•••

A thin Major Hale enters the regiment's headquarters three days later on June 16. His face is wan, but he smiles as he sees Isaac and Stephen.

Isaac returns Hale's smile. "Major Hale, it's good to see you back, sir."

"Thank you, Quartermaster Frye. I could lie about no longer. The rest helped, but it chafed me; though I was sorely ill, to be abed for so many days." Major Hale gazes about the room taking in the arrangement of desks, and his eyes come to rest on a vacant desk. "This is my desk?" he inquires, and Stephen confirms that it is.

Colonel Reed enters the house less than a minute later. "Major Hale, I thought I saw you come in as I was approaching. I am pleased to see you well again." He turns to Isaac. "Any news, Quartermaster?"

"Yessir. A wagon of shovels arrived with orders for us to guard them until further notice. All of the ammunition we've received has been distributed. It seems similar preparations have been made at Roxbury. Though I cannot for my life figure where General Gage will go if his troops can punch through. We outnumber them badly."

"Thank you." Reed strides to his desk. "I was thinking, perhaps you should pay Colonel James Frye a visit. He commands the Tenth

Massachusetts, and he is your cousin, is he not?"

"He does and is, sir."

"See what you can learn from him about these shovels. If they are to dig fortifications, I'd like to know where. Make sure the wagon is out of sight of the enemy."

Isaac stands and salutes. "Yessir, and the wagon is already behind a house, so no chance of it being viewed by the enemy."

•••

Isaac walks into the camp of the 10th Massachusetts Regiment fifteen minutes later. The encampment is on the outskirts of Cambridge, among the closest of the Massachusetts regiments to Winter Hill. The part of the encampment near the house James Frye uses as headquarters is buzzing with activity like a beehive shortly after being struck with a stick. Men are rushing about, dressing while rushing into their company's place in the regimental parade formation,. Isaac finds his cousin coming out of the rambling farmhouse that serves as his headquarters. Colonel James Frye is in his late sixties and is walking with the support of a cane.

Isaac quickens his step, waves, and calls out, "Colonel Frye!"

The older man stops and turns slowly. "Isaac?" He catches himself and smiles, and clears his throat. "I mean, Lieutenant Frye. I'm afraid some of my men are mustering and I haven't much time. Do you need something?"

Indicating the sturdy rosewood cane, Isaac asks, "Sir, your gout again?"

"I'm afraid so. Damn bad, today of all days." He clears his throat with a wet cough. "Could barely get my damn boot on."

"Your regiment is marching?"

"Yes, a part." He motions Isaac to come closer, and in a in a low voice meant only for Isaac's ears, pronounces, "Sending some of the companies to fortify Bunker Hill tonight. Make sure your regiment keeps a good watch. We want no surprises."

"In that case I won't tarry. I had a free moment and thought to visit, mostly to see how things are with you, and to have any news from Andover."

"Hopefully, you'll have another such moment soon and I'll be able to catch you up on all of that. But for now, I must see to my regiment."

"Thank you, and good day, sir." Isaac salutes smartly. His cousin returns the salute with a smile that says he is proud to see Isaac doing his part. Isaac turns and heads back the way he came at a brisk pace.

•••

That evening, just as the sky turns fully dark, Isaac and Stephen exit their headquarters to stand in front of the house, observing several bodies of troops marching from behind Ploughed Hill. They count nearly a thousand men who have quietly arrived.

Stephen nudges Isaac and motions toward one of the officers marching by. "That looks like Colonel Prescott of Massachusetts in command of these troops."

Isaac closes his eyes for a moment, to help his night vision come faster, and looks again. "I suppose so. I don't know the man very well. Look—there in the rear. They've got artillery, just like I predicted, and my cousin says they go to fortify Bunker Hill."

"I see. Looks like they've got four pieces. I hope this doesn't go as badly as I've worried it could. If they can fortify the hill by morning, we will have the high ground, and our reinforcements will be close by. If not..." Stephen leaves the consequences unspoken.

Isaac, keeping his voice low, asserts, "I think it's a good strategy. We won't be able to reach Boston with the artillery, and maybe not even Charles River where they've got their gunships, so it should be seen as just tightening the cordon, but not so much as to become over-extended or be seen by General Gage as an outright provocation."

Stephen weighs his friend's words. "Let's hope that's how General Gage sees it. I forgot to ask about your cousin. You said his regiment is sending some men with this group tonight. Is he going, too?"

"I don't think so. His gout was bothering him today. I hope he wasn't going tonight. He doesn't need much sleep, but he's nearly seventy and the gout doesn't get better with activity."

"Nearly seventy!" Stephen whistles softly. "Is he fit to take the field?"

"For him, it's mind over matter. He's as stubborn and sharp-tongued as they come, and on top of that he has two sons and a son-in-law in the Tenth. He won't want to let them down or show any weakness."

"He sounds irascible. You speak as if you know him well."

Isaac, with a little wistfulness creeping into his voice, explains, "I spent a good deal of time at his inn after my father died. My mother remarried a few months later. I was nine. By the time I was twelve, I didn't much like being at home. I was the youngest. My brothers were grown and spent time serving in the French and Indian War. My sisters were older as well, and both married within a few years. While my brothers were still living in Andover, I spent time with them, but Simon moved to Fryeburg with my Uncle Joseph, and Abiel moved on. I got used to being on my own, or at least that's what I thought when I started spending time at the inn. James owns it. He decided I should earn my keep, and paid me to clean the place and take care of the stables, and whatever else came up. Later I learned my mother had asked James to make sure I was safe."

"Sounds as though she had your best interests at heart, in spite of your inclinations." Stephen pauses. "How is she now?"

"She died six years ago. I made my amends with her for not being a dutiful son. That isn't my nature, and she and agreed on that. My Elizabeth made sure I had done that even before we married. I am grateful for that, as my mother and I enjoyed each other's company for more than a year before she died."

Stephen nods and wipes his brow on his shirtsleeve. The evening is warm, and the cool sea breeze that usually makes this time quite pleasant has not arrived. "It's good all that turned out well for you. Strains on family ties are always difficult."

"I am lucky to have Elizabeth for my wife. She has a knack of helping me see the world rightly."

"I know the feeling; my Hannah does the same for me."

The two stand in silence for a minute, watching the troops quietly file toward Bunker Hill, before Isaac predicts in a subdued tone, "I think there will be a clash tomorrow." His breath catches. "I am surprised I said that aloud. But my gut says there will be fighting tomorrow."

Stephen agrees. "Mine too. That's not another supper of pork and biscuits talking, either. Let's get some sleep. If we're right, it will be an early morning."

•••

The boom of cannon around four o'clock in the morning on June 17 jolts Isaac from a deep, dreamless sleep. For a moment he doesn't know where he is, and reaches out, finding the side of his tent, which resets his mind to the present moment. He grabs his hunting knife and then cautiously crawls out of his tent. The northeastern sky barely glows where the sun will begin to show in ten or so minutes. A second report sound far too close for comfort, but Isaac sorts the fact that he does not hear the crackling whistle of a cannon ball closing in anywhere nearby. His ears more than his eyes tell him to look down the hill, past Charlestown's millpond. There he can see that a pair of gondolas, which are smaller gunboats carrying cannon that fire smaller balls, have moved into place. Another of the small cannon flashes brightly, followed shortly by a boom. Isaac ducks down, even though his eyes tell him the cannon is aiming at a position near the center of the Charlestown Peninsula.

Isaac looks to the left and sees that Stephen is also out of his tent and peering into the pre-dawn shadows. For a few seconds, they strain to see what is happening. To the right of Bunker Hill the foreground is far too dark to make out details. Isaac can see no movement there, or atop Bunker Hill. Other men have come out of their tents, though none report anything of use.

"I cannot see our men. But look there—" Stephen points just past the millpond and the gondolas, to a warship now moving into position.

Stephen shudders. "We're almost within long range here. Another hundred yards and I'm sure we would be. But there's something amiss. They should be firing upon Bunker Hill, and their aim looks to be over the top of Charlestown itself."

"You're right; I think the other ships are firing to the interior of the peninsula. That makes no sense. My cousin said they were to fortify Bunker Hill."

Stephen shakes his head. "With this light, we cannot see. We need to get some eyes on this from the other side of the river, to learn the situation."

Isaac looks quickly towards the Mystic River and then back to Stephen. "Let's go before we're missed. We will be back in less than two hours." He starts back into his tent.

"Wait. I've got a better idea. Find Captain Crosby and ask for Hawkins. Get Sergeant Stone as well. Colonel Reed will certainly miss us, but he won't miss either of them. Tell them to make note of all positions and fortifications."

"You're right." Isaac turns back toward his tent. "I'll meet you at headquarters in a few minutes."

By six o'clock that morning, Colonel Reed and all his staff officers are present in their headquarters. Reed is particularly impatient, pacing from the door to his desk. "What is keeping them? From what I can see, last night's detachment did not fortify Bunker Hill as they had orders to do."

There is a rapid knock on the door. "Enter!" Reed's voice is gruff and tense.

Sergeants Stone and Hawkins enter the room. Both appear energized and hyper-alert. Reed looks each in the eye to get some idea which of the two appears most capable of giving a brief factual report. He settles on Hawkins. "Sergeant Hawkins, what did you learn?"

Hawkins is ready, clearly having thought of what he might say as he returned to headquarters. "Sir, they didn't fortify Bunker's Hill. Not at all. Not even the lower part on the other side of us. They dug in on top of the smaller hill overlooking Charlestown. I believe it to be called Breed's Hill. They are taking cannon fire, but it looks like their earthworks are sufficiently deep and they are continuing their work. The northern half of the peninsula looks as ordinary as it did yesterday. The—"

"You mean there were none of the King's ships or gondolas approaching on the Mystic?"

"No sir. We asked a local from that side of Medford. He said Admiral Gage has never come up the Mystic to take depth measurements, only the bays and on the Charles River."

"Thank you, Sergeant. Do you have anything to add, Sergeant Stone?"

"Just that our fieldpieces didn't seem well placed. I would have thought they would be protected, but at the moment they're in a field, almost like they have been forgotten. At least, I think they are out of range of the ships."

In an instant Reed is in deep thought. He paces a while, then remembers the sergeants are still in the room. "Thank you both. You're dismissed."

The officers are silent until the sergeants leave. As soon as the door closes, Reed spins toward Gilman. "Colonel Gilman, get this information to Colonel Stark, General Folsom, and General Ward. Omit the part about the position of the cannon, as I believe it is not material. Colonel Gridley will have plenty of time to move the cannon into position, should that become necessary." Not waiting for a response, he turns to Hale with further instructions. "Major Hale, make sure our men are ready to march within the hour." Then to Isaac. "Quartermaster Frye, ascertain whether there is any more ammunition available to us."

Isaac is on his feet immediately. "Yessir."

Together Gilman, Hale, and Isaac salute. Isaac hurries behind them out the door.

The War Has Begun

5 BATTLE OF BREEDS HILL

"The officers placed their men in as good shape as they could, but they were a motley looking set, no two dressed alike. Some were armed with fowling pieces, some with rifles, others with muskets without bayonets."

Andrew Leavitt of Amherst, New Hampshire, describing Captain Crosby's company two weeks later on July 2, 1775, just prior to being reviewed by General George Washington.

Nearly three hours later, outside Colonel Reed's headquarters, the 3rd New Hampshire Regiment is assembled in a column, four men abreast. Isaac and Stephen are with Colonel Reed, who is not mounted, as the regiment will travel on foot. They can see other regiments, not far away, on the Cambridge side of Ploughed Hill, ready to march. In the other direction, they see Colonel Stark's regiment paraded in a similar formation on the road alongside the Mystic River.

Reed looks up and down the length of his regiment's column. "Quartermaster Frye, were you able to acquire more ammunition?"

"No more could be had; we now have at least nine cartridges a man, and most have ten. That includes what we had on hand for guarding the Neck."

Reed sighs. Isaac is not sure whether it is disgust or

disappointment. Reed asks rhetorically, "So little? Very well, it is what we have, and we will make the most of it. You and Lieutenant Peabody go fall in with Captain Crosby's company. We will march following the Massachusetts regiments—" He points toward the Cambridge side of Ploughed Hill. "—and will follow Colonel Stark's regiment." He points to the troops along the Mystic River road.

Isaac takes in what Colonel Reed shows him. "Yessir."

Isaac and Stephen stride over to the second of Reed's nine companies and fall in with Captain Crosby's lieutenants at the rear of the company.

Fifteen minutes later, the New Hampshire regiments are still in the same locations. A rider canters in from the road out of Cambridge. As he draws near, Isaac recognizes him as Major Samuel Osgood, one of General Ward's aides-de-camp. Osgood canters his horse up to Reed, and dismounts.

"Colonel Reed, General Ward orders your regiment to remain here, as we have yet to ascertain whether General Gage will attack through Roxbury to Cambridge, or directly upon the works Colonel Prescott's men have put up."

"Thank you, Major Osgood. Is there anything else?"

"Can you direct me to Colonel Stark? We will be sending some of his men over to assist Colonel Prescott."

Reed points out Stark's regiment. "He is over there on the river road."

•••

Almost two o'clock, and no news or orders.

Colonel Reed and his staff officers have moved into the regiment's headquarters to keep out of the hot sun that is sapping everyone's energy. Lieutenant Colonel Isaac Wyman from Colonel Stark's regiment is waiting with them. Every few minutes the sound of cannon fire from the ships in the Back Bay can be heard. There is a knock at the door, and before anyone can respond, Major Osgood enters.

Reed was out of his chair at the first knock. "Major Osgood, I trust we have at last gained an understanding of what General Gage intends. Do we finally have orders?"

"Yes. Yours and Colonel Stark's regiments are to march immediately, and General Ward has placed both your regiments under the command of Colonel Prescott. General Gage has just landed a sizable force at Moulton's Point, on the far side of the peninsula. Prepare your men to go into battle, Colonel Reed." Nodding to Lieutenant Colonel Wyman, Osgood continues, "Colonel Wyman, I presume you are here for the purpose of learning this same information on behalf of Colonel Stark."

Wyman nods. "Undoubtedly, Major Osgood. Thank you. We will be marching within minutes." Wyman is immediately moving, gathering his coat and hat.

Turning back to Reed, Osgood wraps up his briefing. "I've already given orders for several Massachusetts regiments to cross the Neck, they should not delay you, as I expect they have begun marching by now."

Reed and his officers, having gathered their coats and hats while the major was speaking, stand ready. Reed thanks Osgood, then turns to his staff officers. "Gentlemen, let us be on our way. The liberties we have staked our honor upon require our action on that field. They wait for us to wrest them from the hands of our oppressors." The colonel's words cause each man to look to the others. Isaac sees only unshakable resolve.

Ten minutes later, the order to march finally comes. Stark's regiment passes by, but soon stops for over a minute before continuing. Isaac, marching next to Stephen, mutters, "I wonder what that was all about." He cannot help noticing that the Massachusetts regiments have stepped aside, giving way to the New Hampshire regiments. "I would love to have heard what Colonel Stark told those regiments that made them give way so quickly. I thought they were supposed to march ahead of us."

Stephen turns with a slight grin. "Me too. I hope things up ahead are better organized than what Sergeants Hawkins and Stone saw earlier. I heard Colonel Stark was here on the peninsula just after dawn, confirming what we learned, and that there was much work still needed to complete the works."

The column is marching at what seems a deliberate pace, given the gunboats in the Back Bay continue to fire upon them. The shots consistently fall short, and the men take heart from one another's continued good health. Both regiments cross the narrow part of the Neck without suffering a single casualty.

After they pass the Neck, the column turns toward Bunker Hill.

Isaac nudges Stephen. "I'm glad I wrote Elizabeth last night, given our predictions for today proved accurate."

"Aye. I must have been writing to Hannah at the same time."

They lapse into silence again as the column continues marching. The day is hot and muggy, with hardly a breeze. Isaac keeps his focus on the back of the man in front him. Without realizing it, he starts counting his steps as they turn onto the road that leads up and over Bunker Hill.

Stephen takes in the scene as they come to the top of Bunker Hill. The recently cut hay in the field before them lies in neat rows; the smell of it is pleasant. Nearly a mile away, the long boats carrying the enemy soldiers from their ships land on the shore. Their bright-red coats create a sense of incongruous and stark contrast with the greens, browns, and blues of the landscape.

Stark's and then Reed's regiments pause upon the crown of the hill to allow their men to orient themselves to the lay of the land on the Charlestown Peninsula. As Reed's regiment halts at the top, Isaac finally looks up and mentions to Stephen, "Six hundred and fifty-seven paces to the top." The order comes to continue marching, now down toward the center of the peninsula

"I suppose it was. Oddly, I don't remember much of it. Such a beautiful day and place. I dread," his voice turns rich with irony, "we are about to turn this quiet scene into pure hell."

As they march, Isaac continues to takes in the scenery. "It makes me miss my own farm."

Stephen murmurs in agreement, then sets his jaw as they continue the march down in silence. They are nearly to the base of Bunker Hill when they receive the order to halt.

The air is hot, with little breeze, and shimmers as the thick grass dries under the midday sun. Isaac wipes his brow on his sleeve, and looks up to see the sun still nearly directly overhead. He puts a hand on Stephen's shoulder, and offers, "Let us be sure to watch over one another so we both can see our farms again."

Stephen, with a serious look, nods in agreement. "I pray we both will enjoy those liberties that now seem so precious."

Ahead, at the front of the column, Isaac sees Colonels Reed and Stark conferring with Colonel Prescott at the crossroads near the bottom of the hill. The conference breaks up and Stark leads his regiment off to the left. Reed orders his regiment forward, but calls a halt at the crossroad. Isaac can see him speaking again with Prescott, then Reed calls out, "Captain Crosby! Attend us."

Crosby strides out to meet the two colonels. He listens for a few moments before they dismiss him to walk back to his company.

Instead of falling back into place, Crosby commands his company to face to the right, march forward twelve paces, and halt. Crosby motions to the other captains, and they order their companies forward, closing the gap.

Crosby addresses his company in a clear, strong voice. "Men, we have been ordered to guard our right flank from within Charlestown. Once there, we will break into squads, each with an officer, and will take positions with the purpose of affording an advantage to fire on redcoats as they advance towards Colonel Prescott's works. Quartermaster Frye, you'll have charge of the Wilton men; Adjutant Peabody, the Mont Vernon men; Lieutenant Wilkins, with your brother's squad; and I will split the rest of the Amherst men with Lieutenant Maxwell." Crosby steps back a few paces and barks, "Company! To the left face! Forward march!"

Crosby's company marches on the road that soon becomes the main street through the built-up portion of Charlestown. They pass by the patriots' cannon positioned in a farmer's field a hundred yard from Charlestown's outer buildings. Isaac mentally traces an arc, which if correct, is aimed into Boston at the enemy's battery on Copps Hill. A dozen steps later the big guns from the HMS Cerberus on their right, with her twenty-four nine-pound guns, and the HMS Somerset, with her seventy guns, ahead of them send more than a thundering volley of balls toward Breed's Hill. The shock of being so close and well within range causes many to duck involuntarily. Between houses Isaac catches glimpses of the impacts on the newly dug earthworks a few hundred yards away on Breed's Hill.

It is nearly half past two o'clock when they reach the west end of Charlestown. They meet two Massachusetts companies also tasked with guarding the flank formed by the outer buildings and homes of Charlestown. Crosby confers with the other captains while the British ships continue to send cannon fire over their heads. A private in the rank ahead of Isaac mutters, "Feels like we are not expected to be here." In under a minute Crosby returns to address his company.

His tone is less public now, and he makes eye contact with many of the men he knows. "Gentlemen, we will be in the center of the northern side of town. Captain Wheeler will be on our left. Our job is to fire into the enemy's ranks as they march by us. Aim for their officers, if possible. Be as annoying to their discipline as possible." He glances at the ground, deciding what more to say. It is my privilege to lead you—each of you, whether I've known you for years or just these few months. We are fighting for our homes, our families, and our livelihoods." His gaze turns to steel and his voice hardens to iron, pounding out each word on an anvil. "These are our fields. These are our homes. Gage uses the regulars as instruments of injustice and oppression. He sets aside natural law and our rights and liberties. We will not have it!

Isaac and several others take the cue and shout, "Huzzah!"

Crosby immediately barks back. "We will not have it!"

This time all shout a resounding, "Huzzah! Huzzah!, Huzzah!"

Crosby takes a step back and comes to attention. The men do the same. Crosby raps out his orders. "Break into the squads I assigned earlier and take positions. Let us go defend our country, our land, and our liberty!"

Isaac finds the men from Wilton, who are led by Corporal Eleazer Kingsbury, mid-twenties, a farmer with a steady dependable manner. With him are the Greele brothers—Jonathan, age twenty, and John, who is just seventeen. Their father lives along the same road as Elizabeth's parents. Their cousin Nathaniel Greele is with them—a farmer in his early thirties who also hails from Wilton. Other Wilton volunteers include Archelaus Kenney, the solidly built seventeen-year-old middle son of Wilton's blacksmith; Nathaniel Sawyer, in his mid-twenties, one of the two storekeepers in Wilton; and completing the squad is Jonas Perry, a farmer who is of an age with Isaac.

Isaac adopts a hard look, doing his best to imitate Captain Crosby's intensity. "Everyone have their ammunition? Nine or ten cartridges each?"

Most are nodding their heads, though the Greeles are smiling a bit too broadly. The younger Greele explains with a big grin, "We brought us a few extra we didn't exactly tell you about, Quartermaster. It's ours and we wanted to be the ones to use it."

Isaac shrugs. "Put it to good use. I'll not be counting or writing anything today. Let's find a good position to fire from."

•••

Isaac and the men he has charge of take turns surveying the fields below Breed's Hill through the rear windows of the upper floor of a house on the north side of Charlestown. Each has the chance to learn the lay of the land before them. It is shortly after three o'clock. To their left is the summit of Breed's Hill. A little over two hundred yards away they can see the freshly dug fortification built by Colonel Prescott's command overnight. The sun is still high and directly opposite the works, making details difficult to discern. Occasionally, they glimpse movement atop the fortification as men peer out over the top of earthworks.

Isaac checks to the right and realizes with an involuntary spasm that the redcoats are almost upon them, less than two hundred yards away. In his mind, Isaac runs through the sequence of commands he will give to direct the men's firing. Then he steps back and motions for Kingsbury and the Greeles to get a look. Isaac closes his eyes for a few seconds, fixing the image of the last time he saw Elizabeth and his sons. After a deep breath, he opens his eyes, and has another look at the approaching regulars. If their course holds true, they will soon pass within forty yards of the house! Now they can hear the firing of shots by the Massachusetts company similarly hidden in the eastern portions of Charlestown.

Isaac whispers to the men in the room, "They look to be the Forty-Seventh Foot and then marines. Probably the same regiments who attacked at Lexington and Concord."

Nathaniel Greele growls, "Then let's make them pay for their misdeeds."

Jonas Perry's countenance has turned hard. "I was born and lived in Lexington before coming to Wilton with my brothers. We knew some of them who were killed. An eye for an eye."

Isaac holds his hand up so he can continue. "Shoot as far as you dare. The more redcoats we drop, the fewer bayonets they will have with which to charge our works. Make every bullet count. Fire at a small angle along their ranks to minimize your chances of missing. Four of us will fire, then back away and reload so the other four can fire."

Corporal Kingsbury waits for Isaac to finish before adding, "Wait 'til the Quartermaster gives the order. Watch for any who break ranks or are ordered to deal with us. We will need to attend to them quickly."

Isaac looks around. "Everyone loaded?" In low voices they all indicate their readiness. "Less than a minute now. The Greeles take positions with me, and fire on my order. Corporal, you command the others as we withdraw to reload."

Kingsbury confirms the order. "Yessir."

At that moment, they feel and hear the tremendous concussion of mass firing from the other side of Breed's Hill. A few moments later the first rank of British marines marches in line with the house, then a second and a third.

Isaac, in a calm and measured voice, gives the order, "Take aim... Fire." Four shots fire simultaneously.

Before stepping back from the window, Isaac tries to see through the smoke from their firing, which has immediately obscured the view. There is no way to discern whether it was his eyes or his mind playing a trick, and the image of two redcoat marines falling becomes a memory fragment, disjointed from the memory of his voice giving the order to fire. In the same measured tones, he repeats, "Change positions... Reload." One of the Greeles mutters to one of the others moving into place, "It's damn hard to miss."

Four more shots ring out and more marines fall. They repeat this sequence four times. As they fire, the room gradually begins to fill with gun smoke. Then they hear a loud pelting. It sounds like bursts of big hailstones striking the roof and eastern wall of the house. The noise is loud enough to break their rhythm. Isaac and the Greeles fire once again, and again the house is pelted hard with what sounds like hail.

Kingsbury levels his musket. "Take aim..." But he comes up short, his eyes dart left and right to locate the source of a sharp whiff of something unexpected. He turns to Isaac and the Greeles to announce, "I smell wood smoke."

Isaac orders the younger Greele, "Jonathan, check below. See what's happening on the front of the house."

Jonathan Greele rams a cartridge home, replaces the rammer, and moves purposefully to the stairway.

"Fire!" yells Kingsbury, and four more musket balls blaze out towards the ranks of redcoats.

Less than ten seconds after leaving, Jonathan Greele bursts up the stairs. "House on fire! Get out fast!"

Isaac turns to Kingsbury and calmly requests, "Corporal, lead the way. John and Nathanial, cover him. It could be a trap. I'll bring up the rear."

Coats and hats forgotten, the men move quickly down the steep staircase. Smoke roils from the east wall on the first floor. As they emerge from the house, they see flames licking around the sides of the house and engulfing the roof. Kingsbury motions them to the west side of the house. "The enemy's cannons are firing hot grapeshot to burn us out."

Isaac calls out, "Keep low—"

Two thunderous volleys of musketry cause them to turn towards Breed's Hill, where about a hundred yards away the British marines exchange their first close volleys with the Americans behind Prescott's earthworks.

Pointing to the west, Isaac shouts, "Get around the next house, quick! Cover and reload."

Once they have reloaded, Isaac points to Kingsbury. "Corporal, take Sawyer and Perry and go house-to-house. Make sure our men know the town is on fire. Count to five after each load of grapeshot lands, then move. Use the buildings for cover. Kenney, stay with us and we will keep firing."

Another volley of grapeshot rains down, coinciding with another exchange of musket fire on the hill. A few seconds later Kingsbury, Sawyer, and Perry start running as Isaac shouts, "Go!" Each man heads to a different house. Isaac points to the next house to the west, and starts running, keeping low, motioning for the others to follow. They take shelter beside this house.

Isaac yells to be heard over the noise of musketry and screaming from the battlefield, which is only fifty yards in front of them, "Take aim! ... Fire! ... Reload!"

Isaac peers around the corner of the home to see Stephen striding purposefully toward him from the center part of Charlestown. His face is marked with smears of soot and gunpowder, but his eyes show him to be the man in charge. "Isaac! Get your men ahead and cover our retreat. Then join with Colonel Wyman. His men are guarding a fieldpiece outside town." Stephen points in the direction just left of and behind Prescott's earthworks.

Isaac shouts, "On our way!" Then turning to his men, still having to shout, he urges, "Let's go! They've stopped firing grapeshot. Don't fire unless some of those marines break away and come for us."

Isaac notices Kingsbury rushing toward him from between two buildings, with Sawyer and Perry ten steps behind. Isaac waves them to come rejoin the squad. Hot winds from the fires are picking up. The eight of them back away, covering the retreat of Crosby's company as well as the contingent from Woodbridge's Massachusetts regiment.

In the two minutes it takes the three companies assigned to Charlestown to escape, the buildings become a conflagration, with flames soaring over a hundred feet high. To Isaac, it seems the shock of the towering flames and smoke signals a lull in the battle. Soon the roaring flames drown out all other sounds. The men coming from

Charlestown hurry, keeping low, towards the position held by two companies under Lieutenant Colonel Wyman, on the lower slope of Breeds Hill. Wyman commands a pasture about fifty yards below the west side of the main fortification. His troops are deployed in a line designed to cut off any route the enemy could take to gain access to the rear of Breed's Hill, where the entrance to the fortifications is located.

•••

Within ten minutes Crosby's company and the others who retreated from Charlestown more than double the number of troops at Wyman's position, five hundred in all. Crosby and his officers stand behind their men, who stand two ranks deep, ready to defend against any flanking maneuver. Just over two hundred yards to their left they see the ranks of redcoat marines advancing again, in full gear, on the redoubt. The heat of the day, intensified by the flames engulfing Charlestown, seems more likely to deter a flanking movement than Wyman's augmented command.

Captain Crosby checks his cartridge box and finds it empty. He turns to Isaac. "Quartermaster, check with the other squad leaders and find out how many cartridges our men still have. Half of my squad is out; the others only have one each."

A few minutes later Isaac reports back to his captain. "Sir, the two squads who were on this side of Charlestown have two or three left, those who were on the east have one or none. Adjutant Peabody's squad still has one or two cartridges each. In all, about one hundred cartridges."

Crosby thinks a moment. "Have the men with three rounds give one to Peabody's men and any others with just one. I will use those who have two cartridges to check any advance of the enemy. Be ready."

As they watch the advancing redcoat marines, Isaac states to Stephen, who stands to his left, "For the life of me I don't understand the stiff, fool-headed notions of those redcoat officers. The only way we will lose is running out of ammunition. Why don't they put off the packs and coats? Their men are half dead from the heat when they come into our range. It is a cruel sort of butchery they force us to do."

"Aye. I've no love of slaughter or battle." Stephen shakes his head in grim disappointment. "You did good getting your men to warn the others of the fire. I was only a minute ahead of you. Your corporal had found most of Crosby's men already, so we were able to move away from our positions earlier."

"Did we lose any men?"

"John Cole was killed, and James Hutchison wounded badly; both from Amherst."

"Goddammit!" Isaac's knuckles go white around the barrel of his musket as he grinds it into the toe of his boot. In the foreground, the *en masse* exchange of musket fire signals the battle has again commenced, with the redcoats stopping to fire, then advancing once again on the earthworks. None look to be moving toward Wyman's position.

Stephen goes on. "We carried them out. The company from Woodbridge's regiment fared worse. They bore the brunt of the grapeshot and were under fire from the first. The redcoats had found their discipline again by the time they marched by us. How—"

Another tremendous volley of musket fire from the earthworks interrupts Stephen. The volley repeats every few seconds as the two sides exchange fire. They only catch a glimpse before smoke from the exchange obscures their view and rolls on the wind in their direction, prompting Captain Crosby to realize their possible danger. "Keep low! Take a knee," he shouts to his men, who immediately drop down. He continues, "Keep quiet. Watch and listen for flankers."

Now that the conflagration in Charlestown has died down and the men are still enough to hear everything, the cries and screams of wounded and dying men on the battlefield predominate their hearing. Broken by the volleys of musket fire, the screams turn guts, set jaws, and close some eyes. A few men cover their ears attempting to shut out the agony obscured by the smoke on the field in front of them.

•••

A little over an hour later, the field in front of the earthworks is nearly quiet. The British marines move forward again, this time with no packs or heavy wool coats to sap their strength. Lieutenant Colonel Wyman, who has just come from the earthworks, calls the officers from the three Charlestown companies to meet.

"Gentlemen, the word is the marines opposing us have three regiments of reinforcements. The men in our works have little ammunition left and cannot expect to hold the ground. We are to cover their retreat. We will do so back to the base of Bunker Hill, and we must check the redcoats there to ensure our men are off the field safely."

Isaac asks, "Sir, is there any news of how Colonels Reed and Stark fared?"

Wyman turns grim. "The slaughter of redcoats on the far side of the redoubt was far greater than in front of us. It appears we have won that side of the field as no redcoats advance there now. They have all concentrated on the works above us. Stark's and Reed's men only have one cartridge for every three men." He pauses and turns to Crosby. "My men have the most ammunition left, and so we will offer the first check in covering the retreat. Position your men at the base of Bunker Hill just past the cart path connecting Main Street and the center road."

Crosby nods. "Yes. Understood, sir."

Wyman instructs the two other Charlestown companies to cover the retreat of the artillery and to assist in moving them if needed. Wyman scans the faces of the officers. "Any questions?" He waits a few seconds. "Very well. Captain Crosby, move your men now."

Fifteen minutes later, at the base of Bunker Hill, Captain Crosby's men array themselves in one wide rank, positioned to cover the entire field of retreat. The men are still organized into the squads used in Charlestown, though the men with two rounds of ammunition are positioned on the right where they most expect the enemy to pursue the retreating patriots. Several companies evacuate the redoubt, moving down the road that runs through the middle of the peninsula to Bunker Hill. The men in Crosby's company can see the redcoats topping and overwhelming the earthworks, where there are still dozens of brave men repulsing them to buy time for those who are retreating. Lieutenant Colonel Wyman's men begin actively firing at flanking companies of redcoats, initially halting their attempt to get around to the rear of the earthworks, but within two minutes they are outnumbered and forced to slowly give ground.

"Isaac!" Stephen is pointing to a figure riding from their right toward the earthworks. "Your cousin?"

Isaac turns to see Colonel James Frye riding toward the retreating men just as a company of redcoats pushes Wyman's troops back by dint of superior numbers.

Crosby sees the situation. "Peabody! Frye! Take your squads and give Colonel Wyman some relief."

Isaac tells his squad to follow Stephen's marching orders. Stephen barks out his orders in a quick, even beat. "At a quick step. March!"

The sixteen men march out rapidly. About forty yards short of Wyman, and with Colonel Frye having stopped not far away, directing what must have been men of his own regiment toward the road that would take them by Crosby's position, Stephen shouts, "Detachment, halt!" Without waiting, he follows quickly with, "Poise firelock! ... Cock firelock!"

Wyman's men are now running, passing around and behind the detachment commanded by Stephen. Pursuing at a quick march is a company of about fifty redcoat marines, who halt thirty-five yards away. Colonel Frye, who waited for the last of his men to move off to safety, finally turns back to see he is closer to the redcoats than the men covering his regiment's retreat.

Stephen, not missing a beat, commands, "Take aim! ... Fire!" Nearly a dozen redcoats fall, including their commander.

Again, Stephen does not wait. "Poise! ... Half cock! ... Handle cartridge!"

The redcoats haven't yet realized that their commander is down. They stand at attention, waiting for orders, and looking more nervous by the second.

Stephen continues calling out the commands the men have drilled for months on. "Prime! ... Shut pan! ... Draw rammer!"

One of the redcoat sergeants realizes what has happened and steps out, confident in still outnumbering the sixteen rebels by three to one. He starts his own sequence of commands. "Poise firelock!"

He is interrupted when Colonel Frye discharges his pistol, firing at the sergeant, but missing. Colonel Frye turns his horse and follows his retreating men.

Stephen— "Ram cartridge!"

The redcoat sergeant keeps his focus. "Cock firelock!"

Stephen— "Return rammer!"

The redcoat sergeant directs the attention of two of his soldiers towards Colonel Frye, then commands the company, "Take aim!"

Stephen, seeing that their lives now depend on speed, skips the command to poise firelocks— "Take aim! Fire!"

Only a few of the New Hampshire men were ready to fire. They fire a ragged volley. The redcoat sergeant is among those struck. The redcoats ordered to fire at Colonel Frye fire anyway, despite the loss of their sergeant. Their shots are followed by the remainder of the volley from the New Hampshire squad, whose accuracy breaks the discipline of the redcoats. The front rank turns and pushes through to the rear, and the others don't like the odds and begin falling back with their firelocks leveled in the direction of the patriots under Stephen's command.

A ball strikes Colonel Frye and passes through the fleshy part of his thigh. He slides off his horse. Barely able to stand, he pulls the saddle aside and plucks the ball from his horse, where it was wedged, not breaking the animal's skin, beneath the skirt of the saddle and behind the fender. Holding it high, he shouts with contempt, "The regulars fire damned careless!" The pain of being shot does not outweigh his anger as he shakes the bloody ball at the retreating redcoats.

Isaac recovers his wits. "Sawyer! Perry! Assist Colonel Frye. Get him behind Captain Crosby's line! Nathaniel—" He points to the older Greele. "Get the Colonel's horse."

The two run to Colonel Frye and form a chair with their forearms, which the Colonel leans into, and they are easily able to lift him. They carry the still-fuming colonel rapidly back through Captain Crosby's line. Within a minute, they are able to staunch the bloodflow, wrap the wounded colonel's leg, and help him back into his saddle. Captain Crosby assigns Nathaniel Greele to lead the wounded colonel's horse to his regiment's camp.

Stephen, seeing more redcoats emerging from the right side of the earthworks, orders the detachment to fall back to Crosby's line. They do so in a ragged line. They wait several minutes as the last contingents of patriot defenders from the earthworks make the run to pass through their line. The sounds of fighting in the redoubt subside. There are no challenges yet coming from the redcoats, though several marine companies are now formed up near Stephen's detachment's last firing position. Crosby orders his company to form columns and quick march to the center road, where they can make their way back over Bunker Hill and to safety.

•••

A little over an hour later, just after six o'clock in the afternoon, most of Colonel Reed's officers are present outside the regiment's headquarters. Their clothes are stained with smoke and some blood. Stephen, already returned to the job of adjutant, is taking information from each of them when Major Osgood rides up, dismounts, and approaches Colonel Reed.

Osgood's features are hard with determination as he salutes. "Colonel Reed." He hands a sealed packet to the colonel. "Looks as though you're already taking a count of the losses. General Ward has ordered your regiment back to Winter Hill immediately. You'll need to locate to the rear of Colonel Stark's encampment. Tonight, if possible. The redcoats are already on Bunker Hill, and if they get a fieldpiece up there, you're in range."

Reed nods grimly. "Yes, I see. Thank you, Major Osgood."

Osgood's tone changes from that of a professional soldier to one of brotherly concern. "How fared your regiment?"

Reed, sounding tired, but still with some strength, responds, "The men of New Hampshire accorded themselves as expected. We fought like bears defending our territory." Reed's face flushes with indignation. "The regulars be damned for their pride. We didn't just stop them, we cut them down every time they came at us. Entire companies fell before us. They'll not come at us anytime soon."

"Everywhere I've ridden tonight I hear the same. A peaceful night to you and your regiment. I must be on my way; I've still got orders for three other regiments."

Reed nods as Major Osgood mounts and turns his horse toward Winter Hill. "Thank you, Major. General Ward will have his reports later tonight."

Half an hour later, Reed and the staff officers work rapidly to pack their paperwork and desks. Their faces and clothes are still smoke-stained. Major Hale's shirt is spattered with blood. Isaac and Stephen have black-powder streaks on their hands and on the sides of their faces. None have spoken for a few minutes, each intent on organizing the work that must be accomplished.

Isaac breaks the silence. "I took the liberty of asking Sergeant Stone to bring us some supper."

"Thank you, Quartermaster," Reed replies. "How does your cousin fare? I hope the wound is not serious."

"He insists it was a flesh wound, tearing some muscle. He says he'll be fine—no worse than gout. I worry his mind is tougher than his body."

Lieutenant Colonel Gilman continues, "I hope he recovers quickly. What was he doing, coming onto the field alone during the retreat?"

Isaac sighs. "I think not being on the field during the battle drove him to act. To be of use to his men drives him. I know that's what he tells himself. I believe worry for his sons may have also driven him out onto the field today. At least one son was in the battle, maybe two. He said he was in courts-martial all morning, and finally had enough of them. His men said he arrived at the redoubt about half past two."

Stephen adds, "In a way, it was lucky for us. He provided a distraction and gave us the two seconds we needed to get our volley off before the redcoats. If not for that, we might have lost several more men."

After a few moments, Reed stands and leans forward with his hands on his desk for support, then speaks in a solemn voice.

"Gentlemen, we should all stand to hear this." Everyone stands at attention. Reed stands straight and tall. "Lieutenant Peabody. Our losses?"

Stephen reads from a sheet of paper. "For the regiment the totals are twelve killed and twenty wounded." He pauses a moment. "None from Fitzwilliam, sir. One of the men killed and one of the wounded were from Captain Crosby's company." He turns to Isaac. "Two men from Wilton were wounded."

A tentative knock is heard and Isaac moves to the door. "That's likely to be Sergeant Stone with the food." He opens the door, revealing the expected sergeant with a basket in each hand.

"Let's eat quickly," says Reed, "then get all this to Winter Hill. After that, let us be out and about, visiting the wounded. Encourage all the men to keep their spirits up. The regulars may have taken the ground, but by God, we took their pride and beat them with it!

•••

A little after nine o'clock that evening, most of the 3rd New Hampshire Regiment's camp is packed and wagons have already carried most of it behind the works on Winter Hill. Isaac and Stephen are by their tents as they finish packing their gear into wooden chests.

Isaac exhales forcibly. "I don't know if I'll be able to sleep tonight. My veins are so full of anxiousness. I suppose my mind knows it's only an echo of the action this afternoon. Even so, I cannot force my body to stop the sensation of it."

Stephen straightens, turns, and looks into the distance at Bunker Hill, now nearly black against the deepening twilight. "I feel something similar. My mind won't quiet either." A short pause. "We were lucky. We didn't see the worst of it. Colonel Reed told me he watched as Stark's line mowed down the entire Royal Welsh Fusiliers. Mowed them down to a man, Isaac. More than two hundred men in just two or three volleys. Not even half a minute. I could see he was still just as shocked to tell me of it as he was when he saw it. I've never read or heard of such madness and devastation on any battlefield. I'm dumbfounded. I know it happened, and I cannot, for the life of me, make sense of what it will mean."

Isaac shakes his head, his hands clenching and unclenching with nervous energy. "They could have surrendered. They should have surrendered. Couldn't they see?"

Stephen shakes his head. "It happened so fast. We took their officers first, so there was no chance. Frankly, I don't think the king's generals could see past their pride and presumptions. Colonel Reed says we followed Stark by doing nearly the same to the King's Own Fourth Regiment. Maybe only a company left of them. It was if the hand of Heaven guided our men's aim today."

Unconsciously, Isaac's hand moves over his heart. "Aye, a lot of men said divine providence was our lot today. I say it was simpler: our colonels knew their business, and our men know their firelocks even better." Isaac shuts the lid on the chest he has just finished packing. "I don't know what was worse. Until the retreat, every shot I fired was at a man who could not see me."

Stephen's voice takes on a tone of acceptance. "It was butchery today, and there's no point in dwelling on how it was done."

"I suppose you're right. Though I fear I will not easily forget the ease of killing, or hearing the awful cries and screams of the wounded."

Stephen shuts the lid of his chest and closes the fastener. "I don't think any of us will."

A moment later, Isaac blurts out, "Dammit!"

Stephen turns and raises his eyebrows. "What is it, Isaac?"

"I just realized I left my coat and hat in that house we were firing from. Damn! Damn! Damn! Elizabeth made that coat. She was so proud! Now I've gone and lost it and let it get burnt up."

"I'm sorry, Isaac. Though I expect she will understand. My blanket and an extra shirt went up in the flames, too. Strange what I thought I'd need if we were the ones occupying the ground tonight." Stephen exhales a long, slow breath. "I heard Doctor Warren was killed at the end. He and Colonel Prescott were among the last to leave the works. A sorry shame. I hear Warren was the one who sustained the men's spirits when he—the president of the Massachusetts Congress—

insisted on fighting as a private soldier."

"I heard Major McClary from Stark's regiment was killed by a stray cannon shot, well after the battle. He was still on the peninsula, near the Neck, but those damned rascals on the gondolas got off a lucky shot. They hadn't hit anything all day. A pure shame to happen well after the main action like that. Far too many men—good men—gone today."

"Isaac, I fear that's the least of it." Each of the next words come with increasing emphasis. "We have just started a war." Stephen's eyes show a moment of panic in the mind behind them. "Entire regiments of redcoats died today. Every hand in New England has blood on it tonight. King George and Parliament will be howling for our heads."

"Perhaps you're right, Stephen. Well, now that you say it, I believe you *are* right. But, I am even more certain that if we don't get our things back to Winter Hill and write to our wives tonight, the king and his ministers' howling will be nothing compared to what those two women will do to us. I for one am not going to let the news of the battle reach my wife first."

"Yes, first things first, and you're right about getting those letters written. Let's be on our way. The sooner we get to Winter Hill, the better." The two go back to work packing the rest of their belongings in earnest.

Charles E. Frye

6 A LESSON IN PATIENCE

Medford, the 24th of June, 1775
"Gentlemen—
Inclosed I send you a memorandum of sundry articles that your General
thinks very much wanted here for the use of the New Hampshire forces,
and should be glad if you think best that the horses maybe forwarded
here as soon as may be, as there is scarcely any such thing as getting
Teams here and likewise Carriages with them. Salt provision is very
scarce here...The men are very uneasy for want of a months pay that was
propos'd to be given them. I hope you will forward it as soon as possible
and likewise some Cash to me as I am left here and as many People
calling on me as is sufficient to put a man of my patience allmost
Distracted. I always shall obey your Directions with pleasure. I am,
Gentlemen, your very humble servant."

James McGregore

Written to the New Hampshire Committee of Safety

The inhabitants of the most populous city on the continent, and those living in surrounding towns, witnessed the carnage during and after the battle. In the days afterward, the enormity of the battle, in particular the toll in lives lost, sinks in. On both sides, that knowledge fuels an unhealthy fear of an attack. On the night of the battle, the regulars begin fortifying the northwestern part of Bunker Hill. The regulars work while dead and dying remain on the field.

Thousands of militia arrive in the next days to support the army around Boston. The regulars and their general learned respect for their American counterparts. Within the army surrounding Boston, hard-won confidence buoys spirits. The stalemate continues.

Just before eight on the morning of July 4, 1775, the day after General George Washington took command of the army around Boston, Isaac is in Colonel Reed's new headquarters, another farmhouse, this one a quarter mile east of Winter Hill but still within what all regard as the camp on Winter Hill. Colonel Reed and Lieutenant Colonel Gilman are present. Stephen has taken the day off to rest, as he was up two days and nights preparing documents for the colonel to have ready by the previous afternoon, when General Washington inspected the regiment.

"I expect General Washington will wish to organize the army in a way that differs from our present arrangement," Reed expounds to his staff officers, "because the Continental Congress has finally voted to raise and organize a proper army. That includes paying the soldiers and commissioning the officers. We would be called the Continental Army, though we shouldn't get too excited, as it would take weeks to organize."

A knock at the door interrupts him, and a man in his early twenties, with light-red hair, pokes his head inside and removes his hat.

Reed instantly recognizes the visitor. "Come in, Mister McGregore." To the officers he explains, "Mister McGregore has been assisting General Folsom for the past week." He turns back to McGregore. "Or is it now two weeks?"

McGregore comes in and closes the door. "It has been two weeks already, though I'm kept so busy, it goes by quickly." McGregore looks around the headquarters to see who else is present before continuing, "Colonel Reed, sir. I have a letter from the Committee of Safety for you." McGregore reaches inside his coat and pulls out a small, sealed letter and offers it to Reed.

Reed breaks the seal and unfolds the paper. Apparently it is brief, as Reed finishes reading it in just over a minute. He sets it down on his desk and looks up. "Well, Lieutenant McGregore. It seems I have a new adjutant."

Isaac and Gilman look up sharply. Gilman catches Isaac's eye and motions for him to hold off speaking.

The newly assigned adjutant gives Reed a smart, military salute. "Sir, I hope you will find me adequate to the task."

Reed nods. "I hope I will, and that you enjoy your duty. In fact, you are just in time. In a few minutes, the guard needs to be paraded and inspected to ensure the ammunition is accounted for prior to changing over to Captain Crosby's company. Order the guard to parade, and perform the inspection. Twelve men should each have ten cartridges; one hundred and twenty in total."

McGregor salutes again. "Yes, sir." He turns on his heel and leaves the farmhouse.

A few seconds after the door closes, Reed picks up the letter and looks to Gilman, shaking the letter as he speaks with an icy tone. "I will not countenance dishonesty or ignorance, when it comes to disrupting the operation of this regiment." He looks to Isaac, who is obviously disturbed by what has just transpired, and his voice returns to its usual, confident, in-control tone. "Not to worry, Quartermaster. I already have a remedy for this unexpected news, though you will need to hear this to perceive my intentions." Colonel Reed reads the letter aloud.

Exeter, July 1, 1775
To Colonel Reed of the 3rd New Hampshire Regiment,

Sir—The Committee without knowing that you had in actual service or in your eye any person as Adjutant of your Regiment, have commissioned Mr James McGregore, a young man we imagine very suitable for that place. If any person you judge suitable, is disposed to act as a volunteer without pay, in that capacity, we have no objections, unless it should plainly appear to us that he would not answer the end. But you will easily perceive the unsuitableness of recalling the Commission from Mr. McGregore for no reason on his part & commissions & paying a person of whom till was appointed we had not so much as recommendation. You may assure yourself that so far as the publick service will allow we shall take pleasure in gratifying you or the Regiment or any individual; But although we should be willing to make use of any & the best information, we must insist upon it, that our appointments should take place, as the contrary might be attended with boundless difficulties.

By order of the Committee

Gilman shrugs. "That is peculiarly direct and defensive language considering the lack of understanding the author has for our situation."

Reed cocks his eyebrow toward Gilman. "Yes. It's a shame Colonel Sargent hasn't continued as a member of that body, as I cannot think of but one or two who have been here to see our situation. That said, I expect an exasperated lieutenant will be coming in yon door very soon. Quartermaster, please summon Captain Towne, as I will need him to order the guard to parade."

It takes a moment for the colonel's expectations to make sense to Isaac. His mouth opens, almost shuts, and then forms an O-shape, then his eyes turn mischievous as he grins before he responds, "Yessir. I will have the captain here shortly. Should I explain the situation to him?"

Reed nods, a twinkle in his eye. "Yes, as I do not wish for him to berate a lieutenant he will not recognize for attempting to order his men about."

Fifteen minutes later, Isaac returns, trailing Captain Towne; and not seeing the guards parading outside, they enter the headquarters. They are just in time to hear Lieutenant McGregore's frustrated tone, "...the sergeant snarled and told me he would not obey me, nor any officer not of his command. I informed him that sergeants must obey all lieutenants and all superior officers."

Reed, with a calm, kind look, quizzes, "Did the sergeant move the guard to parade or not, Lieutenant?"

Realizing his failure, McGregore looks at his feet. "No, sir. The sergeant told me to move along or he would arrest me."

Reed now looks toward Towne. "Captain, would you order your men to parade? I want to be sure they are not drunken, or suffer from any other disability to recognize their superior officers, or obey their orders." Towne salutes and leaves.

Turning back to McGregore with an air of unflappability, Reed apologizes. "I am sorry to find so simple a duty has proven disagreeable to you. Let's wait a minute and see if Captain Towne has any success with that rascal of a sergeant. In the meantime, I'm curious how it is you thought my regiment to be functioning these past weeks without an adjutant?"

McGregore looks around the room at Gilman and Isaac. "I suppose your quartermaster did some of it, and the rest was split between Colonels Gilman and Hale?"

Colonel Reed corrects him, continuing in the same kindly, agreeable voice. "It is *Major* Hale, and I would that it could be done so easily. Come, let us check to see if Captain Towne has succeeded in getting the guard to parade."

"I'm sorry, sir. Major Hale. Thank you."

Isaac reaches the door first and holds it open for the others. In the open space in front of the headquarters, the guard stands at attention while Captains Town and Crosby inspect the hand-off of the cartridges. The men behave in a smart, military fashion.

Reed turns again to McGregore. "Well, it seems the guard is in order. Therefore, I think it best you return to the service of assisting General Folsom. I will put in a good word for you, if you wish to continue in the service with your commission." McGregore is on the verge of interrupting, but Reed holds up a hand for him to keep his silence. "I would also counsel you," adds Reed, "to do your utmost to learn the officers and staff of the New Hampshire regiments if you harbor any expectations of succeeding in the service. I will thank the Committee of Safety for their concern regarding the staffing of this regiment, and I will have to disappoint them regarding the regiment's need for an adjutant. Do we understand one another, Lieutenant?"

Isaac can see that McGregore at least has the good sense to look embarrassed as he tells Colonel Reed that he understands perfectly.

•••

Isaac and Stephen walk back to Colonel Reed's headquarters from General Washington's headquarters in Cambridge early on the morning of July 16. Stephen rifles through the various documents they have picked up, scanning the upper sections. With Washington in command, a new routine has emerged that includes top-down communication each day. "Here is something new. In today's general orders we are given notice that Congress has decreed next Thursday to be a day of... and I quote—

"Public Humiliation, Fasting and Prayer; that they may with united Hearts and Voice unfeignedly confess their Sins before God, and supplicate the all wise and merciful disposer of events, to avert the Desolation and Calamities of an unnatural war."

"General Washington orders that day... and I quote again—

"...to be religiously observed by the Forces under his Command, exactly in manner directed by the proclamation of the Continental Congress: It is therefore strictly enjoin'd on all Officers and Soldiers, (not upon duty) to attend Divine Service, at the accustomed places of worship, as well in the Lines, as the Encampments and Quarters; and it is expected, that all those who go to worship, do take their Arms, Ammunitions and Accoutrements and are prepared for immediate Action if called upon."

Stephens waves the paper in the air and asks, "What do you think of that?"

Isaac is silent for a few moments and looks troubled. "I am a little exasperated. I mean, we have little time to get much done, and now we are to take a full day—that is not a Sunday—off. I've never been especially religious, but it seems like this shoe doesn't fit me very well."

Stephen laughs. "How so?"

"I find divine logic to be conveniently unfathomable, and the time spent questioning it or oneself could be put to better use."

Stephen nods. "Aye, conveniently true for some people, some of the time. Though I think the intention of Congress is more than each of us contemplating our part in what has happened. Calling upon us to unite in the manner they did, strengthens our sense of humanity, which we risk losing in troubled times like these." Stephen looks Isaac in the eye. "Thinking of such a day pains me to realize I am not with my family, and yet I can see them at home in observance of the same order, and I suppose that brings me a little peace."

Isaac raises one eyebrow, and then nods in acquiescence. "Leave it to you to find the wisdom in words that others like me might dismiss or become annoyed by."

Stephen shrugs. "I saw sense in looking for the good in what Congress asked of us."

"Aye, true. I need to think more like that myself, even when I am bothered and have what seems like too many things to do."

"I don't know when, but I learned to try to see a thing the way others might see it." Stephen's look sharpens. "Now that I'm thinking about it that way, I don't see this day of prayer as being devoted to divine guidance, so much as it is practical and politically motivated."

Isaac shakes his head. "How so? I mean, the words from Congress were pretty specific."

"Yes, but consider that you and I have been involved in the events others are only just reading about, and those words may be too few, or not from the right mouths, to be believed. I think the wisdom that some of the members of Congress have applied here is in realizing it takes time for a large number of people to understand a thing when they are not prepared to learn of it. Ergo, a day for people to talk and spread the news of what has happened here. Sure, some will pray and fast, but others will talk, and that will do much to bring the other colonies around to understanding what we know.

The two lieutenants are approaching Reed's headquarters. Isaac, now looking much less troubled, admits, "That is quite clever. I think you've got the right of it."

Stephen smiles. "I hope so, and if nothing else, I for one could use a break from the routine we've fallen into these past weeks."

...

Late in the morning of July 19, Colonel Reed and his staff officers are working at their desks. The door and windows are open, allowing what little breeze there is to circulate as the day becomes hot.

Reed finishes the letter he has written and clears his throat. "Quartermaster, I realize we have not mentioned the affair regarding Mister McGregore since the day it occurred, though I trust you informed Adjutant Peabody."

Isaac smiles. "Yessir. I mentioned the details of it to him that evening."

Stephen gives Isaac a wry look before answering. "Quartermaster Frye did inform me. And, sir, he fully explained your kind and patient handling of that delicate situation. Have you more news on that topic, sir?"

Colonel Reed stands and walks to the window where there is a bit more light and breeze. "No news. However, I have just now composed a response to the Committee. Would you gentlemen care to hear what I have written?"

The staff officers give their affirmatives, and Colonel Reed reads aloud:

"Camp at Winter Hill, July the 19, 1775
Gentlemen—

I received your letter of July 1st and note the contents. You say, Without knowing that I had in actual service or in my eye any person as Adjutant of my Regiment, have commissioned Mr McGregor, a suitable person, etc. I doubt not but McGregor is a worthy and suitable Gentleman for an Adjutant and is agreeable to me and I wish he had been so to the Regiment; but to my surprise when he order'd the Guards to be paraded I soon learnt they refused to appear; I was under the necessity to order their captain to parade

84

them and they immediately obeyed. You may be assured I have done everything in my power to have made Mr. McGregor's duty agreeable, but this happened at a time when no officer was in commission nor the soldiers sworn, it was not a time to enter into a dispute, the difficulties are better known than expressed. I must beg leave to inform you that not a single day's duty in a regiment can be done with propriety without an adjutant and if ever the duty of an Adjutant was Necessary it was before the late action as well as soon after. How can you imagine that I could do one day without both adjutant and quartermaster?

You say if any person I judge suitable is Disposed to act as a volunteer in that capacity without pay you have no objection unless it should plainly appear to you that he would not answer the End—to which I answer, I hope in time my conduct will convince you that I have the service more at heart than to be partial in the matter. I do easily perceive that it must be very disagreeable to the Honorable Committee and the worthy Gentleman Mr. McGregor to be disappointed but hope you will provide for him some other way. I heartily thank the Honored Committee for their friendly paragraph, which is —you say—You may assure yourself that so far as the public service will allow you shall Take pleasure in gratifying me or the Regiment or any Individual—this is the sole motive why Mr. Peabody is continued as Adjutant and I presume the voice of the regiment will make this manifest, which is the Best information the nature of the thing can admit of.

James Reed"

The men all wear satisfied smiles.

"That was well said, sir," Stephen says approvingly, "and I very much appreciate your approbation and support for my commission as adjutant."

Reed crosses over to Stephen and shakes his hand. "It is my honor to serve with you, Adjutant, and you are without doubt well worth the effort."

Stephen thanks his superior officer and the two go back to their desks.

Within a few moments, Stephen looks up as if he has just thought of something unexpected. "Colonel Reed, sir. I like to think of myself as being prudent and willing to give others the benefit of the doubt. However, I must say, you have me at a comparative disadvantage. How did you know to give Mr. McGregore the opportunity to prove himself?"

Reed grins fiercely. "In the beginning I knew one fact, which is: Mr. McGregore is from Londonderry, the same town where lives the President of our province's Congress—the much-respected Mr. Matthew Thornton. I figured there was some personal correspondence behind the letter I received making the appointment. I wanted to be certain, so I instructed Colonel Gilman to make some discrete inquiries as to when our Mr. McGregore arrived in camp. It was two days after the battle, and while the lad was earnestly working on our behalf to help secure supplies and medicine, I suspect his lack of knowledge for our situation shielded him from fully appreciating the large effort we have all undertaken, and were in the midst of just two days after the battle."

Stephen, who had been nodding slowly throughout Colonel Reed's explanation, smiles with understanding. "Thank you, sir. It would have been too simple to conclude the man to be a damned fool with an underhanded nature."

Reed shrugs. "He was something of a fool for not assessing the situation here, but such is often the case with young, ambitious men. I believe his intent was good, and I believe he learned a measure of respect for his troubles."

"Thank you again, sir."

"You're very welcome, Adjutant."

7 AT HOME

"Isaac Frye, Quartermaster, April 23 1775
5s for 60 miles traveled,
3£ = Rate per month
10£ 19s 4p Amount of Wages plus travel
Less advance of 3£.
7£ 19s 4p total paid"

Excerpt from "Pay Roll for Col. James Reed's Reg't from the time of
their engagement to August 1st 1775"

A pair of large, heavily laden wagons, each pulled by a team of two horses, trundle south on the Mason Road an hour before sunset on a late August evening. The horses are sweaty from the half-mile climb from the Souhegan River. Soon Isaac, who is driving the lead wagon, signals they will turn east onto a narrower road that runs between three farms.

Isaac calls back to Sergeant Ephraim Stone, the driver of the second wagon, "The farm on the left is James Gray's. He is with the army now."

After a hundred yards, they crest a rise just past the Gray farm, and Isaac points to the next farm on the left. "That's my place. That's

Benjamin Rideout's farm on the right."

Stone looks over the fields and farms. "I like the look of this land. You're a lucky man to have a farm here."

About halfway down the slope to his farm, Isaac catches sight of Sarah Holt in the garden. She squints, then shades her eyes a few seconds before recognizing Isaac, and leaps out of the garden, rushing into the house, calling for Elizabeth.

Isaac turns his wagon into the farmyard and then toward the barn in the rear. He is beaming from ear to ear as he sees Elizabeth emerge through the back door, holding an infant in her arms. The new baby does not register with Isaac as he calls out, "Ma'am, have you got enough room for a couple of tired, hungry soldiers for the night?"

Elizabeth, beaming as well, nods her head vigorously. "I think we might, although you'll both need to wash before coming into the house."

Isaac hops down from the wagon, and with a big grin takes a couple of steps toward his wife.

She raises her eyebrows, glances down at the baby, and offers another big smile.

Isaac's mind finally reconciles what his eyes have told him; that the baby is a newborn. He does a double take and his eye go wide. Elizabeth looks only a little different from when he left, and he is extremely confused. "Oh, my darling! When did this baby arrive?"

Elizabeth smiles proudly at the new baby. "Two days ago."

Isaac's eyes go wide. "Looks at least a week old, and so healthy." Isaac takes a few seconds to carefully look Elizabeth over. "You look well, too. How are you?"

"I came through fine. Sarah and young Isaac have done the work on the farm that needed doing. How long can you stay?"

"Just the night. We took delivery of some tents and flour in Amherst and some iron from Deacon Baldwin. We had a half a dozen others from Wilton with us. They have all gone and found their homes for the night. We are expected back in three, no more than four days, and by the look of the clouds tonight I fear it will rain at least once to slow us."

Isaac starts, looking a little embarrassed, then extends his right hand back toward the other wagon. "I was so surprised, I forgot my manners. This is Ephraim Stone, the regiment's quartermaster sergeant.

Elizabeth smiles and nods. "It's a pleasure to meet you, Sergeant Stone."

"I am pleased to meet you as well, Missus Frye. A hearty congratulations to both of you on the birth of your..."

"Oh! I almost forgot. It's a boy." Another big, uncontrollable smile comes over her face as she looks at her new baby and then to Isaac. "We have four sons now, husband."

Isaac beams. "That's wonderful! What a homecoming!" He turns to Stone. "Ephraim, let's take the wagons back beside the barn."

Isaac and Stone bring the wagons alongside each other beside the barn. Isaac jumps off his wagon and walks to Elizabeth, who is still moving slowly. Isaac wraps an arm around her shoulders and uses his other hand to help raise his new son's head so he can see him closely for the first time.

"I've missed you, dear wife. One hundred and twenty-nine days since I last saw you. And this young fellow... I was worried I might not meet get to meet him."

Isaac sees his three older boys standing in a line like soldiers on the step below the back doorway, saluting, and waiting for their father to return their salute. Isaac snaps smartly to attention, and returns their salute. The boys clamber off the step to Isaac who kneels to catch them all in a fierce hug. Mother Holt is standing behind them. "Those boys have missed their father. They've spent the past months observing the militia at drill on Sunday. Abiel Abbott taught them to salute, and told them that you'd expect one the next time you saw them."

Isaac looks up to Mother Holt, then to Elizabeth. "I recognize them, but just barely! They've grown so!" The boys thoroughly enjoy the attention and arch their backs to grow even more.

Sarah comes out of the house. "Isaac! What a surprise to see you!"

"I am pleased to see you as well, Sarah. I bet Elizabeth and the boys have kept you busy, and we are grateful for your help."

Elizabeth turns to her mother. "Mother has been here helping me for the past few days."

"Mother, I am pleased to see you as well. Mother—Sarah—over there is Sergeant Ephraim Stone; he is our regiment's quartermaster sergeant. Sergeant Stone, this is my wife's Mother, Elizabeth Holt, and my wife's youngest sister, Sarah."

"It's a pleasure to meet you ladies. Our quartermaster has spoken highly and often of his family and how they've been helping his wife while he's been in Medford with the army."

Isaac adds, "Sergeant Stone and I will see to the oxen and then get cleaned up."

"I'll take care of the teams, Quartermaster. Please, you get cleaned up and spend some time with your family."

"Thank you, and Ephraim—call me Isaac here."

"Much obliged, Isaac; I need a break from all the military discipline General Washington brought upon us this past month."

Isaac laughs. "He certainly has, and a break will do us some good."

A few minutes later, after washing, Isaac steps outside to stand beside Elizabeth who holds the new addition to their family while enjoying the late afternoon breeze. "May I hold him?"

"Yes, he is starting to nod off."

Isaac brushes the back of his index finger along his newest son's cheek. The softness that comes from touching a new life washes over him as he relaxes for what seems like the first time in weeks. Gently, Isaac takes his new son and cradles his head in the crook of his arm, silently marveling at the lightness of a new baby as he takes in his son's features. "He has your ears." Isaac smiles as he looks up to Elizabeth.

Later that evening, after dinner, Isaac's kitchen is full of people. Elizabeth's other sister, Hannah; her husband, Richard Whitney; and Timothy Sr. have come to visit. Elizabeth is rocking the new baby to sleep, and the others sit in the kitchen or stand around the edges of the room.

Timothy Sr., after hearing Isaac tell of James Frye's confrontation with the redcoats, remarks, "I cannot believe James Frye went riding onto the battlefield. The man's at least ten years older than I am!"

Isaac, looking a little chagrined, responds, "I'm afraid I haven't had the chance to ask him since the battle. I suspect it was his wanting to see his regiment show their worth on the field, particularly his sons. You know how that's important to him."

Timothy Sr. nods. "Aye, he is uncommonly keen about that sort of thing."

Isaac continues, "His gout kept him holed up at headquarters in Cambridge, and he was put on a courts-martial trial that morning. He didn't make it onto the peninsula until well after the battle had begun. His regiment was where the fighting was thickest at the end." Isaac's expression is weary as he goes on, "The retreat was such that no companies came off the field together, or in good order. I think he was riding back and forth to lead portions of his regiment, when he could find them, to safety. I also wonder if he knew whether his sons were safely off the field. Frederick turned fifteen the week prior to the battle—"

"Goodness!" Mother Holt interrupts. "Only fifteen! I'll never understand that compulsion boys and men have for battle and bloodshed." She shakes her head as if to drive away uncivil images of children on battlefields. "Sarah, you know Frederick, do you not? Not even three years younger than yourself."

"I do. I cannot believe he could have been in such a battle. It sounds horrible. He wasn't much more than a little boy when I last saw him."

"Well, he's not a boy anymore," Timothy Sr. adds, somewhat severely. "Has James recovered?"

"It's been over two months and he is still changing bandages daily. He is old, and the wound isn't healing rapidly. It's Frye stubbornness keeping him upright and cursing, and the same trait, I worry, will keep him from caring for the wound as he should."

Richard is anxious to turn the conversation to his own interests, and switches the topic. "What of George Washington? He's a southerner. How does that sit with what is mostly a New England army?"

Isaac nods. "Yes, from Virginia. A plantation owner."

"How do you find him to be?"

"I've not met him. The little I've seen shows him to be every inch a commander. All six foot five inches of him. When he came into Cambridge last month, all the regiments paraded for him to inspect. His horsemanship and bearing were that of a nobleman. He certainly does well in looking the part of a commander. The day after he arrived, and to what I believe is your point, Richard, we had orders for the regiment saying we were all part of an army for the United Provinces of North America, and we should lay aside all distinctions of colony."

Ephraim Stone adds, "He's a disciplinarian for sure. A man can get flogged, or worse, for any little thing now."

Isaac nods with certainty, although he cocks an eyebrow just slightly to Timothy Sr. to show he thinks General Washington's strictness is for the better. "Quite true. Though so far he shows himself to be evenhanded and fair about that business. Since he took command, he got the Continental Congress to pressure the provinces to pay us. So, my opinion of the man is quite high, for now."

While the others think on that, Elizabeth changes the subject. "It seems this business will go on into next year, then?"

Her father responds first. "Yes, I would think so. The Continental Congress has only just appointed a commander for this newly unified army. The king is only just hearing about the latest battle. Even if the king sues for peace, it won't be resolved until well into next year."

"Peace." Richard spits the word with some anger in his eyes. 'Not a chance. It seems a true stalemate now. Gage cannot afford another battle and our army has no leverage in the form of ammunition to pry him out of Boston."

Isaac, sounding resigned, admits, "Aye. True enough about the lack of powder, though we will do our utmost to make a long, miserable winter for General Gage. We realized this was our lot shortly after leaving the battlefield. To that end, we expanded and improved our fortifications on Winter Hill, which is now a fortress for New Hampshire's men. Most of us in the army see more hope than fear or worry. I suspect General Washington has plans for setting up powder mills. I think, as more time goes by, we will become stronger, and General Gage can only become weaker. We've got a line of credit from the Committee of Safety, and I expect the Continental Congress will add to that. I've got contracts to supply tents, iron, and other goods for the army. It's coming from Exeter, Amherst, Andover, and some others of our New Hampshire towns where the people needed the business."

"That is good," Timothy Sr. says with a positive tone. "We need the commerce, even if it is to make war."

Richard, deciding he is not completely satisfied with what he has heard about the army's new commander, persists with his line of questioning. "Tell more of Washington, Isaac. How has he changed anything?"

Isaac shrugs and laughs a little. "You may find all this unremarkable, but since you're asking, I'll do my best. It's meant the most mundane tasks have taken on higher priority. For instance, keeping our store of pikes greased and clean. They must be, to quote the General's order, always fit for service. Before the General took command, nobody said a thing about pikes, or any of a dozen other items an army might need. Then there are all the new appointments in the army. A little over a week ago, he appointed a quartermaster general, a fellow by the name of Thomas Mifflin, which I'll admit has made some sense. Then he appointed a commissary general for the army, and if that weren't enough, the artillery was given their own commissary general, and it goes on and on. With each new appointment, we—to wit, Ephraim and I," Isaac nods to Sergeant Stone, "must count every bit of equipment our regiment has, all over again. I sincerely wonder when it will end."

The others laugh in sympathy and Ephraim bristles dramatically, as if slighted. "I tell you, it's no laughing matter. By the time we return, there'll be half a dozen new duties, and we'll be—" He starts laughing. "—nine days behind!" Everyone laughs even more.

Isaac holds up his hand. "I almost forgot. Bringing up all the appointments reminded me. The New Hampshire regiments have been brigaded under John Sullivan, who has been appointed a brigadier general. I have to say that makes a good deal better sense than General Folsom, who looks the part, and certainly for his past military accomplishments deserves the respect of ranking a general. But General Sullivan is far more actively concerned with prosecuting a war than administering an army, which I must say I like, though with one exception."

"What's that?" asks Timothy Sr.

"Well, we have a brigade major now. Major Scammell by name, and it's his job to parade the regiment on a regular basis. From what I can tell, it's only to waste nearly an hour each day to prove we exist. Washington himself assigned that duty to every brigade major."

Richard winks to Isaac. "I do believe this General Washington is turning our militia into an army."

"Aye, that's true enough, I suppose. Though one thing that vexes me some is that Colonel Reed prohibited me from taking commissions on our supply contracts, as most of the Massachusetts quartermasters have been doing. It seems unfair, as quartermasters are the lowest rank of officer, and so we are the lowest paid. At least because of having to transport supplies from towns like Wilton and Amherst, where the Army has contracts, I'll be able to visit every month or so throughout the winter, and that's a lot more than most men will be able to do. I'll try to arrange it so I can spend more than a night."

Ephraim clears his throat. "That's a good deal better than those redcoats are getting too, what with the smallpox breaking out in Boston."

Mother Holt, a little startled, exclaims, "Oh, my! I hope it stays right there in Boston! I've heard of armies spreading that disease into their enemy's camps on purpose."

Elizabeth, keeping calm, says, "I'm so glad we got inoculated last year. That's the only way to be sure of surviving if it gets out of control."

Isaac adds, "As we well know, but I don't think the generals trust the men to keep inoculations under control. There's worry about enough men self-inoculating that most of the army would be too sick to defend their posts."

Timothy Sr. concludes with, "Probably wise, though an awful choice to have to make. To follow orders and risk getting a full blown case, or engage in deception and get the inoculation against orders." He yawns. "Mother, I should get going."

Richard pushes himself off the doorframe he was leaning on.

"We'll walk with you, Father."

Mother Holt rises. "I'll go with you tonight, since Isaac is here. I need to get a few things and I'll be ready to go."

Hannah's expression brightens. "Oh, good! I haven't had much opportunity to talk with you of late."

Everyone rises as the four guests locate their hats and belongings.

Timothy Sr. shakes Isaac's hand and clasps his shoulder. "Isaac, keep yourself safe, and we hope to see you as often as possible in the coming months."

Richard adds his well wishes, and they take their leave of Ephraim as well.

The house is quiet after the four leave. Ephraim heads for the barn, which he says will do fine, given it's got a roof that doesn't need to be un-staked and folded in the morning. Sarah and the boys retire to the bedroom, leaving Isaac and Elizabeth together in the kitchen.

Elizabeth stands, holding the baby. "I'm so glad fortune and providence smiled on you during the battle and brought you home to me, husband."

Isaac crosses the room and embraces them both. "As am I. To be greeted by a new son makes it even better. With all the excitement on the day of the battle, I must admit I wasn't able to think of home until much later in the day. Stephen was worried the king would take the news of the battle badly, and at that moment I realized you would, too, if I didn't get some lines to paper that night."

"Isaac, tell me, what was it like?"

"What was what like?"

"The battle. Did you—"

Isaac gently cuts her off. "I shall not speak of it."

"We've always shared our thoughts, Isaac, and I'm scared. I've heard how being in a battle affects men, and it's never for the better."

"I would not wish anyone to have to see what I saw and heard that day, especially you. Each man must make his own peace with what he saw and did that day. I've made mine." Elizabeth's face looks more worried as he talks. "Telling you—my gentle, loving wife—about such things seems morally wrong to me. Those memories are my burden that I expect time will lighten for me. Carrying that burden is my duty, just as it is my duty to see through what I helped start. I believe liberty is worth the effort."

"Isaac, I... I see. If that is your will, then so be it." Her tone is disappointed, but not sullen. "Please take care that this is not pride masked as honor. It's bad enough that you were there. Take comfort that you are not alone. I am always here."

Isaac holds Elizabeth and the baby closer for a few moments longer. "I will keep with me the memory of the older boys on the step today. It made me so happy to see them and you. I'll also remember what I feel now. I will carry these good memories with me to balance against anything this war may show me."

•••

Isaac and Stephen come to stand outside Colonel Reed's headquarters, sipping from near-full cups of rum on the evening after Isaac arrives back at Winter Hill. Stephen claps Isaac on the back with a hearty, "Congratulations on your son's birth."

"Thank you. I was lucky to get to see him."

"Yes, and we were lucky Colonel Reed offered some of his personal stock of rum. It's a good deal better than we get for our daily ration."

Isaac looks up at the clear night sky. "Now I wonder how often I will get to see him. We may be at this for the next year, or whatever time it takes."

"I wonder how long, too." Stephen sighs. "I strongly doubt this will end soon. Today I heard news that the colonies are sending delegations here, made up of members of congress, or governors, to discuss how to organize this army."

"Every time a delegation comes, a month goes by, and then we realize we are no closer to resolving this situation. They've appointed a general—what more is needed?"

Stephen chuckles wryly. "Yes, I do see what you mean about delegations stopping things until they've had their say. I believe this will be about how to spend the funds Congress has secured for the army's use. Pay, in particular, needs to be equalized by rank across all provinces. A captain cannot be worth more just because he is from

Connecticut."

"I hope these delegates don't get any ideas to pull their support away."

"They've not seen or heard first-hand of either of the battles. I believe it's good they are coming. I strongly suspect we will have their full support once they realize the significance of what has happened here."

"Good, because I worry King George and Parliament are calling in favors and raising a big army to put us down. All of us, especially the officers and Congress, have risked much already. Do you think it would help if a few of us found and waved one of those 'Unite or Die' flags to welcome them?"

Stephen chuckles softly under his breath. "I think they are already aware of the stakes, and know funding the army will cost far less than any offer or punishment from the king."

"Well, good."

Stephen finishes his rum. "Well, I'm done for the evening, and I need to write a letter to my wife before getting some sleep."

Isaac glances unhappily into the sparse office. "I wish I was done. I am likely to be another half hour. Then I'm going to visit my Uncle Joseph. He is here from Fryeburg. He's been a general for nearly two months now, and I've hardly seen him. I'll see you in the morning."

•••

Timothy Holt Jr. and his wife, Hannah, sit at the table in the main room of their home in North Andover, Massachusetts. It is late afternoon in early October, and they drink from steaming mugs of mulled cider.

Timothy is Elizabeth's older brother by two years. Like his sister, he has a fair complexion and dark eyes and hair. Hannah is six years younger, twenty-three, and also has fair skin, but with blond hair.

Timothy sets his cup down. "I stopped by the hatter's shop this morning."

"Why? You don't need a hat. I don't imagine we could even afford one."

"All true, but the reason I stopped was because I saw Isaac Frye there and wondered what he was doing."

Hannah becomes intensely interested. "Did you speak with him? I presume he is still in the army that surrounds Boston."

"Yes, I am certain he is still in the army. But, no—for no reason I can explain, I stayed back until he and his squad of guards had moved on with their wagons."

Hannah leans in a little, her eyes widen as she fixes Timothy with a look that indicates she thinks her husband has acted in an odd way, then says, "I don't understand."

"Once they were gone I went in and asked the hatter what business the army had with him. He said they ordered three dozen hats, and to me he seemed pleased to have the business. He went on to say they ordered heavy felt for winter. I asked how much such a hat would cost, and—" Timothy pauses with a glum look. "Well, you're right, we cannot afford one."

Hannah at first looks uncertain, then a shrewd look comes into her eyes. "I bet it's a high price Isaac's paying. I heard that quartermasters from some of the regiments do that. I am shocked to hear myself say this, but it seems our brother-in-law is adding his own commission on to the price of those hats. I heard it said that adding such a commission was about making a fair bit more money than a lieutenant's pay."

Timothy draws back and stares at the table for a moment, showing he does not want to make any accusations. "Well, I don't know for sure, but it is possible. I don't think many people have been buying hats since the port was closed. Besides, Isaac always struck me as honest. Though I know the last two years were hard on him and Elizabeth. Almost as hard as they've been on us. Maybe the army is supplying him with a convenient means to pay off his debts."

Hannah's nose crinkles and her brows knit into a glare that says he should get his priorities straight and agree with her. "Husband, it's bad enough your father and mother moved to Wilton three years ago. They are nearer to both of your sisters and their husbands. Your parents help them a good deal more than they do us. What about us?"

Timothy turns defensive. "We have this house and land."

"We don't own it. Isaac and Richard both own their land and homes, and yet your mother and father left Andover for Wilton to help them."

"Yes, that's true, but Wilton is relatively new and unsettled. Andover must be a hundred years older and is now established and comfortable."

Hannah's remains cross. "I still say: what about us? You can't join the army. The three days you were gone for the alarm was more than long enough!" Hannah turns to pouting. "Who would take care of me, or this land?"

"There's no need to worry, dearest. I'm not joining the army like some glory seeker, only to end up dead, or worse. My place is here, with you, and we will make the best of it."

•••

Isaac and Elizabeth sit in their kitchen on a late-October evening. Outside the air is chilly, with the promise of another freeze in the early morning. The kitchen is warmly lit with oil lamps and a fire in the fireplace. There are several lit candles on the table, as well.

Elizabeth looks worn as she looks around the room. She sounds disappointed. "You haven't been paid since August, and that was only for one month. Why?"

"I wish I knew. I think things have gotten confused between the Continental Congress voting to take over and make one army out of all the militias, and whatever agreements each colony had with its soldiers. As I understand things, our committee of safety authorized paying us for one month, and that was in June, before the battle. In July, General Washington ordered that we be paid all the way up through August. Most of the colonies paid their troops as the general ordered. New Hampshire did not, and at the end of August, General Sullivan wrote to the committee asking why not."

Elizabeth rolls her eyes. "At last, someone thought to do something sensible."

Isaac cannot help himself, and lets out a bitter laugh. "Well, the answer he got was that the committee had no idea about General

Washington's order, and that they had agreed to pay us the one month, and the balance once we disband. They expected us to be organized into a new army, paid by the Continental Congress, which would effectively mean we'd been disbanded and could get paid. So, they've been waiting, we've been waiting, and now we are all waiting on these delegations from the colonies. General Washington and Congress called them to help organize the army in early September. They finally all arrived about a week ago, and were still meeting when I left. I think word of their task spread in the weeks before they arrived, and more details about the administering of an army were found to debate than there were soldiers in camp."

Elizabeth shakes her head incredulously. "At this rate, your enlistment will be up before they figure anything out."

Isaac nods in agreement. "I know, and from the little I've heard they are talking of how to pay and reorganize the army for next year. Nothing about this year. I hope to hear better news when I get back."

Elizabeth sighs. "I hope so, too." Then she has another thought. "Is there a chance you'll be paid more? It would offset the unreliable nature and infrequency of when you are paid."

"I know better pay was high on the list of topics for the delegates to discuss. I heard some colonies are paying differently for the same rank, and if we are to be one army, it must be equal for all. There was also talk of the officers getting better pay in general, so I hope the delegates listen to that. Though I fear none of it will take effect until next year."

"Will you serve next year? You said the current enlistment would be until the end of this year. I suppose I may have heard what I wanted, and I took that to mean that you mean to be done then."

Isaac takes her hand. "This has been difficult, and now I worry even more for you. Many are sacrificing much more than we are." Isaac sighs; an exhale that relieves him of some unspoken pressure. "I will see this duty through. Stephen Peabody and I have spoken on this subject nearly every evening of late. Quitting now would be a disgrace. If enough men quit and the remaining army is defeated, I fear what I have already done will not be forgotten. The king will use his army to find the members of Congress, the officers, and likely the men who fought—and hang us." He shakes his head emphatically. "No man wants to die on a gallows in shame when he can fight for his liberty. Especially now, as I think there will not be another time when so many will commit to the fight."

They lapse into silence for a minute before Isaac continues. "If you add King George's habit of allowing Parliament to tax the colonies to pay his war bills, the king will shackle everyone left with debts and taxes. Also, those who supplied provisions for the soldiers will lose the value of those provisions and any hope of recompense. I strongly think we must see this through. I do not see another choice."

Elizabeth's eyes show disappointment and resignation. "I won't beg. You know I would prefer you to be here." She glances up as if for help from above, then looks Isaac in the eye. "I know your duty is to finish what's been started. I just hope it will be finished next year."

"As do I."

Elizabeth stands and puts her hands on her hips, looking around the kitchen. "At least we've got food for the winter. The garden was good this year. It was hard carrying John and doing all that work, but with Sarah's help and help from my mother and father, we made it through."

"I wish there was something we could do to repay your family for their help."

"They wouldn't take anything, Isaac. Write them and thank them. My father likes to hear what is happening, even if he doesn't like the idea of being at war."

Isaac smiles. "I will."

Elizabeth begins pacing and wrings her hands in frustration. "Oh! I wish they would pay you regularly; we need to stock up for the winter before everything is picked over. It would make things a little more tolerable here." She pauses a moment, straightens her apron, and glances guiltily at Isaac. "I am sorry. I shouldn't place demands on you. You didn't create this trouble."

Isaac turns his chair, rises, and steps in front of her. "You're right. If we're not going to be paid, then there is little point in staying with the army past resolving the current situation. If we are not paid by the time the enlistments are up, then I will not re-enlist, though I fear there will be pressure to do so as soon as I return. I do believe the Continental Congress will support the army, and pay us regularly. Last week in camp I learned the colonies agreed to a budget of two million dollars for Congress to use to pay and feed the army. So, once the organization of the army is determined, I expect we will be paid soon after."

Elizabeth's features finally soften. "I hope so, Isaac. This is only the second day I've seen you since the alarm, and to spend even a minute talking of frustrations seems a waste."

•••

Two days later, Isaac travels to the hatter's shop in Andover to take delivery of several dozen hats for the regiment. Sergeant Stone is waiting outside, with half a dozen privates, to guard a pair of wagons laden with supplies. Two of the soldiers load the stacks of hats onto the wagon while Isaac finishes the transaction with the hatter.

Isaac hands the hatter a signed promissory note. "Thank you for completing the order so quickly."

The hatter examines the note, then smiles at Isaac. "Not a problem Isaac—I mean Quartermaster Frye. This was your father's shop once, and I'm pleased you remembered me."

Meanwhile, two buildings down and across from the hatter's, Timothy Holt Jr. watches the exchange from around the corner of a building. He is able to see the exchange though the large window at the front of the shop. The look on his face is one of dark irritation.

Isaac nods. "Aye, true, and you set a fair price. That makes it easy to help friends." Isaac scans the main room of the shop and smiles wistfully. "It's been nearly twenty years since my father was a hatter here. I remember helping stack hats when I was a young boy. Hard to believe so much time has passed."

The hatter smiles. "It has. It doesn't seem possible, but it has. Well, I hope those hats help keep your regiment warm when they're on guard duty this winter. Stop in anytime you come through Andover. I was glad to get some firsthand news from Cambridge."

"I will. Good day to you, sir."

Isaac and the hatter both walk out to watch the men tie off the canvas cover that holds the load in place. As they do, Timothy Holt turns abruptly away and disappears between the buildings.

Isaac catches sight of him and asks the hatter, "That's Timothy Holt, right?"

"Sure is. Strange he's just walking off and not even saying hello. He was in here not too long ago, about the time you placed this order. I figured he was in the middle of deciding whether to get a new hat." The hatter shrugs.

Isaac is puzzled. "Aye, that is odd. Well, I shouldn't tarry here any longer. I've got to get these loads back to Medford tonight. Otherwise, I'd take a few minutes to chase him down and see what he's about." Isaac shakes the hatter's hand. "Good day to you, and I hope good business continues coming your way."

"Good day to you as well, Quartermaster Frye."

Isaac climbs onto the wagon seat, waits a moment as three of the privates take seats on the back of the wagon, then snaps the reins to start the oxen moving. Sergeant Stone does the same in the second wagon.

•••

Late in the evening, Isaac is in his tent writing a letter by the light of an oil lamp.

"Camp on Winter Hill October 25, 1775

My Dear Wife,

After my kind Love to you and Duty to father and mother Love to Brother Whitney and Sister and Brother Timothy if he asks after me. I have nothing remarkable to acquaint you with more than what you have heard of before now or for affairs hear they remain much as they were when I was hom only last Fryday Night. I was almost floated out of my tent such a rain I have not known this grate while before and it was for sum days very uncomfortable indeed but it is got to be pretty good doings now though I cannot help thinking of home where I may have more comfort then we can

hear in the cold, mud, and rain. But I comfort myself that my time is almost out and then if it be tho will of Providence that I should live I intend to come home for the season. I know not what to do with them for I cannot get Mr. McGreger to take them now and the county People throng the Cattle down in South Groves. And so you must keep them till I write to you again I should be glad if Father would contrive to get the remainder of them Syder Barrels down to Chelmsford when he carries them to Andover and buy sum Syder and get it put into a seller and so we can get it home by sledding and I will send up the money to pay for it and you must remember the cow I wrote to you about the last time and get a good one if you can anyways you must take 20 shillings a week for them large oxen of Mr Henlays and 7/6 a week for that other and So I must Leave of writing for I have wore out my pen and got almost to sleep and So no more at Present but I Remain your Loveing husband till Death do ath parts.
Isaac Frye LT

I take notice that Brother Timothy Don't take so much Notice of me as to Send me a Letter or even his look."

Isaac lets the ink dry a few moments, folds it, and seals it with wax.

(Author's note: the above letter has been transcribed from the original document found in Isaac's house late in the twentieth century.)

•••

Elizabeth holds her youngest son, John, who is alert and casting about, his attention pulled from person to person as they make their way home from the services. It is the first Sunday in November, and it is a warm, sunny, Indian-summer day. Most of the trees have lost their leaves, expanding the horizon around the meetinghouse.

Elizabeth speaks with a group of neighbors: Sarah Parker, her daughter-in-law Phebe, and Sarah Rideout, who is about the same age as Elizabeth and likewise holding a new baby.

"It makes me happy to see you at church again," says Phebe to Elizabeth. "I know with the new baby, and Isaac gone with the army, you haven't had much opportunity."

"It has been hard. My sister Sarah and I are doing the best we can. Isaac has been paid only once since June. To make that worse, his colonel forbade him to take commissions like so many other quartermasters have been doing. I know it's morally right, but—"

Sarah Parker cuts in, "His colonel has the right of it. The money the army spends is limited by whoever agreed to back their notes."

Phebe folds her arms as if to ward off a chill. "That scares me. Everything could collapse if the wealthy Whigs decide not to fund this fight."

"I agree," says Sarah Rideout. "Please tell Isaac that Benjamin agrees. We know he is doing what is right. Besides, I will be able to visit more, now that there's less work to do outside."

Elizabeth smiles, gratitude showing in her eyes. "I know, and I am so glad you both have offered me rides to church. It means so much for me to get out and see everyone. I know Isaac is getting the best prices he can. He's always been a good deal maker."

With a sympathetic look, Sarah Rideout adds, "Oh, we know that. It's good we are in this together and simply do what it takes to help each other."

Phebe clears her throat. "Speaking of helping, Josiah has a little room on the wagon if you need to send anything to Andover. He's leaving in the morning. There will be more room on the return trip. Do any of you need anything from Andover?"

They all think a moment, and Elizabeth remembers, "Just some raisins. Isaac likes them. Everything else I will have my sister get next week when Richard makes the trip he has been planning."

Phebe's attention shifts when she sees her husband waving to her. "Josiah's ready to get going. Try as I might, I cannot seem to forget how much there is to get ready before he leaves tomorrow."

Sarah Parker turns to go with her daughter-in-law. "I'll see you off." Turning back to Elizabeth and Sarah Rideout, she adds, "I'll be right back to ride home with you. I won't be long."

Elizabeth waits a moment until Phebe and Sarah Parker are out of earshot. "Do you think I was too obvious?" she asks her friend.

"Maybe, but I doubt it matters. I think Sarah likely caught on right away. They will tell Josiah, and he's a talker, so your brother and his wife will hear."

"That's a relief. It's so difficult to say anything directly to my brother, and if I do, Hannah sees it as prying. Josiah is goodhearted and honest, so if he's the source, no one will be the wiser. It's even better that he saw Isaac last time Isaac was here getting supplies."

Sarah Rideout nods. "There are almost as many Parkers left in Andover as there are Holts and Fryes, so word will spread. In fact, I bet Richard will hear of it when he is there next week."

Elizabeth laughs. "I hope so. I think you're right—it will be fine."

Sarah Rideout looks up to see Sarah Parker walking back in their direction, and speaks a little louder for the older woman's benefit, "Do you have enough cloths for little John, here? I've got extras."

"With three older brothers, he has extras. Babies grow so fast."

Sarah Parker joins them and addresses the younger Sarah. "Your husband is ready to leave. I saw him waving."

"Well, we best be on our way," says Elizabeth, "for as nice as the day is, there won't be much left by the time we are home."

•••

On the afternoon of Thursday, November 23, Isaac is with the men from Wilton in their encampment behind the fortifications on Winter Hill. The Massachusetts Provincial Congress declared this day to be one of thanksgiving and prayer. They have just come from a sermon by Reverend David Osgood, who is minister of Medford's First Congregational Parish. Owing to the New Hampshire troops encamping on Winter Hill in Medford, Reverend Osgood is also their chaplain. The men meet in the part of the encampment belonging to Captain Walker's company, where half of the Wilton men have been garrisoned since their reassignment from Captain Crosby's company in early June.

The day is brisk, with some clouds, but not so cold as to drive the men to gather inside their cramped barracks. They share a keg of cider and a bundle of jerked beef as they talk. Isaac is in a group with the other officers, which now includes Ensign William Adrian Hawkins, promoted for his bravery during the Battle of Bunker Hill.

Lieutenant Brown has become grizzled, the gray in his beard and sideburns more prominent than when they left Wilton in April. He takes a drink of cider before speaking. "I don't know about you gentlemen, but I found the Reverend Osgood's speech this morning a good deal more cross and raw than his usual bluntness."

Lieutenant Pettingill laughs. "At least with that and his impassioned way of speaking, a man can easily pay attention for hours. Not like those honey-tongued types who get into a rhythm, and before you know it two hours is gone, and not a word, thought, or even the nature of the homily can be recalled."

Ensign Hawkins, who generally wears a calm, almost serious expression, nods. "Reverend Osgood speaks with structure, unlike our own Reverend Livermore, who seems not to mind seizing on whatever thoughts come to mind in the midst of his speaking."

That thought causes them all to laugh. Isaac surmises, "Though Reverend Livermore is genuine in his concern for our spiritual affairs, it does seem he cannot preach an idea at face value; he must know that it is true, or digress until he finds the truth."

Brown grins. "That he does."

"For more than an hour on several occasions," adds Pettingill. "I think he even surprises himself with how far afield his digressions take his sermons. It's good he is not a chaplain. We'd miss battles for having to listen to him find his way."

The officers all laugh again. After another drink, Brown speculates, "I think you're right. Reverend Osgood is much better suited to the role of chaplain. I suppose it was Providence that placed us here in Medford with a Congregationalist reverend willing to see to an army's needs."

Isaac raises his cup. "Aye, true, and here's to our Reverend Livermore staying at home where Wilton needs him most." The men raise their cups and laugh a bit more.

Ensign Hawkins changes the subject. "Have all of you re-enlisted for next year's campaign?"

All but Brown nod or say they have enlisted. Brown's gaze encompasses the group as he explains, "My place in this will be at home. In case you all haven't noticed, I am likely the oldest lieutenant in all of New Hampshire. I still have the fire in my belly, but this old back and these old legs feel something else. So, you boys will have to take heart that James Brown will be feeding you. The Army's paying good for hogs and I've got a dozen to sell this coming year, and more if they're needed.

His compatriots, unsure of what to say, lapse into silence a moment, before Isaac raises his cup again. "You came with us this far, and you will be missed. I, for one, am glad to know that a veteran like you is at home, keeping our farms safe." The others raise their cups in salutation.

Brown offers a toast in return. "To the Continental Army and its brave, steadfast officers from New Hampshire."

In unison they bellow, "To liberty!"

8 SPIRIT OF '76

"...Commissions in the new Army are not intended merely for those, who can inlist the most men; but for such Gentlemen as are most likely to deserve them. The General would therefore, not have it even supposed, nor our Enemies encouraged to believe, that there is a Man in this army (except a few under particular circumstances) who will require to be twice asked to do what his Honour, his personal Liberty, the Welfare of his country, and the Safety of his Family so loudly demand of him...And every man who inlists shall be indulged in a reasonable time, to visit his family in the Course of the winter, to be regulated in such a manner, as not to weaken the Army or injure the service..."

Excerpt from General orders for the Army, October 31, 1775

Provided to discourage men from seeking ranks of officers for reasons of higher pay or other base motivations.

One evening in early December, in Colonel Reed's headquarters, Isaac and Stephen are finishing their paperwork. The room looks considerably more lived-in now. Stacks of supplies, half-eaten plates of food, and an empty bottle of wine lie abandoned on the other desks. Colonel Reed's chair is lined with two blankets that drape over the back. A moderate fire burns quietly in the fireplace, adding to the light from the pair of oil lamps that Isaac and Stephen are using.

Stephen rises and walks slowly, rubbing his hands, to the fire, where he begins to warm them. "Have you told Elizabeth that you've re-enlisted?"

"Yes, in a letter with the pay we got two days ago, and with a reminder that the balance—five months' worth—is due at the end of this month, when our enlistments end. In her last letter, to my relief, she wrote she was able to get credit on my behalf a couple of weeks ago, and get what she and the boys needed for winter, I just wish it had come sooner."

Stephen turns away from the fire to warm his backside. "You know, in a way, it was better getting our pay later. It meant nobody spent it ahead of winter and now most will have what they need to make it through."

Isaac laughs. "You sound like my older brother Simon. He was always the prudent one. My Uncle Joseph says he was that way even as a young boy."

Stephen smiles. "I'll take that as a compliment. Everything I've heard of your brother speaks to his superior character." Stephen returns to his desk and begins another entry in a ledger before continuing, "How do you think your wife will take the news of your enlisting for next year?"

"We spoke of it when I was home in October. She knew it was likely. I also told her I would leave the army if we didn't receive our pay. The pay—and the fact that it will be increased next year—is a mixed blessing for her. I feel bad, but the truth is she's done well with the farm, and until the fruit trees are larger, we need hard money more than labor."

Stephen looks up from the ledger. "That sounds well-reasoned, although I expect you'd rather be home."

Isaac's expression changes from carefully neutral to ashamed, and his shoulders slump a little. "Making my reenlisting about pay was a rationalization. I couldn't tell her I signed on again because I feel blood on my hands every night before I go to sleep. I don't know if I could live with myself should I walk away and not finish the fight. I joined because I believed—and still do—that liberty is worth fighting for." Isaac takes a deep breath and lets it out slowly. "I wish I could explain to her how inescapable this sense of duty has become; that it is not just pride and honor. I just haven't thought of the right words."

"I think we all feel something like that, though each in his own way. At least you've told her the necessary part, even if it lacks those details. None but those who were on the battlefield can fully understand such things." Stephen pauses and takes a deep breath. Knowing there is no easy way to say it, he plunges ahead. "I have some news of my own for you. Nahum Baldwin, from Amherst, was commissioned a colonel, and has asked me to be his regiment's major. I accepted conditionally; General Washington must approve it before I can take the post."

"Congratulations!" declares Isaac with a broad smile, clearly impressed. "Deacon—I mean Colonel—Baldwin couldn't have chosen a better man. Though I'll be sorry to see you go. You have too much talent to be stuck as a regimental adjutant on a lieutenant's pay."

"Thank you, Isaac. I expect you will see some opportunities, too. I hear Captain Crosby has decided to resign. That makes sense. He's not as young as many of the regiment's officers. So, perhaps some positions will open up. Of course, you've done quite well as quartermaster, and I expect Colonel Reed may not wish to break in a new man. I know he trusts you."

"I hope so, but if nothing else, at least the pay will be much better next year. It will make being away another year a little easier for Elizabeth to bear. As for Colonel Reed's trust, I appreciate having it, but Elizabeth and the boys don't get much out of it."

Stephen rubs his jaw. "Aye, I suppose you've got a fair point there. Stay the course. You've been proving yourself invaluable, and that will lead to better things. I'm sure of it."

•••

A little over two weeks later, Isaac is home again. It is evening, and extra lamps and candles brightly light the main room of his house. Elizabeth's parents are sitting at the table, and sister Sarah is rocking in a chair by the fireplace, holding John. All enjoy steaming mugs of butter rum, laughter, and cheerful conversation.

Elizabeth, exceedingly happy, finishes refilling her mug and turns back to the group. "This is the first night since the alarm that I haven't felt desperate about what will happen next. It feels so good."

Her mother laughs. "Well, Isaac having all his pay come in over the past six weeks likely helped."

Elizabeth replies, "That makes a big difference. It gives everyone a reason to trust."

"My pay will more than double next year," says Isaac merrily, "and I'll be a full lieutenant, as well. Congress decided not to distinguish between first and second lieutenants, because in most colonies—ours included—they were doing the same work."

Timothy Sr. asks, "Still the quartermaster, right? That's been good for you, with being able to come home more often than the other soldiers."

"Yes, still quartermaster. At least I know the job, though I had hopes for more."

Mother Holt changes the topic. "How is James doing? Has his wound finally healed?"

Isaac closes his eyes and takes a deep breath before looking back to his mother-in-law. "I'm afraid it's worse. The wound won't heal. It's taking a toll on him. His sons James and Fredrick are seeing to his care now. The burden has fallen mostly upon the older son, since Fredrick is so young, though I think his company does more to elevate his father's spirits."

Mother Holt pales at the news. "Oh, my. Why is that man so hard headed? That must be difficult for young Fredrick."

"I expect so. I know what it's like to be young and watching your father... I was younger, but I don't think it's easy at any age."

Elizabeth adds, "It's not an easy thing to bear witness to. At least his brothers are there."

Timothy asks, "Are James's sons all in the Tenth Regiment?"

Isaac concurs. "Yes, as are his son-in-law, Samuel Frye, and Samuel's brother Theopolis, as well."

Elizabeth raises her mug in homage. "No one can say the Fryes aren't doing their part for liberty."

Isaac raises his own in return. "A good many Holts, too."

The others join the toast, and Timothy adds, "Glad to hear we are doing our part, too." He downs a hefty draught, his Adam's apple bobbing with each swallow. "Where do you think this business is heading, Isaac? Have you spoken with your Uncle Joseph, now that he's a general?"

"I've seen him a couple of times in the past weeks. He thinks we will break away from England. When the king's navy burned Bristol and Falmouth this year, it showed everyone it wasn't just a Boston and John Hancock problem. Those attacks strengthened our resolve." Isaac takes another pull from his mug and wipes the excess from his lip with his sleeve. "Uncle Joseph's logic is hard to fault. No matter how badly some would like it, nobody has a plausible scenario for reconciliation. Well, except for some Tories I've heard about, but that doesn't end with us keeping our heads." Isaac rubs his neck and cringes, and the others laugh. "Though I admit the army is certainly not the place for serious talk of reconciliation. I suppose it means New Hampshire may become its own country... or perhaps join with the other New England colonies to form a country. Of all things, that gives me more hope for the future than I had when we started this business."

Timothy Sr. sets his mug down. "I have to say I like that. Though I do think we should be careful what we wish for." He smiles slyly. "New Hampshire would be the poorest little country ever conceived. Let us hope we are a part of a united New England."

Elizabeth takes her father's mug and refills it. "That does sound good; though maybe call it America...or anything. Not England." She brings the steaming mug back to her father. "I wonder if it would be strange to not have a king?"

Mother Holt murmurs, "Strange indeed." Then more loudly, "Though I suppose the king hasn't mattered quite as much as the governors have."

Isaac shrugs dismissively. "Unless you count the king who agreed to Parliament's taxes, appointing his own governors, and sending an army to ensure commerce is diminished to the point that every man, woman, and child feels their king's lack of respect for their liberties."

Timothy chuckles. "Yes, there is that king. I cannot imagine him letting the colonies go, at least not without a full fight. But I suppose he could try to drive a wedge between us and the southern colonies."

Isaac takes another drink. "John Adams, I hear, was behind preempting that scenario by cajoling Congress to approve Washington as commander-in-chief. I think you have it right, Father; a lot must happen before we determine how to govern ourselves."

Timothy Sr. raises his mug. "That's the truth. A toast: To America governing herself!"

All raise their mugs with a rousing chorus of, "To America!"

•••

Later that night, with Sarah at home watching the children, Isaac and Elizabeth decide to get some fresh air. They walk down to the bridge to see the river and get a view of the stars on the clear night. They stroll in silence until reaching the end of the cleared field and the path leading down the hill to the bridge.

"Husband, when I received your letter telling me you had enlisted again, I was surprised. I worry your sense of duty to the cause of liberty outweighs your duty here."

Isaac waits a moment before answering, choosing his words carefully. "I was wondering when we would talk of this." He remains silent for several seconds as they walk, crunching along the frost-hardened edges of the earthen path. "It has become a war. Whether we like it or not, the side we chose has made sure of it. In camp, refusing to reenlist was made out to be as bad as changing sides. For the officers, there really was no option. General Washington made sure of it by supplying the men with noble notions nearly every day in his general orders. No officer who was fit for duty resigned."

Elizabeth's curiosity is piqued. "What did General Washington write in his orders that was so compelling?"

"It started with how commissions in the army were for gentlemen, not just those who could recruit the most men. He went on about how no man with any honor would need to be asked twice to do his duty to secure his personal liberties and the safety and welfare of his country and family."

Elizabeth smirks. "Very persuasive. I suppose if he winked and smiled prettily, no man would ever leave General Washington's army."

They both start laughing. Isaac adds, "Well, perhaps for some, but it is good that my wife is far kinder and prettier than General Washington."

They continue down the path in silence, reach the gate by the road, and then walk out onto the bridge. They gaze at the heavens, lost in their own thoughts for what seems like several minutes. The unusually bright half-moon splashes the few clouds to form a luminous melody accompanied by the stars' brilliant staccato counterpoint. When they look at each other, Isaac's only warning is the flare of Elizabeth's nostrils.

Her voice is firm, but still contains a note of appeal. "I need you... we need you here." With more force, "You have changed. You keep your thoughts to yourself. I..." She emphasizes the next words. "I don't want this war to come between us."

Isaac sets his jaw and nods. "You're right. There are some things I do not wish to tell you. Some of it, perhaps, I don't even admit to myself."

"Such as?"

"Such as, if the king sends a much larger army, it won't be to squeeze taxes from the people of New England; it will be to forcibly take control. The life of every officer in our army will be forfeit. There is no turning back."

Her chin juts forward angrily. "Damn you for a prideful fool, Isaac Frye! The army won't miss you. I need you here!" She looks at him intently as if trying to see behind his eyes to whatever is wrong with him.

Isaac reacts with a pained look. "You don't know how bad it has become!"

"Tell me!"

"There are still people who say we can peaceably resolve our differences. None of them saw what happened at Lexington and Concord, or on Breed's Hill. Perhaps they didn't believe the stories. The hay and stubble on Breed's Hill was coated with the blood of a thousand dead and dying redcoats! Since the alarm, almost half as many from our side have been laid low, bleeding out in fields and on the sides of roads. When the redcoats retreated from Lexington, they killed some unlucky souls in their homes, just for poking their heads out of their own windows at the wrong moment. This will not end without a much larger fight. These battles have only made people on both sides angrier and more determined to shed one another's blood."

The force of Isaac's words and the wildness in his eyes take Elizabeth aback. "What about you?"

Isaac continues, his voice a low, growling, intensity. "I'm not angry, and I'm not out to just kill redcoats. But in all the ways I can think of, I find myself down a path I cannot turn away from. If we quit, there isn't a Frye in New England who won't be hunted down. There are at least a dozen of us in Washington's army now, and we are hardly the only such family. If we quit now, there will be no one to stop the redcoats from coming here and doing the king's justice to me, or worse—to you and the boys—for what I've done in the name of liberty. Mark my words. They will do it for the blood already on my hands!" Isaac swallows hard and grinds his teeth. His voice quiets to a dreadful hoarseness. "There was so much blood. It was on everyone's hands. More than in any battle anyone could remember." Isaac's voice is shaking as he finishes. He looks Elizabeth in the eye and composes himself, again sounding resolute and sure of his decision. "There is no honorable way to quit, and even if there was, I don't think I could live with myself, because there was no honor in what I had to do."

Elizabeth is trembling, her anger gone. "I'm sorry. I... I forced myself to lighten your part in this so I could have hope you would come home and stay. I am sorry, husband." She hugs him, and he returns the embrace. They stay there for many minutes before the cold night reminds them they would be warmer if they were moving.

Isaac finally says, "I am sorry too. I gave my word to support a cause when I hardly understood what doing so would mean. Can you forgive me?"

"Yes. But only if we start walking home now. The butter rum may still be warm."

...

Nine days later, with Isaac back at Winter Hill, Elizabeth is taken with a desire for some fresh air and walks to the top of the hill to get a better view of the sunset, while still keeping her home in view. It is late in the afternoon, a few clouds are high in the sky, and the sun is beginning to set. As she nears the top of the hill, she sees Sarah Rideout walking toward her.

Elizabeth stops at the crest of the hill and enjoys the sunset while waiting for her friend. "A fine evening to you, Sarah," she calls out.

"To you, as well, Elizabeth. I've seen you come out here on occasion and I decided I would join you today. That is, if you don't mind the company?"

"I don't. I come up here for the fresh air and hope of fresh perspective. With Isaac gone... gone to war..." Her voice falters. Regret and uncertainty play across her features. "I've had trouble admitting to myself that he has gone to an army and to a war, and that those things pull on him more than I can. I want to think of him as just away somewhere, and that he will be home soon."

Sarah stands beside Elizabeth and links her arm through Elizabeth's. "I see why you come here. If nothing else, the view from the top of the hill might set your mind to a more peaceful state."

"When Isaac was here, I confronted him about enlisting again. I suppose it was ill conceived to do so. In many ways, he confirmed my worst fears. He was in the battle, and as he put it, has blood on his hands. I don't want to lose 'us' to this war, yet I desire liberty as much as he does. I'm so afraid it may have already cost too much."

Sarah, who is only a few years older, is silent for a few moments. She turns to face Elizabeth, then rubs her hands together vigorously to warm them, but also to break the seriousness of the moment. "Life and living change us every single day. But those changes do not break bonds. You and Isaac are quite obviously committed to each other and to a good future for your children. I see nothing to doubt."

"Thank you, Sarah. It's good to hear another voice say those words." Elizabeth smiles. "It makes them sound reasonable and true."

Sarah laughs wryly. "I hadn't thought of it that way, but I do believe what I said to be true."

They watch as the last of the sun disappears behind the hills. In a few seconds, the day fades to twilight.

Sarah looks over her shoulder to her house. "Worrying is a great deal of effort. You've got too many other things to spend your time doing." She shrugs. "I suppose, in some strange way, I came out here tonight because I thought you were troubled, and I wished to tell you I think everything will be fine. That and I needed a break from little Joshua. He is colicky, and sometimes I haven't enough patience. Thankfully, Ben doesn't mind holding him for a little while."

"I'm glad you came out here tonight. I'm grateful my little John is a good baby. He takes everything well. He seems to want to make me happy. It was a beautiful sunset, too. I do feel better. Thank you."

"You're welcome. We must all care for each other if we are to get through these times."

9 WINTER ON WINTER HILL

"The Regimental Quarter Masters, and their Sergeants, are to cause proper Necessaries to be erected at convenient distances from the Barracks, in which their men are lodged, and see that those necessaries are frequently filled up, any person who shall be discovered easing himself elsewhere, is to be instantly confined and brought before a Regimental Court Martial--They are to cause also the Filth, and Garbage, about the Barracks, to be removed and buried, In short, it is in a particular manner the duty of the Quarter Master, to see that the Barracks are kept clean and sweet; the Victuals properly prepared &c..."

Excerpt from General Orders for the army, January 5, 1776

A loud knock disturbs Colonel Reed, Gilman, Stephen, and Isaac inside the regiment's headquarters on Winter Hill, mid-morning on January 5, 1776.

In a crisp tone, Reed commands. "Come in."

A man whom none of them know, enters. He deduces Colonel Reed as the senior officer, walks to his desk, and presents himself in a military fashion. He is a few inches shorter than Isaac is, with dark-brown, nearly black hair, and dark-brown eyes. He carries himself in a business-like way. "Sir, I am Lieutenant James Otis and am reporting for duty as your regiment's new adjutant. I'm told I am to fully assume the duties within the course of a week."

With one eye narrowed, Colonel Reed gives Otis an appraising look. "Very well." Then he raises a quizzical eyebrow. "You wouldn't be related to the attorney, James Otis, would you?"

"I am his nephew, sir. My father is Colonel Joseph Otis of the Barnstable Regiment of militia, though I've heard he has been promoted to Brigadier General recently."

Colonel Reed nods and seems pleased. "Excellent. You come from a talented family. Let me introduce you to Lieutenant and soon-to-be-Major Stephen Peabody."

Stephen stands and extends his hand. "I am pleased to meet you, Lieutenant Otis."

"I am pleased to meet you, as well."

Stephen, looking as though he finds something familiar about Otis, asks, "Where are you from, Lieutenant?"

"Westfield, out in Hampden County. It's on the far side of the Connecticut River."

Stephen nods. "I've heard that's good land there."

"I think so. I suppose you could say I've bet my life on it—"

Reed interjects. "If you will excuse me, Lieutenant Peabody will acquaint you with your duties."

Both lieutenants thank the colonel. Stephen locates an extra chair and offers it to Otis. As they sit and begin going over the duties of the regiment's adjutant, Reed returns to this desk to finish writing the letter he had been working on.

Ten minutes later Reed sets aside the finished later, rises, and approaches Isaac. "Quartermaster Frye, it's been a few weeks since I heard anything on the condition of your cousin, Colonel James Frye. Have you any news?"

"I'm afraid the news is not good, sir. I went to see him yesterday, and he was quite ill, though thankfully he was lucid. I learned this morning that he got a bad fever in the night. The wound has gotten worse. Festering now."

Colonel Reed sighs, shaking his head. "I am sorry to hear such. He's a good man and a well-respected commander. How well do you know him?"

"Quite well. I've known him for most of my life. I sold my land in Andover to him before I moved to Wilton. I worked at his inn for a few years before leaving Andover, and he taught me quite a lot about commerce and how to get a good deal."

Colonel Reed adopts a hopeful attitude. "I pray his condition will improve today."

"Thank you, sir. I intend to visit him again tonight."

•••

Three days later, in the early afternoon, Colonel Reed is writing at his desk, while Isaac and James Otis are at work on the regiment's inventory with Sergeant James Blanchard, the regiment's new quartermaster sergeant. There comes another knock on the door. Reed gives permission to enter. A captain pushes open the door and makes his way to Reed's desk.

"Colonel Reed, sir. I'm Captain Sawyer from the Tenth Massachusetts Regiment. I have a request for you from Brigadier General Joseph Frye." Captain Sawyer extends a sealed message to Colonel Reed.

Taking the message, Reed responds, "Thank you, Captain Sawyer."

Captain Sawyer waits a moment. "Sir, the general asked me to wait for your response."

"Very well." Colonel Reed opens the message and reads it. "My response is yes."

"Thank you, sir. I will relay your response."

As Captain Sawyer turns and leaves, Isaac notes that the colonel has kept his expression unusually blank. A minute later, after Reed has put some papers away, he gets up and walks towards Isaac's desk. "Quartermaster Frye. Could you come outside with me for a moment?"

"Yes, sir."

The two leave the building and walk a few paces away. Colonel Reed begins, "I'm afraid there was some bad news to prompt that request from your uncle. Your cousin James died late this morning.

Your uncle requested a furlough for you to accompany his body back to Andover for burial."

Isaac shuts his eyes and clenches his jaw for several seconds before taking a deep breath. The news comes as quite a shock for him, despite having seen in the past few days that the end for Colonel Frye was unavoidable.

"My deepest condolences," says Reed with genuine compassion.

"Thank you, sir"

"You're welcome. We will see you in a few days' time."

"Thank you again, sir. I have a few things to complete, then I'll show Sergeant Blanchard what needs to be done while I'm gone."

•••

A large fire blazes, yet does only a little to heat the draughty room. Colonel Reed, Gilman, and Isaac wrap themselves in blankets as they bend over their respective desks. Reed is reviewing the regiment's latest muster roll, Gilman is writing the orders for the guard duty assignments, and Isaac is tallying the latest inventory of pots, kettles, and utensils. James Otis enters the room, with a rush of frozen air whooshing in around him, causing the others to quickly bend low covering their desks to keep their papers from flying away. After he closes the door, they pull their blankets tighter and give the adjutant looks of tired annoyance. After he replaces the rolled-up rug along the bottom of the door, he stands and turns, out of breath with excitement and exertion. He takes a moment to catch his breath, and turns to Colonel Reed, who is now looking at him expectantly. "Sir, finally some good news."

Reed, continues adjusting the two blankets wrapped about his shoulders, and still irritated by the cold air, sarcastically snaps, "It better be about the warmer weather that's right behind you."

Otis glances back to the door and shrugs. "I am afraid, sir, such a change—or even news of it—is well above my position, but I was at headquarters in Cambridge, and there learned that Colonel Knox has made it to Framingham with the cannon from Fort Ti. They will be here in two days."

Reed's demeanor immediately improves. "Well, that is excellent news! Of course, we still need powder."

Gilman shifts his blankets. Whether due to the cold or general impatience with the army's situation, his tone is ill tempered. "If there was ever a good reason to call in the powder given to the colonies for their militias' use, this is it. I hope General Washington does so."

Reed rubs his hands together. "I hope he does, too. Though that will take another month. But this is good; we may finally get past this business with General Gage."

Having caught his breath, Otis asks, "Sir, what do you believe will happen once we have taken Boston?"

Reed exhales slowly while he thinks. "That will depend on what the king and Parliament decide to do in response. I expect we will put effort into protecting the ports so the raids on Bristol and Falmouth are not repeated elsewhere."

Gilman, his tone less surly, adds, "Once we drive General Gage out of Boston, Congress will have some decisions to make. They have made arrangements thus far, but longer term, we will need something more than committees of safety and correspondence. What do you think, Colonel Reed?"

"Yes, and I fear King George will send an even larger army, and will have the backing of the Parliament to borrow immensely for it."

Gilman gets up and retrieves another log to put on the fire. "That leads me to wonder how many more armies King George can afford to send."

Before Isaac can stop himself, he says, "One or two at the most, sir."

Reed turns and cocks an eyebrow. "How do you figure, Quartermaster?"

Isaac offers, "Well, sir, I cannot imagine the king has revenues, much less reserves enough, given that the colonies must have diminished the crown's income via the boycotts on imported goods."

"I suppose so, but two armies the size of General Gage's, or quite likely larger, would, I think, be too much for us in New England. We will very much require the other colonies to furnish troops with at least the same commitment as New England has shown."

Otis whistles in amazement. "Until now, I had more or less presumed this was a New England matter. Pulling the other colonies into the struggle seems unavoidable, given that logic—but to what end?"

Isaac answers, "My uncle believes we may form separate nations, or maybe the New England colonies will unite to become a new country."

Gilman puts the log on the fire, then turns to warm his back before concurring, "I have heard similar ideas." He raises his eyebrows and grimaces skeptically. "Though I don't believe any are actively being entertained by Congress."

"Nor do I," concludes Reed. "And now, gentlemen, I believe we have digressed long enough. Let's be back at our work."

•••

A few weeks later, in late February, Isaac is back in Wilton. This time with the regiment's new quartermaster sergeant, James Blanchard. Blanchard is tall, in his mid-twenties, broad-shouldered, and has thin, light-brown hair and green eyes. With them are Timothy Holt Sr. and Isaac's two older sons, Isaac Jr. and Abiel. They all step carefully, to avoid slipping, downhill through the snow-covered woods above Isaac's house and barn. It is still early in the morning and they have been tapping maple trees. The air is cold, well below freezing, causing their breath to create small clouds.

As they come out of the woods Timothy Sr., who is hold Abiel's hand to keep him steady on the steep hillside, asks, "How large is the army these days? I assume quite a large number of the men have been given time to visit their families."

"Last month," explains Isaac, "the army was half the size it was in June, although our numbers are rising, now as men come in from the last of the winter furloughs."

They reach the barn and go inside to find Elizabeth and her mother. They've just finished feeding the cows. Elizabeth, seeing that the men only carry mallets, and no taps, smiles to Isaac. "It looks like you were successful."

"Yes, we tapped two dozen trees, so you should have a plenty of sap soon."

"Good," replies Elizabeth. "That leaves us time enough to change and easily make it to the meetinghouse."

Twenty minutes later, all but Elizabeth, Sarah, and the boys are outside waiting beside the wagon. Mother Holt's head comes up with a sudden start. "Isaac, I had forgotten to tell you, Father and I met Stephen Peabody's wife, Hannah, last month when we went to Amherst. We enjoyed meeting her. How is Stephen?"

"I think he's well, though I have not seen him for several weeks. He got a major's commission with Colonel Baldwin's new regiment, although we are not certain when the men will be raised to fill their regiment. Stephen is a good man for that job, and I imagine could command a regiment himself. I believe he's at home now until their regiment is ordered to muster."

Elizabeth asks, "Who replaced Stephen in your regiment? You wrote it, but I don't recall now."

"James Otis. He's from Massachusetts. A good man, too, but younger, and doesn't have Stephen's calm and organized presence. I like him, though. He is a cheery and affable sort."

"Sergeant Stone—what happened to him?" queries Timothy Sr.

"He got a lieutenant's commission in Timothy Bedel's regiment, which was sent north to Quebec by way of Fort Ti."

"Good to hear. I liked him."

Isaac, realizing an opportunity to bolster his new sergeant's morale, quickly adds, "I did as well, though Sergeant Blanchard here has done just as well, if not better. I'm lucky to have him, as I need all the help I can get." Isaac nods appreciatively to Blanchard, who tips his hat to Isaac.

Mother Holt comments wistfully, "It seems so long since all this began, and yet nothing much seems to have changed."

Blanchard smiles. "I see some hope on that front. We got the cannon from Fort Ti, and General Washington called for the militias to send their powder to Boston."

Isaac adds with a grin, "Not much has arrived yet, but once it does, we will be sure to let General Gage know."

Mother Holt perks up at the news. "Then what?"

Isaac looks thoughtful. "I suppose we secure Boston and the port. I imagine quite a few people would like to see the port re-opened as soon as possible."

Elizabeth leads the boys out of the house, followed by Sarah who holds a squirming baby John, as Isaac finishes speaking.

For having his back to the house, Blanchard doesn't notice and grimaces. "That will be a nasty bit. They've got the pox there, and I don't fancy going into Boston and catching it."

Elizabeth exhibits genuine concern as she walks up, motioning the older boys to climb into the wagon. "You haven't been inoculated?"

Blanchard shakes his head. "No, ma'am. My father thought it was too risky."

Elizabeth responds confidently, "I suppose we thought it too risky not to. We got inoculated, the summer before last. A traveling doctor came through. I had been reading about the inoculation procedure and agreed with the principle."

Blanchard, who is very interested now, quizzes her. "So, it worked? Did you get very sick?"

Isaac picks up Timothy and deposits him in the wagon, then winks. "Not so much sick as thoroughly annoyed by the illness. A few pocks, but not like in the full-blown cases. Still, it was worrisome."

Elizabeth nods in agreement. "Yes, it wasn't until after we got our inoculations that we heard about some poor souls who got full cases from their inoculations. Fortunately, it seems such cases are rare."

Blanchard asks Elizabeth's parents, "How about you? Did you also get inoculated?"

"Yes, and had a similar time of it," answers Timothy Sr.

Blanchard is much relieved. "Well, given the evidence, I think I will get inoculated as soon as the opportunity presents itself." He turns to Isaac. "Do you think Colonel Reed will let me?"

"I'm not sure it will be up to him. I've heard there's been debate amongst the generals. Stephen said there were enough loud voices on both sides to keep a decision from being made. I suggest keeping quiet about it. I won't say anything."

Blanchard walks to the front of the wagon and checks the harness as Isaac speaks. "Good idea."

Timothy Sr. climbs up into the front of the wagon and takes the reins, and Isaac gives Elizabeth a hand up to sit beside her father. Blanchard helps Mother Holt up to sit on the other side. Blanchard and Isaac mount waiting horses.

Elizabeth looks over to Isaac with a warm smile. "There will be plenty of people glad to see you and hear the news from Boston."

Isaac urges his horse into motion to lead the way out of the farmyard. "Let's be on our way then. I am looking forward to seeing everyone."

•••

A little before midnight on March 4, Isaac and Adjutant James Otis—who have formed a brotherly bond in the months since James came into the regiment—are standing beside a mortar placement on the outer wall of the fortifications on Winter Hill. They are looking toward Boston, each holding a cup of rum. For a few moments, a break in the heavy clouds allows the nearly-full moon to illuminate the foreground. To the right of Ploughed Hill, an orange flash signals the arrival, half a second later, of a boom from a cannon. Briefly, the space in front of the cannon is revealed, then indistinct dark-grays collapse onto the cannon and crew of artillerymen. A flash from another nearby cannon illuminates the waves on Charles River, making the scene look strangely festive for an instant, but the view fades as the clouds close together and hide the moon again.

Isaac raises his cup. "Cheers to a successful bombardment tomorrow, and to not needing a general battle to take Boston."

"Cheers to both of those good sentiments." James raises his cup and takes a drink. "That was quite a feat, moving all those cannon to Dorchester tonight."

"Hiding them behind all that hay we piled up outside of Roxbury and into Dorchester now seems divinely inspired. I bet nothing can be seen even from as close as Roxbury. The few times the moon has shown, it only lasted a few seconds, and I doubt anyone in Boston could hear that work, given this cannonade we've kept up all evening on our side over here. General Gage shall be mightily afflicted when he awakens to the surprise we've prepared for him."

"Particularly so, given he likely went to sleep thinking us fools for firing at this range and wasting our powder."

James coughs and clears his throat. "The weather these past few weeks has been so dismal with all the cold and rain. It made me wonder, until tonight, whether the redcoats had gotten out of the habit of looking our way."

In the foreground, another flash of orange bursts from the cannon on Lechmere Point, firing towards Boston.

James takes another sip. "I don't know about it being a waste of powder. I believe this is about keeping up appearances. It would annoy me, if I were trying to sleep in Boston, to hear that noise, knowing it's pointed in my direction. I know the general wants them looking over here tonight. Though I'm not sure they can see any more than the flashes. These clouds make it hard to see the drink in my cup."

"I hope this ruse our artillery is putting on works. I'd hate to wake in the morning to find Dorchester overrun with redcoats. I'm going to take a nap. We've got to be ready before dawn with the boats."

"Sounds like a good idea." James finishes off his rum. "Get me up if you don't see me."

•••

A few hours later, the sky shows the first hint that the sun is rising to the east, down the Mystic River from Winter Hill. Thickening clouds allow just enough light to see the shapes of the hills along the shore above the village of Chelsea. Isaac, James, and Sergeant Blanchard carry lanterns as they inspect one hundred or so small boats of sizes ranging from rowboats to bateaux, which are drawn up high on the bank of the Mystic. The weather begins to take a nasty turn, with gusts of wind blowing sleet, stinging any exposed skin.

Blanchard puts his back to the wind. "Quartermaster, where did we get all these boats, and what's the plan for them?

Isaac, a couple of boats away, turns into the wind to respond, but the wind whips his words away. He walks toward Blanchard, who meets him halfway. Both huddle with their backs to the wind.

"The boats were brought from the towns on the coast, I think from as far as Marblehead, though most came from Chelsea and Lynn. We are to keep them here, hidden from the enemy's view. General Sullivan's brigade is to guard against the redcoats punching through on this side, from Bunker Hill. But if they should attack *en masse* at Dorchester, we will carry these boats over to the Charles River, and cross it to attack their rear or flank."

"Hmph," Blanchard grunts with approval. "Makes good sense, but I hope the redcoats stay in their beds this morning. It's looking like an awful day for a battle. My feet are already soaked and near frozen."

"Aye, true, but we need to make sure none are likely to sink with a load of men on board. We will have to test them all. Go up and roust some of the men to help us. No point in us having all the fun."

Blanchard casts Isaac a grateful look. "Thank you. For a moment I was worried we'd be testing them all ourselves." He turns and heads back up Winter Hill.

•••

Twelve taxing days later, after successfully bombarding Boston day and night to finally achieve the goal of General Gage's surrender, Isaac and a group of the officers from New Hampshire arrive on the crown of Cobble Hill, next to Ploughed Hill, which affords the best vantage point from which to view Boston. It is midmorning, yet they all look haggard from lack of sleep. However, their spirits are clearly high as they eagerly take their turns with the small telescope to see the regulars paraded in preparation to evacuate the city.

The Boston they see before them sags, exhausted and depleted over the peninsula it had thrived on for a hundred and fifty years. Most of the trees are gone, chopped for firewood, and there is far too little activity on the streets.

One of the captains absently renders the view into words. "The greatest city on the continent, withered and sickened, and finally the poison is leaving. Good riddance to the ministerial pox." A few of the men laugh half-heartedly.

When Isaac puts his eye to the telescope, he can make out lines of redcoats waiting to board ships. It is a satisfying sight. Isaac hands the telescope to James. "Well, it finally looks like they're going. Without a battle, too."

While James is taking his turn, he comments, "Yes, it looks as though we are out from under the king's bloody boot heel." James passes the telescope to Captain Towne. "I suppose I feel relief, but I'm so exhausted from the constant music of General Washington's Suite Number Four for Cannons, I could barely drink a toast to our victory."

With a weary-sounding laugh, Isaac puts his hand on James's shoulder. "I am most definitely relieved there was no battle, especially on that first day of the bombardment with the sleet wind. It does feel as though a burden has been lifted. Our families are finally safe, and that feels exceedingly good."

10 THE SICKNESS

In *General Orders, March 16, 1776*

As the weather is so bad, and the roads so mirey, the Regiments and Companies of Artillery, ordered to march this morning, are to halt until to morrow morning.

General George Washington

Three mornings later, on Tuesday, March 19, 1776, Isaac, James, and Gilman are diligently copying orders for each of the captains of the regiment's companies. The orders pertain to the imminent possibility of responding to an alarm. They expect to march, on moment's notice, should an alarm come. Many in the camp believe General Gage will not sail to Canada as he promised, and instead will turn south and land the troops, recently evacuated from Boston, in Rhode Island or Connecticut. A set of tentative knocks sound at the door.

Gilman looks up. "Come in, please."

A man, obviously not a soldier, enters. From his dress, he looks to be a farmer. "Sirs, I have an urgent letter for Quartermaster Frye."

Isaac looks up for the first time, concern showing on his face due to hearing his name in such a way. A second later Isaac recognizes the man. He rises and shakes Amos's hand with a warm greeting. "Amos Holt! I am surprised to see you here." He introduces the man to the room. "Gentlemen, this Mr. Amos Holt of Wilton. He is first cousin to my wife." The other officers nod in greeting.

Isaac looks back to Amos. "You said something about an urgent letter for me?"

Amos wears a pained and grim expression. "I do. This letter," Amos produces the document from inside his coat, "is from your wife. I suggest you read it while seated."

Isaac takes the letter and sits down. It is addressed to him, written in Elizabeth's hand... though not her usual neat and orderly hand. He keeps his expression neutral, despite feeling a little anxious for not knowing the contents of the letter and having three others observe him. He turns the letter over twice, then breaks the wax seal.

Isaac unfolds the letter. The color drains from his face as he reads.

March 17, 1776

Dearest Husband, Today our son Timothy passed into the care of our Lord in Heaven. He became sick a few days after you were last here. I beg you to come home. Your Loving Wife.

Isaac shudders, blinking away tears, and sets the letter face down on his desk. The neutral mask is replaced by immense pressure as Isaac clenches his jaw. His neck bulges, his eyes widen, and he begins to shake uncontrollably.

Instantly concerned, James and Gilman are on their feet. Dismay and alarm play across their faces as they move toward Isaac.

Isaac's tightly balled fists bounce rapidly on the top of the desk as he continues to shake. His face has taken on a deep, frightening shade of red.

James ventures, "Isaac, are you well? I see that letter held no good news."

Isaac cannot respond for several seconds, then when his shaking seems on the verge of a seizure, he exhales raggedly. His voice— choking—provides the tragic explanation. "One of my sons died on

Sunday." Isaac inhales hoarsely, then leans over his desk, his hands pushing with all his strength on the sides of his head. As he exhales, his voice filled with pain, growls, "Noooo."

Gilman starts moving to Isaac's left side, and motions for James to move to the other. "Let's get him some fresh air."

James nods once and they gently pull Isaac's hands from his head and lift him to his feet. He sags momentarily in their grasp, before getting his feet set squarely. They guide him toward the door, which Amos Holt opens.

They stand outside for a minute. Isaac, despondent, keeps his eyes closed. The cool air begins to bring Isaac back to himself. He opens his eyes. "His name was Timothy." Isaac turns to Amos. "I'm stuck here and cannot go. The army is preparing to march."

James spits in frustration. He looks to Gilman. "Surely we can make an exception?" Gilman, wearing a sympathetic but grim look, shakes his head.

Isaac turns to Amos, his arms ramrod straight at his sides as he clenches and unclenches his fists. He shakes his head violently to clear his head. "Amos, can you come back in fifteen minutes? I would write a few lines to my wife and send her something along with it."

Amos bobs his head encouragingly. "I can. One thing more you should know—Elizabeth's mother looked to have taken ill with the same sickness on the day I left. She was staying and helping at your place while your son was sick."

Isaac nods to acknowledge what Amos has said, then swallows forcibly and replies, "Amos. Thank you. I will get this written as quickly as I can so you can be on your way."

Amos begins to leave, but James intercepts him. "Mr. Holt, I can take you to get some food. It's the least we can do, given how far you've come."

"Thank you, sir."

James leads Amos through the door.

Isaac sits and begins writing.

March 19, 1776   Camp on Winter Hill

Dearest Wife, My mind is at a compleat loss upon reading your lines to know what I should tell you. It pains me greatly to convey that the Army plans to move south any day, I know not where. I planned to write you tonight with that news. Thus, I cannot be spared from my duty. My love and prayers go to you, the boys. Give my gratitude to your Mother, Father and Sarah.

--Your loving husband, Isaac.

P.S. Enclosed is my pay.

When James returns with Amos, Isaac has the letter sealed, along with his pay, and he rises to hand it to Amos. "Amos, we expect to march soon. I would very much like to hear from Elizabeth again, as soon as she can write. Can you bring her next letter to me? We will pay you for your trouble. I am grateful for this effort you have undertaken on our behalf."

Amos looks everywhere but directly at Isaac. "I can. Won't be able to start plowing for at least a week, given the wet weather over the past month. Everything is mud."

Isaac presses the letter into Amos's hand. In that instant Amos's eyes lock onto Isaac's features.

The anguish in Isaac's eyes cuts off Amos's chatter. He holds Isaac's gaze "I am truly sorry, Isaac."

"Thank you, Amos. I am glad so many of Elizabeth's family are in Wilton."

As the two shake hands, Amos affirms, "You are most welcome." Amos beings to leave, but turns back to Isaac. "I should make it back to Wilton late today, or at worst tomorrow morning. I came by way of Andover, which is how I am here so early in the morning. I will be going back through Concord. Though if the roads are slow, I will stay in Hollis." Amos tucks Isaac's letter into his coat beside a couple of loaves of bread, and closes the door behind him.

•••

Four days later in Wilton's cemetery, a little over a mile to the north of the meetinghouse, a somber group is gathered. The graveyard is on a hilltop, in a clearing hemmed in on all sides by tall trees that in summer provide a feeling of seclusion and peace. In late winter it has a bleak coldness most visitors take as an invitation to be quickly about their business. The ground quickly turns muddy wherever people walk and gather. The day is cloudy, with gusts of cold wind, and though it rained into the previous night, no rain has fallen since midnight.

The lane along the east side of the cemetery is lined with wagons. Almost four dozen mourners have gathered, including a central group comprising Elizabeth, her father, Isaac Jr., Abiel, Sarah Holt, and Richard and Hannah Whitney. Elizabeth's brother Timothy and his wife Hannah are also present. Several others are nearby, including Henry and Sarah Parker, Josiah and Phebe Parker, and Benjamin and Sarah Rideout. Several other groups of Holts, who live in or near Wilton, are also among the mourners.

The group gathers about two graves—one small, recently filled, and one fresh, with an adult-sized coffin draped in black cloth beside it. A muddy mound of heavy dirt lies nearby. The Reverend Jonathan Livermore, in his late forties, and a man for whom ministering and tending to his congregation is second nature, is speaking. "We ask God for strength in the coming days to shoulder new burdens and to accept our losses with grace. Last, we ask God to guide us and help us to find peace of mind in these troubled times. Amen."

The group responds with Amens of their own. Then some of the men use ropes to lower the coffin into the new grave. While this is happening, Rev. Livermore and his wife, Elizabeth, come to stand with Elizabeth, her father, and her sister, Hannah Whitney. "May my wife and I call on each of you in the next few days? It is my custom to avail myself to those who are grieving."

Timothy Sr. nods. "Of course, Reverend. I would appreciate some company."

Elizabeth barely acknowledges. Her face is devoid of emotion and her eyes dark from crying and too little sleep. "Yes, Sarah and I would like that." She forces herself to show a small, appreciative smile.

Hannah, who is holding her eldest child, a boy of nearly two years, is grateful for the offer. "That would be much appreciated, Reverend Livermore."

The reverend and his wife move on to offer their condolences to Timothy Holt, Jr. and his wife, Hannah.

•••

Late in the afternoon of March 27, James is with Isaac in the regiment's area of the encampment behind Winter Hill, where Isaac is overseeing is the dismantling of one of the barracks. The weather is cold and blustery, and the men do not appear happy to be dismantling their shelter given the promise of a cold night. The men load the salvaged boards into wagons.

James asks, "Where will these boards be taken?"

"To Watertown," Isaac responds. "They were on loan from the public stores of Massachusetts." Isaac points to a pile of rolled up tents. "We brought our tents back on these same wagons this morning."

Isaac turns as he hears his name called.

Amos Holt, walking at a quick pace, approaches. Isaac walks to meet him, and offers his hand. As they shake hands, Isaac says, "Amos, I am most relieved to see you. For the past few days I've worried as to whether I would be hearing from Elizabeth."

"Aye, Isaac. I was hoping you had not yet marched."

"It is a close thing. The regiment is on alert and could receive orders to march at any moment now."

Amos looks worn, more than a little damp, and his boots and trousers are carrying a good deal of mud, and not all of it from the churned ground in and around Winter Hill. "Isaac, I'm sorry. Your wife's letter will explain my delay." Amos reaches into his coat and retrieves Elizabeth's letter, then hands it to Isaac.

Isaac asks, "Will you be staying the night?"

"I was planning to ride back as far as Andover and stay with family there."

"Then I will give you this now for Elizabeth." Isaac takes a sealed letter from within his coat and hands it to Amos. "Amos, you have my deep appreciation for the troubles you've endured to help Elizabeth and me. With our loss, and my duty here not allowing me to come home, I know it has been difficult for her."

"You're our family too, Isaac. Uncle Timothy, as you might expect, wishes you to do your utmost to bring this unpleasant business to an end and come home."

"Thank you, and I will." Isaac hands Amos a small pouch with a few coins. "For your troubles. Travel safely home."

"I will. Thank you, Isaac."

Amos leaves. Isaac opens the letter.

March 25, 1776

Dearest Husband,
I am afraid there is worse news to share with you. The day after Amos returned with your lines Mother dyed of the same sickness that took our Timothy. It has been two days since the burial. Each day is a tryal, and though I try to not dwell on it, so much death is almost too much to bear. I hope to receive some lines from you to make me laugh, for I have not done so in weeks. Your loving Wife, Elizabeth.

Isaac, oblivious to the fact he is not alone, and furious at himself for not reading Elizabeth's letter while Amos was still there, shouts, "Damn!" The outburst startles James and several of the soldiers. Isaac reddens. "I'm sorry. James, I need to chase down Mr. Holt."

James says, "I'll help you find him."

Isaac takes off at a run, heading for the Medford ferry that crosses the Mystic River a few hundred yards away.

Only fifty yards later, Isaac spies Amos Holt standing beside his horse and speaking with Jonas Perry from Wilton. Isaac shouts, "Amos! Amos Holt!"

Amos and Jonas turn to see Isaac approaching at a run, and wait the few seconds for Isaac to arrive. Before Isaac can speak, Amos holds up his hand. "I figured you'd want to send another letter back, so I stopped here to wait."

A little out of breath, Isaac pants, "Thank you." He catches his breath. "I'll just need time to write a few lines. I should have read her letter first. She asked for something particular, and I would give her that much if I could. Can I prevail on you for fifteen or twenty more minutes?"

Amos nods. "Yes, it was going to be dark by the time I made it to Andover anyhow, and it's good to see another Wilton man," he says, nodding at Jonas.

Isaac points to the regiment's headquarters. "I'll be in the headquarters writing. Please come in when you're done visiting. I'll write quickly. Thank you."

Isaac turns to see James heading in his direction.

James calls out, "Sergeant Blanchard is finishing up with the men taking down the barracks, so take your time."

Isaac calls back "Thank you, I'll be in the headquarters."

Back in the regimental headquarters, Isaac writes:

March 27th, 1776, Camp on Winter Hill

Dearest Wife,
It is my hope this letter finds you at liberty to giggle. The business here the men laugh at is unfit for including here. Gather the boys around you, perhaps on the bed, for they must share in the laughter. Tickle young Isaac's belly for me, and blame Abiel. If Isaac doesn't tickle Abiel, then you should, and blame me with a big wink.

James comes in as Isaac lays down his quill. His eyes go wide when he sees Isaac cut four buttons from his coat.

"Isaac what the devil are you doing? Major Scammell has been nearly livid respecting the state of the men's uniforms. Now you're going to hear it for sure when we parade next." James shakes his head.

"If the quartermaster of a regiment cannot procure needle, thread, and four new buttons in an hour's time, we are well and truly lost."

Amos knocks on the door before entering. James offers him a seat by the fire while Isaac finishes writing.

When your cheeks are rosy and you have tired of the tickling. Distribute one button to each boy. There is one for you. I have just cut these buttons from my coat, in the presence of our regiment's adjutant, James Otis. We are on alert to march at any moment. Tell the boys to keep the buttons safe. Thus, wherever I am to go, I am with you, and each of you is with me.
Your Loving Husband, Isaac.

P.S. Send the Boys after Sarah if she misses the first tickling. I am sure she could use a laugh too.

Isaac folds the buttons within the letter and seals it. "Amos thank for indulging me. In trade, I can only offer that the road will be fifteen minutes drier for your trip, and hopefully it goes better for that."

Amos takes the letter. "It will, Isaac. I hope the campaign you are embarking on goes well and you are home soon." Amos tucks the letter into his coat and leaves for the second time.

Five minutes later, a sharp knock surprises both Isaac and James, who were preparing to leave. The adjutant gives permission to enter. Captain Sawyer closes the door behind him and heads for Isaac's desk. "I've got a letter for you from General Frye. He knew you would be busy and did not want to take up your time, but he says you would need to hear the news as quickly as possible." Captain Sawyer hands Isaac a small, sealed letter.

"Thank you, Captain Sawyer. I'm sorry you had to take the trouble to come here just for this."

"It's no trouble. I'm glad to get out and exert myself, even if it is a bit chilly." As Sawyer turns to leave, he adds, "He said there is no need to respond, and he sends his wishes for your continued good health and good fortune."

"I am pleased to have his words, and convey to him that his estimate of my state of affairs is correct."

After Sawyer leaves, Isaac sits at the table and unseals the letter.

March 27, 1776, Cambridge

Nephew,
I regret my tidings are of an ill nature, and sadly add to those you've endured recently. Your brother Simon has also lost a son, five days ago. One of the twins, John, died of what is likely the same sickness as your family. I had the news from my wife this morning.

Brigadier General Joseph Frye

Seeing Isaac's prolonged quietude and deepening frown, James grows perturbed and asks, "If I may, what was the news?"

Isaac sighs in total despondency, then passes the letter across the table. "I would rather not say the words aloud. Please read it for yourself."

James quickly reads the letter. "Oh." With reverence, he carefully refolds the letter and hands it back to Isaac. "I would not have been able to imagine a spate of sorry news the likes of which has found you. I am very sorry."

"I don't know what to think, other than to endure."

"I wish I knew a way to ease your burden." James rests a companionable hand on Isaac's shoulder for several seconds. "They say time helps."

11 MOVING SOUTH TO GO NORTH

"Providence, March 31, 1776, 5 O'Clock pm.

Sir, I have just received an express from Col. Belcher of the regiment of militia on Rhode Island. That one ship of war hast got into the harbor of Newport and that twenty seven more undoubtedly having the Ministerial troops on board are within Sciconet Point within a few hours sail of Newport. As they are undoubtedly destined for this colony, I must urge the necessity of your altering your route and marching into this colony to oppose the enemy. The absolute necessity of this stop will justify you.

I am, Sir, your most obedient and humble servant"

Nicholas Cook, Governor of Rhode Island
(to Brigadier General John Sullivan)

The six regiments under Brigadier General John Sullivan—including Colonel Reed's 3rd New Hampshire Regiment—are in formation, ready to march. The column of four thousand men, stand, halted about one mile outside of Providence, Rhode Island. It is the middle of the morning on April 1, 1776. They are awaiting word as to whether they will be marching into Providence to defend the city, or south toward Norwich, Connecticut, on their way to New York City.

Isaac and James stand with Gilman and Hale, waiting for Reed to return from conferring with General Sullivan and the commanders of the other regiments.

The field beside the road shows a little green as the first spring grasses are emerging. Isaac watches the meeting with a sense of relief, as there is clearly no sign of anxiousness or tension in the way the colonels are carrying themselves. "From the looks of how they're standing, two long days of marching were for nothing."

James scratches the back of his head, deciding how he feels about Isaac's observation. "I suppose I prefer it that way."

Isaac stands looking at the ground through partly closed eyes, his expression morose. He speaks in a low, petulant tone. "I'm of a mind to decide this business once and for all, and the sooner the better." His irritation with not being at home where he knows he is needed manifests physically. His arms both are suddenly itchy, and he rubs the fabric of his coat and shirt vigorously to combat the exasperating tingling.

James cocks an eyebrow at Isaac's fidgeting. "Even if we had another chance at General Gage's troops here, Parliament has likely already approved sending another army to contest us, and they may not arrive until summer." His expression turns sympathetic. "Though I agree; letting Gage and his beaten dogs just leave does not sit well with me. Letting them sail away, perhaps to Canada, didn't justify the effort."

Isaac composes himself. "All the ill news from home has me with a foul mind and with no patience. Logically, I know this won't be over with just one more battle, and it won't fix things at home, but..."

James companionably pats Isaac on the back. "Who wouldn't be out of sorts, given the kind of news you've had? Maybe we will put an end to this business this fall in New York. If the king sends an army, the least we can do is oblige him by sending them home by year's end."

Isaac laughs sarcastically. "We've got enough powder for one or two shots each. I'm not so sure Gage won't just drop the Tories in Nova Scotia and head up to Quebec." Isaac notices that Reed is on his way back. He straightens up expectantly. "Here comes the Colonel."

Reed walks up to the group and reports. "General Sullivan says the alarm in Providence is false. Thus, we will immediately march for New York."

Gilman looks concerned. "Not staying even the night? Just in case?"

Reed shakes his head. "No. General Sullivan had a dispatch from General Washington saying General Greene of Connecticut was a day or so behind us and would send a rider to recall us if we were needed." He turns to Major Hale and orders, "Prepare the troops to march."

"Yes, sir." Hale turns and strides toward the regiment, calling them to attention.

Isaac and James pick their way through the muddy road back to the regiment's wagons. "I hope the road to Norwich is dry," says Isaac with a sigh.

James notes the mud caked on Isaac's boots, breeches, and even halfway up the back of his coat. "Me too," James adds, sounding hopeful. "We spent too much time during the past two days dragging wagons through the mud, but it looks to be better today. But if not, I will ask Colonel Reed to change our regiment's colors to brown."

Isaac deadpans, "Very funny."

The pair arrive at the wagons and Isaac announces with a commanding voice, "Get ready, gentlemen. The regiment will be ordered to march shortly."

•••

Four days later, it is late afternoon and the brigade is crossing the Connecticut River. The men are taking boats across, while the more than fifty wagons and teams use the ferry. Isaac lets the drivers of the nine wagons for the 3rd New Hampshire regiment know it will be much later that night before they cross, and tells them to get some sleep now, while they can.

James struggles, almost losing a boot, through the mud to his friend. He stamps his feet to warm them and rubs his arms vigorously. "I am glad the weather cooperated today," he says to

Isaac. "Could you imagine doing this in a rainstorm? Colonel Reed, along with the other colonels, are to have their wagons cross first so they can begin getting a camp set up. I am to cross with them."

"Yes, I am grateful for the decent weather, and I'll see to it that Colonel Reed's wagon is brought forward. Do you know this area well? You live not too far from here, right?"

James shakes his head. "Not Middletown. Hartford is about twelve miles north of here, and I live half a day's ride north of there. Though I do some business here. Why?"

"Mostly curious. I've never been here. This will be my first time to the west side of the Connecticut River, and this is the furthest south I've traveled as well."

James laughs companionably. "I see. What do you think so far?"

"The trees are a bit different; more cedar, not so much spruce. Seems to be more bogs and such, as well. It seems like it ought to be no different than how the land changes going into Boston, but somehow—I don't know—it's as if the air feels different."

James nods. "I went up to Falmouth once, I know what you mean. For looking similar, that place felt quite different."

"I've seen a good deal more apple orchards, too. I expect the season is longer and milder. Have you been to New York City?"

James tucks his paperwork into a satchel. "Aye, it's smaller than Boston. Well, at least the Boston of two years ago. I expect it's in a good deal better condition than Boston today."

Isaac pulls his collar tighter around his neck and blows on his fingers. "I hope so. Well, I had better see to the colonel's wagon. I'll come over on the next of our wagons. See you later tonight."

•••

After crossing the Connecticut River, it takes most of three days to reach the city at the southern tip of York Island. The march makes good progress each day for being on the main post road, taking them through rolling hills from Middletown to New Haven, and along the Coast through Fairfield and Stamford.

Marching the length of York Island from King's Bridge to New

York City takes Sullivan's brigade nearly half a day. The city occupies the southernmost square mile, though unlike Boston, which is about the same size, there are no heights on the island from which to gain a clear view of the whole city.

The late afternoon air is turning chilly as the 3rd New Hampshire regiment moves off the parade grounds at the edge of the East River, where their march ended less than thirty minutes earlier. The parade grounds are part of the battery on the southeast tip of the island. The battery provides room to stage and deploy over a thousand troops, and cannon emplacements to cover the East River and well into the much larger Hudson River on the west.

Colonel Reed has just dismissed the regiment's companies to take their quarters about two blocks away. Reed and the staff officers congregate on the parade grounds to go over the details about where to store the supplies and provisions.

Isaac can see past several ships across the water to Long Island. Looking back to the ships, he counts merchant ships, mainly brigantines, sloops, and schooners. To his relief, there are no ships of the line, like the H.M.S. Somerset with its sixty-eight eighteen-pound guns, that he remembers patrolling the Back Bay of Boston. The port looks busy, which is a welcome sight compared to the inactivity of Boston's docks.

Colonel Reed points toward a row of warehouses. "There are at least two inns a bit past where the men will be taking barracks. We should take quarters there."

Gilman, taking advantage of the sun's light illuminating the busy docks on New York Island before them, says, "I am pleased to find New York unsullied by his majesty's troops. What the redcoats did to Boston was a crime above everything else."

They all nod and Reed adds, "Yes. We should find it relatively comfortable here. It was quite a march getting here, and I was just now struck at how worldly I believed myself for having seen a good bit of New England. Now I realize it wasn't so much, as I look at this city before us. As we marched, I saw the farms looked to be quite well kept. I hope that bodes well for provisioning our army."

Isaac looks to the green landscape of Long Island. "I spent so much of my energy on making my small farm work these past years. I only sensed the rest of the world was somewhere else. Now I *am* somewhere else. It is a strange juxtaposition to go so far from home to fight for liberty at home."

Reed laughs. "I quite agree. If it helps, we will keep you busy, Quartermaster. We will see this through and go home with our heads held high.

Isaac gives Colonel Reed a wry smile. "I take your point, sir. Regrets won't change what's already happened."

•••

Isaac is alone inside the room he shares with James Otis. The sparsely appointed room is above the main room of the Fighting Cock tavern. It contains one small, round table, and two beds, chairs, and oil lamps. Extra uniform shirts, pants, and coats hang on pegs on the back of the door and over the ends of the beds. A week has passed and Isaac realizes he has not written Elizabeth since leaving Boston. Despite the fatigue of several long days of hard work, Isaac sits at the table with quill in hand.

New York City, April 15, 1776
Dearest Wife,

I am sorry it has taken so long to write. The Army marched soon after I got your lines. I am in New York City now. I also heard Simon's sad news from my uncle. We marched by Providence to Norwich and then New Haven. We marched through many towns like Wilton, with farms and streams and orchards. All made me think of home. I've seen nothing that compares to our land, which I like best, perhaps for it being ours. It req'd over a day for the brigade to fully arrive. I have been kept constantly busy with quartering the regiment, food, etc.

I am otherwise fine. I hope you are bearing up and can find some way to keep your spirits up. I will write as soon as I learn more of what the regiment will be doing. Your Loving Husband, Isaac.

P.S. Please tell me of the farm when you can. Thinking of it takes my mind away from the less pleasant scenes here.

James enters the room and hangs his coat and hat on pegs on the back of the door. "Good evening, Isaac. Is all well?"

"As far as I know, yes. I have just finished a letter to Elizabeth. I can scarce believe it has taken me a week find the time. How are you faring?"

"A good meal tonight has made a difference. I bet your Elizabeth will be glad to know where you are. You remind me that I need to write to my Sarah."

"You should write to her tonight, while you are in good spirits."

James takes off his uniform as he converses. "I'm too tired now. Say, did you have much luck on contracts for rations and entrenching tools?"

Isaac shrugs. "Some. Not like Boston. Everything was easy there. Here, people are cautious. Worried there's a Tory behind every door and outside every window. Just meeting with a merchant is an affair of great drama."

James sits on his bed and takes off his shoes. "They did not experience a fraction of the privation here. New York's port has been open and free of an occupying army."

"Aye, true. That, and no battles. I suppose not many from New York were in Massachusetts at the time of the alarm, but surely some were present to see that we fought in June in Charlestown."

James lies down, stretching his arms overhead. "I hear there are loyalist towns in this part of the colonies. Even within a day's ride of here."

"They should visit New Hampshire. It would change their minds."

"I doubt it would be that easy. In fact, I heard Tories were in charge of this city until not very long ago. They were arrested. Leaders more to our liking were installed."

"That's good. Though it makes me wonder what it takes for some people to see clearly the injustice right in front of them. They must have gotten the news from Boston in some form this year." Isaac sees James is getting ready to sleep, and rises and starts undressing.

James looks thoughtful. "People see what they want to. I think what's happened at home is mostly theoretical to people here. Not so tangible as the Boston Massacre taking place on a street you or I have walked upon many times. Nor did they have the likes of Paul Sargent moving nearby to stir the blood of the citizenry. Since we arrived, I've heard stories of families being split; the Tory sides moving to Nova Scotia."

James wraps himself in his blanket as Isaac puts out one of the lamps.

"That's hard to imagine," says Isaac. "For me, the Fryes and Holts have always known blood was thicker than water."

"Well, you come from one of the oldest families, and one blessed with many sons. You're used to the advantages of numbers. Here, it seems to be every man for himself. We must take care who we are seen talking with."

"Yes, that seems to be how it is here." Isaac puts out the second lamp. "Good night."

"Good night to you, as well."

•••

A week later, Isaac and James are enjoying the pleasure of dinner in the main room of the Fighting Cock tavern. Their meal of squab, potatoes, and carrots, washed down with glasses of ale, is one of the welcome changes being garrisoned in a city offers. They are in a small booth near the back corner, and able to converse in relative privacy. The room is crowded with other officers from New Hampshire and Massachusetts.

Isaac pushes his empty plate away and adjusts to a more comfortable position. His uniform, including a new, dark-brown coat, is clean—free of mud and stains. James notices and cannot resist commenting. "Until this week, I have never seen you in a clean uniform." He takes a drink and then grins. "How do you like it?"

"Very funny, coming from the only man whose hands have more

ink stains than our commander's."

"Touché." James raises his half-full glass to toast Isaac's barb.

Isaac finishes off the last leg from his roast pigeon. "Well, I'm glad we're eating something besides pork and biscuits for dinner for a change. I suppose I'm dressed too well for our usual fare."

James leans in, motioning for Isaac to do the same. "Colonel Poor's boys got orders today."

"Really? Can you say?"

James looks around the room to make sure nobody is paying them any attention. "Sure. It is soon to be common knowledge. They have orders to go north to Canada to support General Arnold. I'm glad it wasn't us. I prefer civilization to military camps."

"I can see you do." Isaac stops and his eyes go wide for a moment. "Though I'm thinking we should enjoy this civilization while we can. One regiment isn't going to change the fate of Arnold's expedition. Mark my words, James. We—and the rest of Sullivan's brigade—will be going north, too."

James draws himself up in a pose of mock urbane civility, his voice affecting a spoiled nobleman. "Don't say that!" Then he gives Isaac a conspiratorial grin. "We've got it good here. The howling wilds cannot be so good as this."

Isaac raises his eyebrows, then sighs. "Oh, I could get used to this, too." His mood shifts in an instant, the joviality disappears, replaced by the weight of responsibilities. "No point, though. Farm and family are my future, and the sooner the better. This could have been a dinner in Boston after selling my harvest. Instead, it's the lucky fortunes of our brigade being sent here for the time being."

James sighs. "You're right, of course. But there's no sense avoiding the opportunities fortune has provided us."

"Aye, true," he replies, thinking of the prospect of being sent to Canada. "Since we're here, let's have another ale."

•••

Three evenings later, at the same table, though dinner has been over for several minutes, Isaac and James are reading letters from home. Isaac's visage is gloomy as he reads.

Wilton, April 19, 1776
Dearest Husband,

I rec'd your lines. It looks like five or six days between us now. New York seems far. Rev. Livermore and his wife have come by twice. It was comforting to have them to talk to. They visited father and sister Hannah too. I'm glad Sister and Brother Whitney live close by to father. I saw Brother Timothy and his wife Hannah. Hannah would not stay in Wilton long. Ben and Sarah Rideout's youngest son Joshua did not survive long into April. This was a harsh past two months.

The work of the farm got started in earnest this week. The ground finally thawed and some plowing got done. The boys help some with the garden, Sarah makes contests of it for them. I will see about Mr. McGregor using the east field for pasture. I hope you continue to be well. We are doing well now. Your Loving Wife, Elizabeth Frye.

As he finishes reading, Isaac sees James, already finished, is waiting. "Did you have good news?"

"Nothing of note," James responds, "though I am mindful that no bad news is good news. How about you?"

"Elizabeth says our neighbors also lost a child early this month. I cannot remember a year with so much sickness."

"New Hampshire has difficult winters. I am not sure I would live there."

Isaac folds Elizabeth's letter and puts it in his coat pocket. "I think I will go upstairs and write some lines to Elizabeth. Lieutenant Butterfield is leaving early tomorrow. Given the supplies we are ordering, I expect we are soon heading north, maybe to Ticonderoga, or even Quebec."

"I wish I could argue with that logic, but I fear you're right, given the urgency Colonel Reed has applied to nearly everything in the past day or so."

"Yes, and Lieutenant Butterfield may not make it back here for ten or twelve days. I suspect we could be moving northward before he returns."

James finishes his ale. "I am feeling social tonight. I think I will find some of my friends from the Massachusetts regiments and see if they have heard news of who is to be ordered to Canada. I'll try not to wake you when I get in."

Isaac stands. "Enjoy the evening. I'll see you in the morning."

•••

The 3rd New Hampshire Regiment is paraded on the grounds at the southern end of New York Island. The nine companies, each neatly grouped into rectangular formations, stand in front of Colonel Reed. Each company's captain stands on the right of his company, and the first lieutenant stands on the left. Lieutenant Colonel Gilman and Adjutant James Otis are in front of the three companies on the right, and Sergeant Major James Gray and Major Hale are in front of the leftmost three companies. Isaac is closest to Colonel Reed, about six paces to his left and ten behind.

Reed is reading aloud orders received earlier that morning. "April 28, 1776. The Second Continental Regiment, also called the Third New Hampshire Regiment, is hereby reassigned to the Canadian Department. We will sail, beginning tomorrow, up the Hudson for Albany. There, we will obtain bateaux and continue upriver to Fort Edward, then overland to Lake George, and then Lake Champlain, and ultimately Quebec." Colonel Reed turns to Gilman and Hale and orders them to make the same announcement to the outermost companies in the regiment. Once they've completed that, Reed bellows, "Sergeant Major! Adjutant! Collect the muster rolls."

James steps briskly to the captain of each company and collects a sheet of paper, each with the same table indicating the numbers of men present and fit for duty, sick, absent on assigned commands, etc. One company's lieutenant—instead of its captain—furnishes the roll. Sergeant Major Gray meets James in the middle of the regiment and hands the adjutant the rolls he has collected. James takes them to

Reed, who immediately inspects them.

About halfway through the stack, Colonel Reed's head comes up, and in a loud, irritated voice, asks, "Why is no captain listed for Captain Wilkinson's Company? Lieutenant Grover, I saw you hand over the muster roll. Come forward."

Grover detaches himself from his company; a young man in his middle twenties, with dark hair and a slightly unkempt look about him, which is a look common to many of the soldiers and a few of the junior officers in the regiment.

While Grover is coming forward, Reed turns to Isaac. "Quartermaster, attend me and witness this intercourse." Isaac approaches and waits as Grover presents himself. Reed returns the salute and in a slightly-too-cheerful tone asks, "Lieutenant Grover, do you know where your captain is?"

To the surprise of everyone who hears the question, Grover, with a wild look in his eyes, responds in an audacious and loud voice, "No, sir, I do not."

Reed points out the captain of Grover's company—who stands mustered with his company—and contradicts the wild-eyed lieutenant. "Yes, you do."

Grover retorts in the same loud, animated tone, "I do not know who my captain is or where to find him, whether in Heaven or Hell!" The last few words are shouted in a defiant, flippant tone. The men in Grover's company all laugh.

Glancing back, apparently emboldened by the men's laughter, Grover assumes a pose mimicking the posture of Captain Wilkinson. "So far as I know, sir, I am captain of this company. For I recruited them, and their agreement is to serve with myself as the commander in lieu of Captain Ogden, who did not join us in Boston."

In the meantime, behind Isaac and Reed, two other Continental Army officers – from Connecticut, by the look of their coats – a colonel and a major, are passing by and overhear the last part of Grover's speech. They change course and come up behind Reed. Isaac notices them, then clears his throat to get the colonel's attention, and directs his gaze to the newcomers.

Reed remains composed, seeing he has more witnesses, though his shoulders and neck are tense and the look in his eyes could flay the insolent lieutenant before him. Reed changes tack and calls out, "Sergeant Major! Major Hale!" Once these men arrive, Reed commands, "Sergeant Major, arrest this man on the charge of insolence and disrespect to his commanding officer."

"Yes, sir!"

Reed continues, "Major Hale, attend the Sergeant Major and the prisoner. Ensure the charges are filed properly at the gaol."

Hale responds in a calm voice, "Yes, sir. I will."

Then Reed greets the newcomers. "Colonel Hartley and Major Trumbull, were you witnesses to the behavior shown to me? You as well, Quartermaster?"

Colonel Hartley answers first. "Yes, his demeanor was insolent and insulting."

Major Trumbull adds, "Yes, obviously quite so."

Isaac adds, "Yessir."

Reed nods. "Very well. Major Hale, do you have the names of the witnesses?"

"Yes, sir, I do."

Hartley interjects, "Colonel Reed, before we take leave of you, what was this about?"

"Lieutenant Grover believes he should be captain since he recruited the men, but His Excellency General Washington and Congress believe otherwise, and furnished a commission for him to rank as lieutenant, and in the same stroke they furnished a commission to Captain Wilkinson over there." Reed points out Wilkinson to the newcomers. "I delivered those commissions last week, though neither man seemed pleased. In fact, Lieutenant Grover, the prisoner, would not accept his."

Hartley nods in understanding. "I see. Thank you, Colonel Reed. We will support you in this matter." He and Major Trumbull move on.

Reed calls out to Gilman, "Colonel Gilman, you have the regiment for now. Before dismissing them, give them orders regarding when and where we will leave tomorrow, then order them to their quarters to pack per the instructions we wrote an hour ago."

Gilman nods crisply. "Yessir!"

•••

The next afternoon, Isaac is overseeing the loading of troops and supplies onto two schooners at the Albany Pier on the southeastern tip of the island. Several more schooners are waiting up river. The day is warm and sunny, and the docks swarm with men carrying provisions and supplies.

James approaches Isaac. "Good afternoon, Quartermaster"

"To you as well, Adjutant. It's good to see we are using first names."

James adjusts the strap of Isaac's haversack, which is twisted on his back. "Good to see a little of your humor returning." I heard you were called to the court-martial of Lieutenant Grover this morning. How was it?"

Isaac responds dryly, "Civil to the point of boredom. I only had to confirm Major Trumbull's testimony. None of the insolent nonsense from Grover, like yesterday. A night in gaol seems to have given him a reason to act with humility and civility. They adjourned until tomorrow, though my part is done."

"That Major Trumbull—isn't his father the governor of Connecticut?"

"Yes. I thought he accorded himself in a superior manner. I hear he is an accomplished painter as well. As good as Copley; maybe better."

James pulls at his chin. "Well, that's something. He's quite young, too. Must be a rare talent, then."

Isaac directs a pair of privates carrying a large wooden box containing Colonel Reed's marquee to one of the schooners. "One thing for certain, I find Captain Wilkinson more than a little overbearing."

"What do you mean?"

"Well, he's got no time for anyone of lesser rank, or apparently Colonel Reed. Yet his behavior to certain other officers of higher rank is fawning and servile."

"Hmm." James thinks a moment before he responds, "A soulless sycophant, yes?"

"Precisely."

With a good-natured grin, James rolls his eyes. "At least he's on our side."

Reed walks by with Gilman and Hale. "Gentlemen," he says, indicating the nearest of the two schooners. "Will you join us? It's time to leave." He motions Gilman and Hale to board ahead of him, then turns to his quartermaster and adjutant. With a serious look, and in a low, quiet voice, he urges, "Be extra vigilant. We've just loaded the brigade payroll. You two are in charge of guarding it during the voyage."

James, in a tone suggesting he already knew of this assignment, replies, "Yessir. We will keep it secure and secret. Sergeant Blanchard and Sergeant Major Gray will be sharing the duty."

Reed, satisfied, claps James on the shoulder. "Very good. See to it." Then he crosses the gangplank.

James motions for Gray and Blanchard to join them. "Gentlemen, let us board and I will explain our additional duty on this voyage."

The four men board the schooner and James leads them to the poop deck. James checks to ensure nobody is within earshot, then whispers, "Gather close. Below us is the captain's quarters. Colonels Reed and Gilman will be quartered there. In there is a chest with not just our payroll, but everything for the Canadian Department of the army. Three hundred thousand. Only us and the other staff officers know. Nobody but the ship's captain and our two colonels are permitted into the captain's quarters. We will take shifts watching. Any questions?"

The men shake their heads, and James explains the shifts they each will take. In the meantime, the crew pulls the gangplank aboard and men on the dock push the schooner back into the river.

Isaac looks up at the rigging and the fine, afternoon sky. "Seems a good day for our travels to start. Hopefully a good omen."

The War Has Begun

12 TO FORT TICONDEROGA

General Orders - New York, April 28, 1776

"...The Articles of war are to be read, at least once a week, to every Company in the Army, that neither Men nor Officers may plead Ignorance against any of the Rules, and Regulations therein contained..."

General George Washington

Ten days later, Isaac and James sit outside their tent, one of six hundred that fill a large field a mile to the south of Albany. A number of soldiers are walking about the encampment, which is surrounded by more pastures and recently cleared lots.

James stands and looks around. "I'm surprised to see how much land in this area is clear. I had always pictured Albany to be a town hemmed in by ancient forests, and savages lurking behind every other tree."

Isaac, his uniform now stained with the splash and splatter of several muddy days, sits on a folding stool and uses a stick to draw in the dirt in front of him. "By the looks of it, this place has been farmed and logged for at least a dozen years. It looks somewhat the same as Wilton did to me when I first saw it seven years ago."

James sighs. "All in all, it's rather quiet here. It seems they were not expecting us. General Schuyler is absent, so perhaps word that five more regiments would be arriving soon was not received. That would explain why no bateaux are ready for us to use to go north."

Isaac rolls his eyes. "But they sure knew we had the payroll. Once word got out that it was paper Continental Dollars, and not hard species, their concern for being paid got placed ahead of everything; as if liberty was one of many potential employers. Never mind their responsibilities as citizens and as men."

James chuckles, though with little mirth. "You're right about that. It seems they are accustomed to every man being for himself."

Isaac scowls and stands, then flings his stick over the tent and into the field beyond. "It gets worse. The bateaux they're now making are of unseasoned wood, and probably will leak for as long as we will use them."

"Better have pails for bailing in every one." James laughs then turns business-like. "How many do we need?"

"Bateaux? Maybe five dozen. I hope not so many pails, but I think we have enough of those. Depends on the amount of supplies we will carry from here."

James laughs, though whether it sounds sarcastic or wry is lost on Isaac. "Well, a few weeks ago you surmised it was probable that we would come north, but that doesn't mean General Schuyler had any of the same thoughts. He may not have promptly received word that General Washington ordered us north. Most likely it didn't matter, because there simply aren't enough men here to make that many bateaux. Your conjecture was logical, though we were not privy to the details that would make it practical."

Isaac shrugs. "It seemed obvious to me. I thought we sent too few men to hold Quebec. Taking it by surprise is one thing, but there really isn't anything to stop General Gage from sailing his troops past Nova Scotia and taking it back with the large force he left Boston with."

James shakes his head. "I'm certain that possibility was discussed. I don't think General Gage could do it, at least not quickly. No army can move faster than its stomach. It's hard enough to plan when you've got enough food in supply. Though General Gage would either be desperate or a fool to expect to find food waiting for his army in Quebec, or in Nova Scotia. It was a long winter, even for those not in Boston. I don't think there are enough farms from Boston to Quebec to feed Gage's army for very long."

"You'll make a fine quartermaster one day."

"Ha! I'll remember you said that. Okay, so how long before our regiment's bateaux are completed?"

Isaac scratches his head, then slaps a mosquito. "Hard to tell. I figure late tomorrow, or more likely the morning after. I'm not sure it matters, since Stark's regiment will need some, and the remaining three of Sullivan's regiments, as well. They cannot make enough for a regiment in a day, so it will surely impact our plans for arriving at and then deploying from Fort Ti. Have you heard any of those plans?"

James shakes his head. "No. I think our commanders are as limited as we are on that topic. My guess is we will move one or two regiments northward at a time." James slaps at a mosquito. "These things are going to make for a long summer."

"Breathe only through your nose. I learned they seem to bother us most when we are at the height of exertions of labor or discourse. I think they smell our breath. Our mouths breathe outward and our noses downward. I've noticed I have less of a problem when I remember that."

James looks thoughtful. "That sort of matches with my wife's advice to eat garlic or onions. She says doing so changes our scent."

"That's a good idea, but you just better get used to them, as there are far more of them than us, and I don't see much garlic."

•••

Two mornings later, Isaac, Sergeant Blanchard, and the Greeles – Jonathan and Nathan – are testing the new bateaux for leaks. Reed and Gilman are onshore, observing. The Greeles are at the oars, while Isaac and Blanchard inspect the boats. The bateau they are currently testing is about thirty feet out from shore.

Isaac is in the front of the bateaux. "This one leaks some, too. You see leaks, Sergeant?"

"A couple. We can staunch most of it with shavings and tar, but add the weight of a dozen men and everything they carry, and who knows where else these will start leaking."

Isaac turns to the Greeles. "Take it back to shore. Let's check a few more and make sure we know what we're in for." The Greeles reverse their oars and pull towards the shore. As the bateaux gets close, Isaac jumps out ahead and points out another to try.

Reed walks up to Isaac while the Greeles are moving to the next bateau. "What say you, Quartermaster? Are these fit for travel?"

"Barely, sir. Bailing will be needed, and I could use a few more men to add weight to make sure we find all the leaks we can, while the supplies to seal them are at hand."

"It's already May ninth. We cannot wait longer. The carpenters are already making more for Colonel Stark's regiment. Test a few more and gauge what we will need to repair them as we go."

Isaac nods. "Yessir. We will be loading within the hour."

Reed turns away. "Very good." He and Gilman leave, moving toward the encampment.

Isaac turns to Blanchard. "Unless it's a major leak, it will have to do. Move any that leak too much to the end, and I will have a few men see to them while the others get going. But first, find any with serious problems and send for carpenters so they can be fixed within the hour."

•••

Isaac and James sit in front of their tent, late on the fourth evening since leaving Albany, reviewing the orders for the following day's march. Sergeant Blanchard and several of the soldiers assigned to him stand nearby, listening. Reed's regiment is encamped on the eastern shore of the Hudson, about two miles south of Fort Miller.

In the light of an oil lamp, Isaac draws a simple map showing the river, some rapids, and the falls. "Just below the rapids, here, is where we will unload the bateaux and carry them past Fort Miller, above the falls. Hopefully the rapids from there to Fort Edward are not so severe that we have to make a second portage."

James nods. "That makes sense. Will there be any wagons to help us at Fort Miller?"

"Maybe, but if they are in use by the men taking provisions north, we'll be carrying our baggage by hand, which is what we'll need to do once we reach Fort Edward, as there is not a good road from there to Fort George."

"How far to Fort Edward, and then Fort George?"

"Ten miles to Fort Edward from here, and fifteen more to Fort George. Tomorrow will be our longest day by far if we make it all the way to Fort George. Though if the river is a problem, or the weather turns against us, we'll need to camp along the way."

James quirks his mouth as a question comes to mind. "Isn't Fort Edward where your uncle earned his fame? He was commander in a battle near there, about twenty years ago, right?"

"Right. My Uncle Joseph was a colonel then. He had command of the provincial regiment of militias. Not the regulars; that was Colonel Munro. But it wasn't Fort Edward; it was outside Fort William Henry where he and his men were attacked."

"Oh, that's right." James slaps at mosquito, "After your uncle escaped, he found his way to Fort Edward, right?"

"Yes. Munro surrendered William Henry to the French. He made a deal that his officers would march first to Fort Edward, and then the regulars, and after them the provincials. My uncle's regiment was in charge of the sick and wounded, and the rest who were in camp. The Indians who fought with the French saw they wouldn't get the scalps they'd been promised and started in on killing the sick, the wounded, and even some of the women and small children, as well. A scalp is a scalp to them."

James, unable to help himself, exclaims, "For the life of me, I can't fathom what must be broken inside a man to cause him to kill children. It's against the laws of God and nature." Some the men echo James's sentiments.

"It was bloody ugly," Isaac continues. "The Indians started sacking the fort when my uncle's regiment was finally permitted to march. The French had apparently backed away from the scene, not wanting to cross their Indian allies any further. The last of the companies had started marching away when the Indians really got their blood up. They were screaming mad about not getting all the scalps the French promised, and Munro's surrender didn't mean a thing to them. They lit out after my uncle's troops, and caught up fast and started killing those in the rear. The column halted and my uncle and the officers went back and asked the French for help. The French were not apparently feeling up to playing the part of gracious victors that day. They said no. The Indians started taking coats and blankets, taunting our men, daring them to fight back. Then they separated the officers from the men. They started shoving and striking some of our men, taking shirts and anything they wanted as trophies. Some of the men didn't take such physical treatment very well and started to panic. Most of the regiment held together and escaped. My uncle was taken prisoner, stripped of his clothes, and given to one of the chiefs, who led him a ways into the woods so he could scalp him. I never quite understood why that chief wanted to go off alone to kill my uncle. Anyhow, Uncle Joseph was having none of it, and broke free and went at the chief with his bare hands and killed him—"

James interrupts. "Damn! I never heard the whole story before. That's why he got the patent for Fryeburg, right?"

"Yes, for his troubles, as he put it to Governor Shirley. He spent three days and two nights in the woods with no clothes, before making it to safety. That it was August and not October probably saved his life. As for the surrender, he says it was the bloodiest day he ever saw, and he'd seen more than a few."

James gives a low whistle. "Some say hundreds of men were killed. Was it that bad?"

Pressing his lips together and slowly turning his head, Isaac disagrees, "I never thought of it being more than dozens. That many was bad enough. My uncle doesn't speak of it often. I heard more of it from men in James Frye's inn, particularly the part about how he escaped. I checked the story with my older brother, Simon, who went with my uncle to found Fryeburg, and he said that was about as much as anybody had ever said."

"How about your father? Was he in the service with your uncle?"

"I don't think he was with my uncle then. In fact, I think he had died by that time. He was a captain with Colonel Williams a couple of years earlier. They were very near where we will march tomorrow, somewhere between Fort Edwards and Fort George. They fought the French under Dieskau. He came back home shortly after that battle. I was a young boy at the time, so didn't hear the stories until later."

"It sounds as though tomorrow will be a long day," ends James with a yawn. "Let's get our sleep while we can."

•••

Early the next morning, Reed's regiment is just south of Fort Miller, a relic of the previous war. The palisade is nothing more than a berm surrounding the remains of the blockhouse, the roof of which is completely collapsed. The regiment is in the process of making the portage around the falls and rapids located just downriver of the fort. Some of the regiment are already loading their bateaux above the falls. Along the banks of the river the land for several hundred yards is clear of trees, this area having recently been logged to provide the king's navy with timber.

Isaac comes to the rear of the column where one of the last groups of men is already complaining. In a tone that tells the men this much is nothing, Isaac tells them, "Gentlemen, knock off the grumbling. It's contagious."

James is trailing Isaac by about twenty paces. "Only twenty-three miles to travel today. You'll be enjoying the victuals Congress has prepared for us as you dine at Fort George tonight, and Lake Champlain two nights hence."

Corporal Eleazer Kingsbury from Wilton is within this group of men. "I found taking shots at the enemy a good deal more satisfying than this labor, good sirs. I believe we all thought we'd be doing a good bit more shooting."

Reaching the end of the column, Isaac reverses his course to follow them. "You got your shots in, Corporal Kingsbury, and you're right. The army offers but a few glorious moments, that I am certain you will share with your grandchildren. Gentlemen, none of you need reminders. We all signed our names pledging our honor to do our duty to gain the liberties rightfully due us. Securing liberty's northern border is just part of the duty. Shoveling, chopping, carrying, and learning to march in a straight line matters just as much as shooting."

At the sound of a trio of horses approaching from the south, Isaac and James turn to see a gentleman in the uniform of a general, flanked by two captains, ride up to the column's rearguard, which issues the challenge. Apparently, the general or his aides know the countersign, as they are permitted to pass. One of the aides approaches Isaac and James and introduces himself. "I am Captain Goforth, aide to Major General Schuyler. Whom do we have the pleasure of addressing, and where might we find your colonel?"

James responds, "I am Lieutenant Otis, adjutant of Colonel Reed's Second Continental Regiment, and this is Lieutenant Frye, our quartermaster. Colonel Reed should be at the head of the column."

Captain Goforth turns to General Schuyler, who nods and responds directly to James. "Excellent. Would you two kindly lead us to Colonel Reed, as I would address the officers and men of your regiment immediately."

James turns to Isaac. "I'll take them to Colonel Reed."

"And I," Isaac begins, "I'll find the captains and subalterns and tell them to parade the men up by the fort."

Ten minutes later, General Schuyler is standing beside Reed, atop the berm of the old fort's palisade, facing the assembled regiment. The area around the fort, recently cleared of brush and trees, also contains a stockpile of barrels of provisions, and several crates of supplies destined for the American army in Canada.

"Gentlemen," announces Reed, "with me is Major General Philip Schuyler, commander of the Northern Department of the Continental Army. He would address us on an urgent matter." Reed turns to Schuyler. "General."

"Thank you, Colonel Reed." Turning to the regiment, he says, "I'll not waste your time with pleasantries. We have a critical situation whereby I have ordered your brigade to halt their march north and assist with the moving of provisions to Fort George, Ticonderoga, and then up the lake to St. Johns. The troops already in Canada have run short of pork and flour, and they have conveyed their distress and anxiety in the past days. If they do not receive provisions soon, they shall be in danger of starving."

Schuyler's words set the men to low murmuring and Reed sharply barks, "Gentlemen! Silence while the General speaks."

General Schuyler continues, "Last night, crews moved the one hundred and nine barrels of pork you can see here." He points to the barrels. "There are no crews to move them to Fort George or Ticonderoga, and therefore you will be pressed into that duty. You will set your heavy baggage aside here, and move the pork, which must reach Fort George this evening, and Fort Ticonderoga next evening. You will encamp outside of Fort George until there are provisions sufficient to support the troops in Canada and your own brigade." Schuyler then turns to Reed. "You and your quartermaster will oversee the loading, and I will brief you on how your regiment will assist in the coming days."

Reed agrees, and dismisses the regiment to begin preparations to load the pork barrels into their bateaux. He leads the general—with Isaac, James, and the aides in tow—to the point where they will load the pork. As they approach the beach along the riverbank, Reed candidly starts, "General Schuyler, we will do our utmost to deliver these provisions to Fort George tonight. We know there is some risk in making the complete trip due to the river and conditions of the road—"

Schuyler interrupts with a dismissive wave. "Yes, yes. I have found that not all men in any regiment are fit for such duty. Pick your most fit men. I calculate that one hundred and fifty can move the pork, and a like number the bateaux, so three hundred should ensure success."

Reed, struggling to mask his irritation, nods stiffly. "Adjutant, let the captains know to send their fittest men forward, thirty-five per company. Assign the others to the unloading of our baggage."

James leaves to do as he was bid, and Reed turns to Isaac and orders, "Quartermaster, stage our baggage where we were paraded. I will send Major Hale to lead the first group forward." He leaves Isaac and walks a dozen paces to confer with Schuyler regarding the provisions that are due to arrive in the next few days. Schuyler also conveys that he must travel to the town of Stillwater, about fourteen miles to the south, to ensure that the transport of provisions begins without delay.

Within a few minutes of Schuyler's departure, several captains approach Reed, who is discussing their route with Gilman and Hale. The captains convey to the colonel their fear that by not taking their baggage with them, particularly tents and kettles for preparing meals, it will not make it to Fort George for days, and the regiment will not function nearly as well to provide the aid that Schuyler has ordered.

By the time the captains make their case, the pork has been loaded into the lead bateaux. Reed strides toward Isaac, with Major Hale in tow. "Quartermaster, our plans have changed again. I see it would be wiser to transport our baggage and as much of the pork as possible to Fort George today. Unload the pork and replace it with the baggage. Set the pork off to the side, and whatever bateaux are left can be used to transport the pork after the baggage is loaded. We can move the rest of the pork in two days, along with whatever General Schuyler sends here next."

Isaac salutes smartly, hiding his dismay at being ordered to oversee a third unloading and reloading of the bateaux. "Yessir." He turns and calls Blanchard over, and gives him the vexing news.

As the men finish the latest reloading of the bateaux, Isaac counts forty-eight barrels left high on the riverbank. James steps over to Isaac and asks, "Do you think we will dine on pork tonight?"

"Ever the hungry humorist, eh? I expect we will eat on the way."

•••

It is late morning at the northern end of Lake George, which is a narrow thirty-two-mile-long tree- and mountain-lined water body covering a little over two thirds of the distance between Fort Edwards, on the Hudson River, and Lake Champlain. Despite arriving at Fort George on the southern end of the lake late the previous evening, the men of Reed's regiment arose before dawn the next morning to convey the sixty-one barrels of pork north to Fort

Ticonderoga. The sky is clouding over, which brings some relief to the sweat-drenched men who have been at the oars for over five hours.

As they near the north end of Lake George, which is about two miles south of Fort Ticonderoga. Major Hale, in the lead bateaux, moves ahead to greet a crew of soldiers just arriving from Fort Ticonderoga. They number twenty men and eight wagons, tasked with hauling the provisions overland to the fort. Major Hale had sent one of the bateaux ahead to make sure there would be a crew to meet them.

Isaac and James wait until their bateaux grinds into the shore, and then hop over the side to stretch their legs. Major Hale calls out for men to eat their midday meal they packed before leaving, and rest for half an hour before starting the return trip. Their detachment consists of half the men who came up to Fort George the day before; the others have been sent back to assist the remainder of the regiment haul the rest of the provisions from Fort Miller to Fort George.

As they sit, a cloud of mosquitoes settles in on James. Unable to fight them off for having of a plate of cold pork and biscuits in one hand and his canteen in the other, and no ready spot to set either on the sloping shore, James gives into frustration. "Christ-almighty, these infernal things are inspired by Satan himself!"

Isaac stands and offers a hand to James to pull him up so they can escape the flying bloodsuckers, by stepping a dozen paces away. Isaac notes evidence of a few bites on the back of James's neck and high on his forehead. "Only minor damage. Though I have to say your choice of words has become more colorful of late. More like a sergeant."

James snorts and snaps back, "Perhaps it's the army that's affecting me. Well, more likely infecting me." Once clear of the flying pests, James takes a couple of deep breaths. "I'm not my usual self. I suppose going to church regularly kept me in line. I miss the comforts of civilization already."

Isaac is thoughtful for a few moments. "Well, the army does lack a certain tranquility. Though I'm sad to say, the army suits me. Between my brothers, my uncle, and our cousin James, I heard a goodly number of tales about the likes of Robert Rogers. I spent a great deal of my boyhood out learning the woods and imagining I was with them. I would be ashamed to tell my wife that. She would prefer me at home."

"How many brothers do you have? I've only heard you speak of Simon."

"Abiel is the eldest. Named after my father. He left Andover once his sweetheart moved to Connecticut. He's a private sort. We don't hear from him much. He's in Pennsylvania now. On the edge of civilization, in place called Easton."

"Pennsylvania seems a long way off."

"It does."

They finish their meal in the next minutes and wash off their plates, forks, and knives. Isaac suggests, "Let's walk around a bit and get stretched out, we'll be at the oars again soon."

•••

Four days later, after two more round trips transporting provisions up Lake George, General Schuyler orders Sullivan's brigade to continue making their way north to Canada. On May 19, Reed's regiment traverses Lake George one more time. This time, on arriving at the northern end they carry their bateaux and baggage overland two miles to Lake Champlain. They encamp to the southwest of Fort Ticonderoga, which sits atop a promontory that narrows the lake such that the fort's cannon can reach anywhere on the lake a mile north or south.

As James and Isaac walk up to the fort, clouds blow in from the northwest, and soon it looks as though it will begin raining at any moment.

James looks up the gentle slope at the fort and admits, "Given how much people talk about this place, I thought it would be grander."

"It does seem somewhat insignificant from this angle. I think its placement is what makes it effective. The lake is narrow this far south, so cannon can hit anything on the water. Anyone wanting to control access to and from Canada must come here to do it."

As they near the fort's entrance, James eyes the fifteen- to twenty-foot walls. "I can see how this place might hold out against men and small arms." A strong gust of wind buffets them. James scans the turbulent clouds overhead and urges Isaac, "Let's be about our inquiries, I think we may need to secure our tent a bit better. The weather looks to be taking on a violent aspect."

"Aye, true. Let's hurry."

The rains start that night, accompanied by strong winds the next day. By mid-morning, Colonel Reed decides not to risk embarking lest the weather cause them to capsize and lose valuable supplies or provisions.

Late that afternoon, Colonel Stark's regiment arrives at Fort Ticonderoga. He sends Major George Reid to Colonel Reed's headquarters tent—where the 3rd New Hampshire regiment's staff officers are already meeting—with news and the latest orders from General Sullivan. As Reed reviews these, he stops and shakes the handful of papers in Isaac's direction. "Quartermaster, it is fortunate we got this order before leaving. I will need you to check all the pork we are taking with us. If any of the barrels are light, do not take them. General Sullivan found the wagoners at Stillwater were tapping and drawing off the pickling to lighten their load. For worry the meat is rancid, General Sullivan has ordered us not to accept or transport any such barrels."

Isaac huffs with indignation, then gives a nod to Reed. "Yessir, where shall I direct the men to send any light barrels?"

"To the commissary at the fort. They will know what to do with any brought in and described as light. Go ahead and get to it, as the sooner we know and can replace any problem barrels, the better."

•••

The lead elements of Reed's regiment push their bateaux into Lake Champlain two mornings later on May 22. They have been joined by Colonel Stark's 1st New Hampshire regiment. Isaac and James are in the middle of one of the bateaux, going over figures for the resupply of provisions, and the timing between each resupply mission.

James seems tense and irritated. "I expect you've heard the pox is all over Quebec now. Not good. You get inoculated?"

Isaac stops what he is doing. "Yes, a couple of years ago." He fixes James with a worried look. "Did you?"

James hesitates a few seconds. "I didn't."

Isaac notes James's eyes are a little wider than usual. "You have a plan?"

James delays a few seconds before responding. "I hear in Quebec General Thomas has ordered no inoculations. I suppose he's figuring we'd all go out and do so on the same day, making the entire army sick at once."

Isaac hears the uncertainty and discomfort in James's voice. "I heard a little differently. Colonel Reed said that self-inoculations are forbidden. I take your point, though; it would be a mess." Isaac pauses a moment. "Aye, if you're already thinking like this, I'm certain half the men are likely ready to panic."

James responds immediately, sounding defensive. "Wouldn't you? Wait, that's not what I mean. I hope the men are not panicking. Last week nearly eighty were already sick and unfit for duty, owing to wet weather. All of them are with us, and I am worried they will be more susceptible, and the situation may get out of hand."

Isaac shakes his head. "Then I hope it wasn't so wet in Canada, because there are a lot more men there."

"Me too." James nods and then looks around the lake. "How long do you think it will take us to reach the fort at St. Johns?"

"Ten days, given the heavy load each bateaux carries. You okay? You usually have details like that marching in neat rows."

"The pox has me spooked, I guess. As soon as I can, I'm getting inoculated. You're living proof it's the right thing to do."

"Me and a lot of others. Maybe it was the pork we ate last night that's got you spooked. The smell of it disturbed me some. Maybe it got to you, too?"

James shakes his head, looking a little dismal. "I could hardly eat."

•••

Just after the services on Sunday, June 16, the meetinghouse in

Wilton is busy with groups of people sharing news, children playing games, the nickering and whinnying of horses, and the creaking and bouncing of wagons. It is a beautiful late-spring day. The elm, chestnut, and maple trees around the meetinghouse are at last fully green, and a warm breeze from the southwest sets them in motion.

Elizabeth and her sisters, Hannah and Sarah, are talking with Sarah Parker and her daughter-in-law, Phebe Parker. Elizabeth is holding John, now ten months old. There are other clusters of people, though more women than men, gathered in the sunshine, enjoying the fine day before making their way home.

More than fifty men from Wilton are now gone; some—like Isaac— are serving in the Continental Army, and others—like Richard Whitney and Josiah Parker—are part of a second militia call-up to bring Fort Ticonderoga up to strength and repair its fortifications. The latter group mustered at the meetinghouse early that morning before marching west to their rendezvous point on the Connecticut River.

Phebe Parker, with her eighteen-month-old son Farwell on one hip and her head seemingly on a swivel to keep track of her other children, bemoans, "I can scarcely believe my Josiah left for Fort Ti today." She turns to Elizabeth. "It's too bad Isaac has already gone to Canada. It would be good for the Wilton men to see one another."

"Yes, it's good for the men see friends from home when far from home." Elizabeth looks up at the bright sky. "The sun feels so warm and healthful today. I wish we would have more days of such weather."

Phebe shakes her head. "Yes, especially after this spring."

Hannah is four months pregnant and just beginning to show. "I hope Richard writes often." Her oldest son, Richard, is playing with his cousins, while Israel, who is two and a half, clings to her skirts. "I already don't like having him away."

Sarah points down the hill at the road. "Is that Lieutenant Butterfield, now?"

The women all turn to look. Elizabeth is the first to confirm. "It is. I wonder where he has been. It's been three weeks since he delivered Isaac's last letter."

171

Butterfield rides up to the meetinghouse and ties his horse near the entrance. He moves as though he is in a hurry, and bounds up the front steps to the porch, then he turns to address the crowd. The congregation gathers anxiously to hear his words.

The lieutenant is young man in his early twenties, with freckles and reddish-blond hair. He calls out in a clear voice, "I have letters from soldiers who were on their way to Canada from Fort George." He pauses to allow people to react and then quiet down again. He retrieves a bundle of letters from a haversack at his side, and shuffles through them, reading the names on each. "Mary Holt—from Lieutenant Sam Pettingill. Phebe Perry—from Private Jonas Perry." The women step forward and claim their letters.

Elizabeth's eyes are bright with anticipation. She whispers to her sister, Hannah, "Sam and Jonas are in Reed's regiment!"

Butterfield continues, "Abigail Hawkins—from Ensign William Adrian Hawkins. Ruth Greeley—from Private Jonathan Greeley. And Elizabeth Frye—from Lieutenant Isaac Frye."

Elizabeth steps up and takes her letter from Isaac. She removes the seal, and reads it.

Fort George - 18 May, 1776
Dearest Wife,

We are to continue north to Quebec tomorrow. It seems the army moves fast and then cannot seem to move at all. We are now five days delayed here waiting for provisions to take north. My pay is enclosed. I won't be needing any myself this summer. Give my love to Father, your sisters and brother. I will try to write again once I am in Canada. Your loving Husband, Isaac

Phebe asks, "What's the news?"

"It's nearly a month old. They went to Quebec. Has anybody heard news from there?"

Nobody answers for a moment. A few shake their heads. Someone says, "They have the pox there. It's bad."

Elizabeth sighs. "Isaac won't have to worry about that, but I have a feeling, from what he has said, it may be a serious problem for the rest of the army. I hope none of our men have any trouble from it."

13 A POX IN QUEBEC

New York, May 15, 1776

"...The Letter from the Commissioners, which you were kind enough to leave open for my Perusal, describes Matters and the Situation of our Affairs in Canada, in so striking a Light, that nothing less than the most wise and vigorous Exertions of Congress, and the Army there, can promise Success to our Schemes and Plans in that Quarter. What might have been effected last Year without much Difficulty, has become an arduous and important Work. However, I hope, all Things will yet go well..."

George Washington
In a letter replying to Major General Philip Schuyler

On May 31, the bateaux carrying the bulk of Sullivan's brigade arrives at Fort St. Johns, about twenty miles into southern Quebec on the west side of the Richelieu River. Isaac disembarks, followed by James. They walk to the fort, which looks to have been hastily refortified. The main defenses are earthen walls topped with a low palisade of sharpened logs. Within the fort, the grounds have been reduced to churned-up, hardening mud. One large blockhouse serves as headquarters, and the second story is tall enough to look out over

175

the walls in all directions.

Isaac, looking around, becoming uneasy. A frown darkens his face. "Far too quiet," he says to James with foreboding. "Should be more men and activity."

"Aye. This isn't good. Let's find Colonel Reed and see what he's learned."

They head towards the blockhouse. Reed exits when they are about twenty paces off. He sees the lieutenants and angles to meet them. "We will encamp outside the fort for the night. I expect we will learn where we are to go tomorrow."

"Yes, sir," James responds. With a look of gloomy determination that reveals his uneasy feeling about the fort, he broaches the dreaded subject. "Sir, it seems awful quiet here. Don't you agree?"

Reed's face is exceedingly sober. "I do. General Thomas has the Pox. He's at Chambly. Morale there, and here, is miserable."

James shudders involuntarily. "Oh, damn... Sorry, sir." He shudders again.

Reed motions them to start moving to the gates, "It certainly is a shock. Let's get back to the regiment." The trio of officers takes quick strides and leaves the fort in short order.

•••

Late in the morning, two days later, Reed calls a meeting of his staff officers and captains. They stand outside of an open fly tent, with three sides up to allow room and shade for the gathering.

"Gentlemen," Reed begins, "I've just come from headquarters at the fort. A dispatch from Fort Chambly came, informing us that General Thomas has died. General Sullivan is now in command of the fort here, and of the whole army in Quebec."

Colonel Reed pauses while the officers take in the news of General Thomas's death. "The most recent reports have it that several thousand of the king's soldiers have marched from Quebec City, and the enemy controls the rivers. Thus, our army will fortify Sorel and Chambly. This regiment is ordered to march tomorrow for Fort Chambly. There will be three regiments moving from here to defend that location. General Sullivan will take the rest of the brigade north to Sorel, which is likely the object of the king's troops. General Sullivan worries they may attempt to move around Sorel and go to Chambly to split us and cut our supply routes. Thus, we shall return here immediately if such a movement is reported."

Reed studies the faces of the assembled officers before continuing. "We are at a further disadvantage due to the enemy having earlier captured much of the powder and fieldpieces our army brought into this country, and for already having their own cannon. Thus, we shall not engage the enemy except on the ground and time of our choosing. Chambly is a little better than half a day's march from here. We will garrison that fort. We need to look our best upon arriving. The morale of the men there is quite low; particularly given it is where General Thomas spent his last days. They need to see a military bearing from us to bolster their spirits. Are there any questions?

Captain Levi Spaulding anxiously asks, "What about the pox? Is it at Chambly?"

Colonel Reed nods. "Presume it is everywhere. If your men show signs of it, separate them. Those who have it from inoculation are to be tented together, and those who get it through exposure must be separated, well away from the others. Is that clear?"

Spaulding looks around to ensure he has support from the other captains, and sees several looking expectantly to him. "The men don't like the prospects already. Some will see marching further north as a death sentence."

Reed nods again. "There is no help for it." Then with a firm, iron voice resolves, "They must do their best to stay active and clean. We have orders to take this country, and until we have orders to leave it, we will do our utmost. That is our duty. We will parade at six o'clock tomorrow morning, then march to Chambly." He looks around to ensure his words have had the desired effect.

Captain Jacob Hinds, whose tense, tightly clenched jaw and narrowed eyes confirm the tension many of the officers look to be feeling, asks, "Do we know, beyond morale, what the conditions are at Chambly?"

"I understand the fort there to be a considerably stronger place than the fort here. Three stories of stone, is what I was told, though it cannot withstand cannon for long, so we shall be adding to a strong defense that ensures no enemy cannon can be brought to bear." Reed looks around at the gathered officers, and seeing no further questions, dismisses them to prepare for the next day's march.

•••

Late that afternoon, the 3rd New Hampshire regiment makes their preparations to move north to Chambly. Isaac and James are supervising men in the loading of a dozen wagons. Captains Towne, Spaulding, and Mann, along with several lieutenants and ensigns, gather nearby. Each are supervising crews from their company, loading the wagon assigned for their company. The privates' uniforms are muddy, their clothes looking well used and showing wear from their journey from Albany to St. Johns. The officers look only a little better.

Ensign Hawkins and Lieutenant Pettingill from Wilton walk up to the gathering. Both greet Isaac, and then Captain Towne asks, "Lieutenant Pettingill, did you have any luck?"

Pettingill smiles. "Yessir, I did."

James overhears and moves a few steps in the direction of this conversation. Captain Spaulding, clearly pleased with Pettingill's news, places his hands on his hips and says, "Good, as I heard some men here already have the pox."

James enters the group, not quite sure how to ask, "I hope you're talking about arranging inoculations?"

The captains and lieutenants look at each other, deciding what to say next.

Pettingill eyeballs a few of the ensigns and lieutenants, then nods and says with a low voice, "Come to Captain Towne's tent after dark. Don't go informing the Colonel about this."

"You've got my word." James sighs loudly with relief. His shoulders relax. Suddenly self-conscious, he adds, "Thank you."

Seeing James relax gives the others the sense that he is genuinely as worried as they are. Spaulding looks around the group, and in the same conspiratorial tone amends, "That's officers only."

Pettingill adds, "Yes. After that, it's company by company for non-commissioned, and then for privates."

The group, realizing they've become a group, break up just in time to allow some privates to move though and continue loading tents, barrels of provisions, sledge hammers, shovels, and boxes of extra flints.

James returns to stand with Isaac, who asks, "What was that all about?"

James covers his mouth with his hand and coughs, then mumbles, "Inoculations."

Isaac smiles, relieved he does not need to deal with that. "I think it's for the better. Hopefully you and the rest will come through with light cases. Do you know how many will be doing so?"

James shakes his head. "No."

Isaac's eyes widen as his mouth goes dry. "I hope for the army's sake it isn't too many."

Early the next morning, the 3rd New Hampshire assembles in formation along with three other regiments; twelve hundred men in all. They are on the west side of the Richelieu River, fifty yards to the west of the fort. Reed is addressing his regiment. "...I will remain here. Colonel Gilman, who is already in Chambly, has command there. You will obey him as you would me." He turns to Major Hale. "Place the regiment at rest until we are given orders to march." Reed turns and rejoins General Sullivan and the other colonels who stand beside a corner of the fort.

Isaac walks rapidly over to where James is posted in front of the regiment, scanning the mustered companies as though something is amiss. "Do my eyes deceive?" he queries in a low voice, "Or are there nearly one hundred men missing?"

James, pale and expressionless, as though he is very tired, replies very seriously, "I've not had confirmation, but my worry is they're sick with the pox already."

"That's not good at all. How are you?"

"Good—so far."

The order comes to march, and Major Hale orders the regiment to attention. Isaac and James hurry to the wagons, climbing aboard as the orders to march are given.

•••

Isaac and Lieutenant Colonel Gilman are setting up their new office two days later in the room designated as regimental headquarters. Fort Chambly is a square-shaped, brownstone fort, with three-story buildings forming the sides and a four-story bastion at each corner. It sits on a small area of land jutting slightly from the west bank of the Richelieu River. The interior yard is a little over one hundred feet on each side, roughly enough to fit one regiment standing in tight formation. Just to the west of the fort is the town of Chambly.

As he works at getting the regiment's paperwork unpacked, Isaac looks up and says to Gilman, "It has just occurred to me this is the first time the regiment has been quartered at a permanent fort."

Gilman looks away from the rolls and guard duty schedules he is organizing. "I was told by General Sullivan this fort is already over sixty years old. He said it cannot withstand a cannonade, but I agree, it is superior to a tent or a farmer's abandoned home. General Montgomery sent only one hundred men to capture it in November. Though I suppose there were even fewer here to guard it."

The headquarters room is a generous twelve feet deep and nearly twenty feet wide, with half a dozen desks, and twice as many chairs. Two small windows that look onto the interior yard flank the door. There is enough room for the staff officers and captains to sleep on the upper floor.

Captain Spaulding comes in from the yard. "Colonel Gilman, sir. We have the fieldpiece in place and the mortars are now securely mounted, as you ordered."

"Very good. How many of your men are fit for duty?"

"About fifteen in my company." Spaulding continues, looking a little sheepish, "Most of the men were not inoculated for the pox. Quite a few found a local source for inoculations."

"Aye. As did our adjutant. Send word to the other companies to have officers who are not sick or under inoculation to come report their situation to me."

"Yessir."

As Spaulding turns to leave, Gilman asks, "Captain Spaulding, were you already inoculated?"

"Yessir. Well over a year ago. Same fellow our quartermaster saw. Colonel Sargent had him come to Lyndeborough and Amherst."

Isaac adds, "He came through Mason and Wilton before that."

Gilman sighs. "I wish he'd been to Fitzwilliam, where Colonel Reed is from. I just had an express from St. Johns. Our colonel has taken ill with the pox. He writes it's a mild case, and expects to recover quickly."

Spaulding grimaces. "I hope his recovery is rapid."

"We all do," Gilman responds. "Thank you for your report, Captain Spaulding. At least we can defend against a sizable body of infantry now. Though if they have cannon, we will be in a bad way."

Spaulding nods and leaves.

•••

A few days later, just after breakfast, Lieutenant Colonel Gilman calls a council of the officers of the regiment fit for duty. Isaac and Major Hale are present, as are Captains Levi Spaulding, Jacob Hinds, Benjamin Mann, James Wilkinson, and Jonathan Whitcomb, plus Lieutenants Pettingill and Farwell, and Ensign Hawkins. All look a little weary, but none show signs of illness. Gilman looks around the room and shakes his head in dismay. "This is all the officers who are fit for duty?"

Spaulding, who has been filling in for James Otis as adjutant, responds, "Yessir. The rest are suffering from their inoculations, though most are not badly off."

Gilman sighs, then with effort his expression regains a sense of purpose. "Very well. Ours is one of two regiments ordered to march to Montreal tomorrow. Patterson's is the other. Our assignment is garrison duty— holding the city as long as possible in the event the enemy attacks. All men not hospitalized will march. We will parade at six in the morning in front of the fort, then march. Dismissed."

The officers begin leaving, but one, Ensign Hawkins, turns and approaches Isaac and Spaulding. "How bad is it with our rank and file? I mean, if better than half the officers are not fit."

Spaulding answers, "Probably about the same."

"What about the other regiments here? Will there be enough fit men to defend this place?"

The captain nods. "Given that two regiments are assigned to Montreal, that leaves three here, though only one in three of those men are fit for duty. That should be plenty, since it looks like the regulars do not intend to attack here. Though I figure if it came to a battle, most of the men here would do what it takes to get a shot or two in." With a tone of thoughtful concern he asks, "How many of the men of your company were inoculated?"

Hawkins thinks a moment. "A little better than three quarters. A few don't believe it to be effective, and the others were already inoculated."

Isaac interjects, with concern in his tone, "Dammit. So, several may have full-blown cases?" Then seeing he has spoken ahead of Captain Spaulding, he says hurriedly, "My apologies, sir. I couldn't help myself."

Spaulding nods. "Yes, this is unfortunate news." Then to Hawkins he says, "You better see to your company's preparations, and if you suspect any men with a full case, get them to the hospital tents."

Hawkins responds, "Yessir," and turns to leave. "See you tomorrow morning."

•••

Reed's regiment and Patterson's from Massachusetts assemble the next morning outside Fort Chambly. Neither regiment is quite at half strength, five hundred fifty men in all. James, however, is among those who are fit today. He approaches Isaac, who is overseeing the preparations of eight wagons. James, looking pallid, with a few light-red spots showing as evidence of having had a light case of the pox, otherwise looks glad to be up and about, and does his best to sound chipper. "Quartermaster, Good to see you this morning."

"Even better to see you, Adjutant. How are you?"

"My fever broke yesterday morning. I feel weak today, but that's it. Only a few pox. So, I'm glad to be upright, and so far, I feel like I can stay that way for the whole day."

"That's good to hear. You've come through better than most. Captain Spaulding and I filled in for you. He will be glad to see you up and about as well."

James grins weakly. "I'm glad we're not carrying heavy loads."

"Yes," Isaac confirms. "I hear there are still provisions for us in Montreal. We are replacing troops General Sullivan ordered to Sorel nearly a week ago. That's where most of the army is encamped."

"I suppose you'd still be happier playing General Sullivan's concerto for musket and mortar in Sorel?"

"Aye, although you make it sound well-orchestrated, and from what I've seen, Canada is completely the opposite."

•••

Midday on June 10, Reed's and Patterson's regiments arrive in Montreal, which is situated on the southernmost of a pair of large islands in the middle of the St. Lawrence River. The city is a quarter the size of New York City and the only access from the south is via a ferry. The few remaining guards under General Arnold direct the incoming soldiers to a pair of warehouses, which will serve as their barracks.

Gilman walks back along the column of men to Isaac and James. "Quartermaster. Adjutant. Both of you are to report to Major Scammell. He is overseeing the remaining supplies and provisions we are to use. He's in the warehouse on the left."

Both answer, "Yessir," and make their way to the warehouse in question, which like the others around it is a long, rambling, one-story building with large sliding doors on either end to allow wagons access. The wagon doors are open. As they enter, they see several dozen barrels and boxes in one corner. To the left is a table serving as a desk for Major Alexander Scammell, who serves as General

Sullivan's aide and as Brigade Major.

Isaac notices the major first, and strides to the table, and offers a crisp salute, followed by James a step later. "Major Scammell, Colonel Gilman ordered us to report to you."

Major Scammell rises and returns their salute, and immediately it becomes obvious he is one of the taller men in the army, well over six feet tall, with a strong athletic build, a strong jawline, and light-brown hair. "Excellent. How many men marched with you today?"

"Close to two hundred fifty with Colonel Reed's regiment, sir, and a little over three hundred with Patterson's."

Scammell looks relieved. "That's good. We will have enough food, with what is left here. If it becomes clear the regulars are intent on coming to Montreal, we will load whatever supplies are left onto boats and take it to Chambly, and the rest will march for Chambly." Scammell's relieved expression becomes one of concern. "How many of your men are sick?"

Isaac responds, "Better than half are sick in Chambly. Perhaps one in five were already inoculated, and better than half of the others were inoculated in St. Johns, including Adjutant Otis here. So half of those still at Chambly are recovering from their inoculations."

Scammell nods. "I see. Well, expect it to get worse—two or three more weeks for those who were inoculated, is what we've seen. So, keep the healthy men here and send any who have symptoms into another of the empty warehouses. I'm just now over my inoculation. Also, you've not likely heard the news: Two days ago, we fought a battle at Three Rivers. Trois Rivieres, as the locals call it. It's nearly two days northeast from here, a little past halfway to Quebec." Scammell's tone shifts from measured to clearly frustrated. "We lost badly; our forces are scattered and some captured."

"Oh, hell!" James reacts. "I thought we would have numbers..." Realizing his coarse manner in the presence of the major, he immediately becomes contrite. "Sorry, sir. I find the news distressing. I didn't mean to—"

Scammell holds up a hand to stop James. "No need to apologize for patriotism. Given the number of sick men, we no longer have numbers in this country. We have word that the enemy has added some ten thousand fresh troops to the garrison at Quebec. Some Prussians, too. They're all hale and anxious to meet us, and frankly I would have preferred to meet them, but on our terms instead of blundering about with our generals being either sick, bull-headed, or badly uninformed. General Arnold chafes at being consigned here, away from the main action, and, I am afraid, at not being in command of our forces in Canada. General Sullivan – despite a grand appearance – is too late, I fear, to set an offensive scheme in motion. And now it appears that even had the pox *not* played a role, and had Sullivan arrived a month earlier and won a victory, any gains would have been short lived."

Isaac takes his hat off and rubs the back of his head. "I see. So, until we know where the enemy intends to strike, we must wait."

Major Scammell smiles grimly and nods. "Precisely. Our cause in Canada is effectively lost. Our efforts now go toward a retreat. Find your quarters and report back here. I could use a hand in planning what must ultimately become an evacuation."

•••

Late that evening, Isaac and James are resting in a small room on the upper floor of a large house that Reed's officers have taken for their quarters. A small oil lamp hangs from a wall sconce between the beds, lighting the room.

James stretches fitfully on his bed. "It was good luck Captain Mann found this house. The owner must have been a Tory and fled to the countryside."

"Even if he wasn't, I don't blame them for leaving. Armies bring sickness." Isaac's tone has undertones of bitterness and sarcasm. "For, most assuredly, we are an army now."

James stares at the ceiling. "It seems like things turned against us so quickly."

"I thought about it this afternoon. Things have been taking turns for the worse in this country for over a month. It was too quiet when we got to St. Johns, and even back when we were at Fort George the situation regarding the food proved to be an omen. Optimistically, I took that to be the usual state of armies, but now I've had my eyes opened."

James raises an eyebrow. "You're right. We all choose to see things how we want, myself included. The moment I saw the state of the muster roll that Major Scammell was completing this afternoon, the truth sank in. The whole army's situation is bad indeed. He didn't have the Canadian volunteers on that roll, and I am certain just as many of them are sick. Major Scammell says it's even worse, because some of those numbers are over a week old and the proportion of healthy men continues to get smaller."

Isaac turns on his side. "I didn't see that. How bad?"

"Out of sixty-three hundred men, over a quarter are sick on Major Scammell's roll, and almost another quarter are scattered. The bulk of those who are fit - about twenty-five hundred - are with General Sullivan at Sorel. The enemy has more than twice - maybe six times - that number, if the news Major Scammell provided is correct about ten thousand more of the enemy arriving."

"They won't be able to hold the redcoats, or even slow them, given those numbers, and we don't control the water." Isaac growls, "Christ! We get sent here to idle, when we could be in St. Johns in two days with safety at our backs and time to make this country even more miserable for the redcoats."

Before Isaac can go on, James shifts the topic. "What did you think of Scammell? Today's the first time I've spoken with him, beyond exchanging packets of papers."

"I didn't pay much mind to him. I'm thinking of home. Not getting letters regularly has me worried."

"I wish we had more officers like him," James offers. "Chafing like a caged bear for being stuck under inoculation and stuck in that warehouse doing paperwork." James notices that Isaac is not paying attention, so he speaks a bit louder, "What has you so preoccupied?"

Isaac shakes his head with despair. "Everything depended on my being there. I didn't realize it until now. We were in a bad way two years back, too. I got hurt in the fall of seventy-three. It was at the meetinghouse raising, and a lot of us fell when a support beam burst. That was bad. A few died on the spot."

James, a little confused, says, "I heard about that. Something like fifty men hurt. Tragic."

In a bitter voice, Isaac goes on, "It was, and I got nothing done all fall and winter, and was weak for some of the spring. We needed things done. Even my sister's husband sued me for the money I owed them. I had to sell fifteen acres. We didn't make any money that year, and owed even more by the end of the year. We were close to getting caught up when the alarm for Lexington and Concord came."

James nods in understanding. "With the redcoats shutting the port, nobody was doing much better. Being behind, I admit, would have been worse."

Isaac continues, "It's odd, but my debts to Paul Sargent are what got me the quartermaster commission. He offered to forgive them if I agreed to the job. I figured if it came to it, being a soldier would pay better. Now, so far away, not being paid regularly, and not working on my farm, I am seeing I may have been wrong."

"I think a good many men figured like you did. Nobody figured on the funds being so scarce."

Isaac becomes more animated. "Right. Now Congress is printing money that nobody thinks is worth anything. I was shocked to find out that's what we were guarding on the way up to Albany. I took you to mean sterling the first time I heard you."

"I bet you did." James grins, "Now there's rumors of the redcoats printing more of our money than we are."

"So being paid in worthless paper and not doing the work of the farm has added up to even less. I worry Elizabeth has it worse than I do now. I very much thought we would be stopping the king's and Parliament's policies by a show of force, and we would have been done and back to farming by now. Instead we got more blood and battles than anyone would have predicted. Elizabeth must curse me for a fool most days."

"From what you've told me, she's got a lot of family to rely on, and a farm and a garden. Even without hard money, she's doing better than us, pinned down in the midst of a plague, day by day watching our pork go rancid, and we've got to share that with six thousand other men. She's not got a fresh army waiting to pounce on her first move." James lies back. "There is no going back in time to change things. Let's get some sleep. Tomorrow will surely come sooner than we like. Maybe by then we can sort out how to share the pox with the enemy."

Isaac turns down the flame in the oil lamp. "Sleep's a good idea. I have a feeling the next few days will be long. I've heard the regulars are inoculated before coming to America. So, I expect we will need to find another way to send them back the way they came." Isaac turns out the lamp.

•••

A day later, a little past the middle of the afternoon, Isaac is supervising a group of soldiers reorganizing the provisions to ensure that the best foodstuffs are saved for last. Major Scammell comes into the warehouse, looks around, and approaches Isaac. "What do you think of our situation, Quartermaster Frye?"

Isaac returns the major's gaze, trying to discern Scammell's intent from his expression. The other man's face is open, inviting Isaac to speak his mind. "Sir, the past few days of inactivity aside, I don't wish to criticize those in command, as it is plain our situation has no easy remedy."

Scammell takes his hat off, and judging from the expressions playing across his face, discards several responses before arriving at one he can use. "Consider this conversation between us, as gentlemen. And I have no wish for you to criticize or speak uncharitably of those who are not here. I am only asking for candor and your insights. You are closer to the problems of the brigade than I am."

Isaac weighs Scammell's words and decides to engage. "I would have inoculated the men months ago, at Fort Edward, or Ticonderoga, safely away from towns and supplies."

Major Scammell nods. "I agree with that." Then turning and surveying the warehouse, remarks, "Some of our generals are such rivals that it makes them rash and ineffectual at times. To make it worse, many of our colonels put on the airs of generals, with their baggage and fine dinners, even here in this country. Do the men respect such pomposity?"

Isaac laughs. "I don't think the men call it pomposity. They see wealth and honor, but it is not the same as the honor they place on honest, hard work, no matter how much liberty they've been promised. The generals and colonels appear to believe that the wealthier they appear, the more others will find them worthy of respect. The men did not very much enjoy hauling Colonel Reed's baggage. He has gained quite a lot of *essential* possessions in the past year. Granted, some of that was the headquarters tent and tables that are still back at St. Johns, so at least they weren't carried here. Either way, hauling all of that into the squalor of the fort at St. Johns did not please them, especially for the little bit of paper money they were paid. But not all the colonels are that way. Colonel Stark seems to be all business."

"I see your point. Well put. I wish Colonel Stark had as much zeal when it comes to sweet-talking Congress. The man should be a general, but he has a habit of pissing on those who aren't military enough for his taste, and the more wealth, the longer it seems he is willing to piss. I wish he could see that winning this war is going to take wealthy men and men like Colonel Stark acting together.

Isaac shrugs. "Somebody ought to tell them. Though I think that even if Colonel Stark was made a general, he wouldn't hold his tongue long. The other generals would run him out. Their numbers make them more powerful and diminish the value of being an effective commander of men in the field. I'm sure you've heard it as much as I, that Colonel Stark was mighty effective at Bunker Hill, and no general—blessed by Congress or not—was on that field."

Scammell nods. "So very true."

Isaac ventures, "You've been here some time now with General Arnold. What do you think of him?"

Scammell's mouth quirks sarcastically. Isaac notices, his eyes widening a little. After a few seconds, Scammell responds, "As to General Arnold, he reminds me of that occasional rooster, who by accident or chance realizes that if the sun is up he can crow any time he wants because the hens come running. This experience teaches him to crow frequently. But if the sun is hidden by the clouds, he can be as glum as an old lame hound, and mean, too.

Isaac almost laughs aloud, and then gives the major a reappraising look.

Scammell smiles and his eyes show his thoughts shifting. "I was wondering, why did you join the cause?"

"I suppose this is irony: it was my lack of wealth." Isaac's expression turns critical. "The king, Parliament, and all their taxes keeping me from a better life. And to double the irony, here I am now with a rather miserable army, paid with paper, and not on my comfortable farm."

"Really? Your family is hardly poor. Granted, their wealth is in land, as I recall. Is lacking more wealth the only reason you joined?

"The Fryes owning land used to be a good assumption. Now much of the land is split up. Blessed we are, with many sons in our families. I suppose the lack of respect from Parliament and the king is at the core. Why shouldn't I have wealth, or the liberty to try to build some wealth for my family and myself? That feeling of disrespect permeates a man, making him either doubt himself or want to fight."

Scammell looks thoughtful. "I think we all feel the disrespect. Each in our own way. That someone far away, who knows us not, so clearly wants less for us, is an affront; and once it is known, it cannot be ignored." He takes a deep breath. "I'm an impatient sort. We could be doing so much more, yet here we sit."

Isaac puts his hands on his hips. "I'm sure we could be doing more. I've been impatient to end this for the past year. The battle at Bunker Hill started something that needs to be finished. The truth is, it was less battle for me than it was killing. I was in Charlestown. We shot men who never saw us. Obtaining our liberties somehow made doing that necessary, and we've fought nothing and gained little in this past year beyond pushing General Gage out of Boston."

"Aye, that has frustrated me as well."

Isaac looks down and scratches his neck. "One of my sons died just before we left Boston for New York. I wasn't home. I was with this army—not fighting."

Major Scammell nods, realizing the conversation has taken a turn.

"I had no idea. For myself, I was chafing at the notion of accomplishing so little. You give me much to consider. We must not take for granted the men like yourself, with families and lives set aside, and who fought at Bunker Hill." He rubs his chin. "What do you think of the quartermaster's department?"

Isaac waits several breaths before answering. "I don't know whether I've quite got a full understanding of the department. There was nothing well organized before the alarm for Concord and Lexington. Once we settled in around Boston and credit was arranged, I suppose it functioned adequately. Though one thing that bothered me early on was the commissions some quartermasters charged. Colonels Gilman and Reed were rightly up front about prohibiting my doing the same. I gained much respect for them and learned how important it is not to abuse, or make presumptions about, the support the public gives this army."

Scammell's posture relaxes a little. "I'm glad to hear you say so. I agree. It seems there is a lot of that going on with the people who supply our army. I heard General Sullivan had to confront the men who were transporting our pork. They had drained off the pickling to make the load lighter. The meat had rotted, yet they still wanted their pay."

"Too many men see only the opportunity to enrich themselves. There's a few thousand of us with knots in our bellies who wouldn't mind setting them straight. But at least the local fare here is far better than what was at St. Johns or Chambly."

Scammell's expression turns serious and determined. "It won't last much longer. Even with just the main parts of Reed's and Patterson's regiments in this city, food is becoming scarce here. It will soon be desperate times. We must all do better for our brothers-in-arms and those who support us." Scammell nods towards the men, who have finished their tasks and are beginning to loiter. "It looks as though these men have everything arranged."

"Yes. If you'll excuse me, I need to get my dinner. Hopefully I will find some and then brief Colonel Gilman."

"Yes, dismiss the men, and I'll see you tomorrow. Thank you for speaking your mind."

...

Orders come the next morning, June 11, to move all the sick back to Fort Chambly, which will only leave about three hundred in Montreal – about half from each regiment. Enough food for four days remains with those who remain at Montreal. Major Scammell has command of the garrison, as Lieutenant Colonel Gilman, Major Hale, and James return to Chambly. Captain Spaulding is in charge of three makeshift companies of Reed's men who are fit for duty.

The men who remain in Montreal are set to work preparing a bridge, to the north of the city, for destruction when the time comes to retreat. Its destruction will force the enemy to choose between taking Montreal or pursuing Scammell's command to Chambly.

General Arnold returns from St. Johns in the early afternoon of June 11, but has no additional orders, and sets the men to watch for signs of the enemy approaching.

Early on the afternoon of June 15, Isaac is with Captain Spaulding and ten men scouting northeast along the river, when from their position on the northernmost point on the Island of Montreal they spot a contingent of enemy ships about ten miles up the St. Lawrence. Their detachment makes a hasty retreat and learns they were not the first to discover the enemy's approach. That news was also conveyed by a rider sent from General Sullivan's command. General Arnold waits as long as possible to be certain the enemy ships are making for Montreal. The ships are about fifteen miles from Montreal when he gives the order to evacuate.

Within thirty minutes of the order, Isaac is stepping off the ferry, after crossing the St. Lawrence. He takes one last look back to Montreal before turning to watch Spaulding's men set fire to the last ferry, effectively disabling the enemy's ability to immediately pursue them.

14 ISLE OF DEATH

Montreal, June 24, 1776

"It is with the greatest pain, I inform you that after our retreat from Canada to this place of which I have given your Excellency an acct thru General Schuyler & after I had Determined to make a stand here , Till I received your Excellency's order That I find myself under an Absolute Necessity of quitting this Island for a place more healthy. ..."

Brigadier General John Sullivan
Beginning of a letter to General George Washington

Three days later, in the early evening of June 18, Isaac arrives some ten miles to the south at Île aux Noix, on one of the last bateaux from the fort at St. Johns. The island is at a widening of the Richelieu River. Within seconds of stepping onto the island, a foul rotting stench greets Isaac; a mingling of noxious odors from the open trenches of waste, of a place too wet, and the strongest note is the putrid tang of sick and dying men. The guards direct him to the headquarters, which lie within the ruins of an old French fort on the south end of the island.

Isaac finds Major Hale on duty. "Sir. I just arrived with the last of the detachment under Captain Spaulding. Have you seen him yet?"

Hale looks haggard in the light of a single oil lamp. "No, though I expect he may be with Colonel Gilman. I imagine that was a hellish bit of work. Do you have anything else to report?"

Isaac indicates a chair. "Do you mind if I sit? The fatigue of the last few days is coming upon me."

"No, go ahead."

"When I embarked from St. Johns, General Arnold and Captain Wilkinson indicated they would ride north to reconnoiter the position of the enemy. It also seems Captain Wilkinson has left our regiment to take the position of General Arnold's aide-de-camp."

"Interesting, I suppose Wilkinson attaching himself to General Arnold is for the best, don't you?"

"Yes. Though I think the satisfaction Lieutenant Grover may take will not be of any benefit to him given the circumstances we have found on this campaign, nor will it make up for his lost pay."

"No, it won't," Major Hale agrees. "I know. He will reap what he sowed. What else?"

"There was little in the way of provisions. Food was scarce when we left Montreal. Whatever was at Chambly was either spoilt or consumed when we burned the fort. We left that place two mornings ago. We burnt the bridges and did what damage we could to the roads along the way to St. Johns, where we arrived late last night. In the morning, we stripped and burned it, though the rain made that more of a chore. The enemy will not gain so much as a useful tent stake."

"Well, I imagine our men have done three days of hard duty."

"Up before sunrise to after sunset, each day. Would you mind showing me where my tent is? I could use a little sleep, or I may wilt."

"Of course. I need to stretch my legs. I've stayed in here too long, circumstances out there being what they are. The adjutant set your tent up last evening. Though this place is anything but comfortable."

"I'm tired enough that it won't matter. It has got to be better than any of the past three nights out in the weather."

Major Hale rises and grabs his hat from a peg. "Have care; there are a great many sick here. Dozens of men died today." As they leave, he gestures to the north and west.

Isaac follows, too weary to take in the details of the miserable camp. "Hard to believe we were on a battlefield, proving our worth, this day a year ago. Now we have been whipped by poor planning and disease." Isaac shakes his head. "Our tails between our legs."

Hale responds, keeping his voice low, "Aye, this is a miserable reversal of fortune. It seems we can do very little that goes as planned, lately. A strong effort usually overcomes poor planning, but the pox made us weak."

"Were not the sick sent on ahead? I could scarcely believe the stench that hit me when I arrived."

Hale lets loose a sigh of frustration. "No. Not enough bateaux were left over, and Generals Sullivan and Arnold deemed the supplies were more important."

"Sorry, sir. I s'pose that's old territory."

They walk for another minute until they arrive at the 3rd Regiment's tents, then pick their way toward the middle, finally stopping at one.

"Get some sleep. You look overdue. Try to keep your tent shut; there're clouds of no-see-ums floating about. It's as if they found religion, and God rewarded them with this army to suck the blood out of. I've never seen the likes of it."

"Thank you, sir. I will."

Isaac tries to enter the tent, but finds it tied shut. He fumbles about the canvas with hands shaking from fatigue, attempting to locate the knots and undo them. "James? You in there? Help me get in."

James, sounding clearly agitated, grumbles, "Oh, shite! Hurry up. I'm helping." The last words are almost a growl.

The opening is soon large enough and Isaac crawls in, dragging his pack, satchel, and firelock. James pulls him toward the back of the tent. "Glad you're here, but let me get this closed again. I'm trying to keep the stench, filth—" He shudders involuntarily, and his voice holds a note of panic. "—disease, and whatever the hell else is flying around out there, from getting in."

Keeping his voice casual to avoid adding to James's fears, Isaac says, "Christ, James. I've never seen you in such a state. You've already had the pox, though I must say I understand about the stench.

It's foul indeed."

James is still irritated. "Yes. The pox is just one of many of the agents of death out there. Agues and fevers and more—I want none of it!"

James lights a lantern and Isaac can see that he looks like he hasn't slept much either. James sees a thin, grimy, soot-stained Isaac. The two look at one another for a second longer in silence.

James sits back. "That's not the worst of it. When I got here, I learned Colonel Reed's case was worse than we knew. He's getting better now, but he's been left blind."

"Hell, that's no good. What a mess." Isaac notices James's eyes darting about with extreme anxiousness. Isaac lets out a long controlled breath, hoping James will do the same.

Instead, James continues, "Aye, a thorough mess. I heard men were deserting rather than spend another day on the Isle of Death. That's what we've come to call this place."

"That may be, but it won't matter 'til I've had some sleep. It looks like sleep will do you some good, too." Isaac begins arranging his pack and blanket.

"Yes," James says. "Maybe you're right. I hope I can sleep." Seeing Isaac settle in, he reaches over and extinguishes the lantern. "You remember seeing this island when we came up?"

"Truth?" answers Isaac. "Not really. Why do you ask?"

"Well, it's no more than a mile long and maybe a quarter mile at its widest. We've got five thousand men here now. Half are sick and dying."

"Major Hale mentioned some of that. What about our regiment?"

"Half of those who left Montreal early are still sick; mostly those who didn't get inoculated. Some of them are sick with the ague and the usual camp sicknesses. Discipline is gone. This afternoon, Colonel Gilman told us that restoring order is to be our job in the next days."

"I'm exhausted. I cannot thank you enough for setting up the tent. But if I don't sleep, I may as well be sick."

"You're right." James sounds resigned. "Lack of sleep has my wits tattered like a sail in a gale."

•••

Three days later, on June 21, a couple of hours past dawn, James enters the tent and ties the flaps shut. Both Isaac and James look gaunt from nearly a week of exertion and very little food.

"Finally, some good news," James begins. "General Sullivan ordered the sick moved down to Crown Point and La Motte. He's sent troops to repair the buildings and set up hospitals."

Isaac retorts with a mix of anger and sarcasm, "Hundreds have already died. That he waited so long completely defies logic."

"There wasn't a choice. Not enough bateaux. Most were sent to Fort Ti with supplies and cannon we couldn't use here, and so they could be reloaded with provisions we do need. The few that were left behind have been used for reconnoitering the riverbanks."

"It's always those damned bateaux! Since the day we arrived at Albany we've been hampered by our reliance on the damn things. And if it's not them, it's the food; either there isn't any, or it's rancid or wormy."

"Easy, Quartermaster. The injustice of that can't be fixed now... or with anger."

Isaac takes a deep breath to calm himself. "More like Shit-n-puke-master," he says. "I don't know how many men we had to order not to shit or piss wherever they pleased. We've dug trenches and vaults for the men to use. So many are sick and wandering about with no sense of decency or modesty. A few are wallowing in their own filth and causing the rest of us to either clean them up or suffer the self-same fate. This island just isn't big enough for ten men to behave so, let alone hundreds."

"Aye, you had a shit-filled day yesterday, though I must say it doesn't sound as though you'd have been much of a doctor or surgeon. Be thankful we have enough shovels and enough healthy men to use them."

"Aye, true. But you'd think some general would have sorted it out, knowing full well we have a quarter of the army—or even as much as half—sick and needing to be sent south. The debacle we've found ourselves in is crushing our morale. A dozen officers resigned their commissions today and left. About a platoon of privates left, as well.

James sputters. "Christ, that best not be true. I cannot believe it. So many? This was such a grand army not so long ago. We've only been here four days, so word of our needs may have only just reached Fort Ti."

Isaac scratches his head vigorously, the cramped and dirty conditions driving him almost to a fit. "You make sense, James, but I see why those men left. Figure they can make their way home, living off the land. This place being so small, with so many men, half of them sick with the pox, dysentery, and God knows what else... There's so little food, and not much of that is fit to eat. The enemy and their Indian allies have harried every hunting party, and some haven't returned. And the water is foul. No wonder so many more men have become ill. It would be healthier not to eat or drink."

James nods. "It seems you may be close to the truth. Well over a hundred of the sick have died these past few days, and despite all the work we've done digging and cleaning, and the army surgeons working night and day, I fear it will get worse before it gets better."

Isaac shakes his head wearily and sighs. "I fear you are right."

The pair sit in silence for nearly a minute. Isaac opines, "It seems to me that Major Scammell would be a better sort to command a regiment. We spend a great deal of effort administering this army, as if there is a right way to do so. Funny, but I used to think armies only drilled and battled. I suppose battles and preparations for them are what historians think we find entertaining. Given the little we've done of either these past months, I am beginning to think we'd be better off fighting. It's that or risk administering ourselves so poorly that we make an even bigger mess by starving unpaid men into deserting in droves. That's only one step better than them being at one another's throats out of sheer hunger and frustration."

"Good points, though what does that have to do with Major Scammell?"

"I found Major Scammell's mind was aimed toward winning the endgame, and not spending so much time putting spit and polish on the army. It's ironic: polish and paperwork, it seems, are all his superiors want from him. He very much chafes at that."

Isaac finds his hat and makes his way toward the tent flaps. "I guess it's my turn to get food and water."

"It is," James agrees. "I thank you, good sir. Rancid pork and buggy flour sound excellent again today."

Isaac plays along. "I'm happy to be of service, sir, but I'm going to hold out for flour and some rum. The pork isn't fit to eat rancid and buggy. The water here is foul beyond even the pork. At least we can sift anything unwanted out of the flour."

"Rum and flour it is. Again. Maybe a barrel of cider if you find one rolling about. Though you'll need to bring all of it to headquarters; I've been assigned duty there today. An adjutant from one of the regiments is to be on duty each day. Lucky me—I was selected to be the first."

Isaac laughs. "I wouldn't get three steps with a barrel of cider. Not sure I'd even get one step inside headquarters. Such a prize that would be! Besides, the rum will be hard enough to get." Isaac gets the tent flaps undone and steps out of the tent. "I'll deliver whatever I can get to headquarters for you. Then I may come back here to write some lines to Elizabeth, in the hopes that a bateau will go to Fort Ti to carry it. Then it's back to cleaning up and haranguing the men to use the newly dug facilities."

•••

An hour later Isaac is back in the tent writing to Elizabeth in a shaky hand.

20 June 1776
Camp of the Northern Army

Dearest Wife,

I am sorry I have not written for weeks. I am fine and have not taken part in any of the actions in this quarter. The part of the Army I am in has traveled all the way into Quebec. Montreal is perhaps the only place I've been that you may have heard of. We are now encamped on an island in a wide place on the Richelu River. This river makes the Souhegan look like a small stream. About a mile wide here, though this river moves very slowly.

We have taken to calling this place the Isle of Death. So many of the men are sick, maybe half. All manner of sickness that has ever befouled an army has found us here. The pox especially. Godly men have sworn never to attend a church again, for how could their God have allowed such suffering and misery?

It is a wonder I am well. I stay active, and am careful not to drink the foul water. There is little hope of us leaving this island for perhaps a week. The men from Wilton fare well so far. I try to keep you and our sons in my thoughts so I will not dispair. Your Loving Husband, Isaac.

Isaac folds the letter, figuring to take it to headquarters where he can seal it and have it sent. He tucks the letter into his belt, exits the tent, ties the flaps, and makes his way to the southern end of the island. The way is already hard-packed mud, and Isaac notes just how much of the island's greenery has disappeared in just a few days, cut, trampled and probably boiled for food. He finds James at work on a report. Isaac takes out the letter, sets it on the field desk, then asks James for a candle and some sealing wax. James lights a candle from the oil lamp and hands Isaac the sealing wax. Isaac starts to move the wax into the flame, then stops, sets it down, picks up his letter and holds it into the flame instead. He holds it while it burns. Once the flames have consumed most of the paper, he drops it and twists his boot over the remains, grinding them into the dirt.

James looks confused. "Why did you do that?"

Isaac sighs. "I can't bring myself to tell Elizabeth what it is like here. I don't want to worry her. She will have to wait until we've left and things are better before I'll write."

James goes back to writing his report, and without looking up says, "I don't blame you. I've not written my Sarah any letters since we were at Fort Ti. I admit I was relieved not to be caught up with General Sullivan, composing his concerto for musketry and mortars, but at least I could have explained that piece of music to Sarah. This dirge with its wailing choir of sick, miserable men is not fit for such ears."

•••

Five days to the hour later, Isaac and James are outside their tent, taking it down. The scene around them has many men doing the same. They all look haggard, gaunt, and move as though they have aged twenty or more years. The ground between the tents is hard-packed mud. In patches where tents once stood, a few feeble blades of grass attempt to recover. In the distance, men are at the riverbank, loading supplies into bateaux. Isaac and James are filthy. They move deliberately, as if trying to conserve energy.

Not bothering to look up, Isaac breaks the silence. "At least we are finally leaving."

"Aye. We finally got some fit food yesterday. First time in eight days for me." James stands up straight, rubbing his aching upper arms. "What a disappointing debacle this campaign turned into."

Isaac continues working a stake loose. "I suppose we should be grateful to still be here, complaining."

"Seriously, it was a protracted, piss-bucket debacle, or maybe it was a shit-hole debacle." James starts to laugh, and then coughs. He spits in disgust. "I wonder if General Washington has accomplished anything with his part of the army. If not, I fear I shall lose faith."

"In our cause?"

"No, not in the idea of it, anyway. Achieving it, yes, I worry we cannot organize ourselves."

Isaac shrugs. "In our cause, I too still have faith. Though I must say, I'm much less certain of my part in achieving it. I think I could build bateaux, or better yet, raise a few head of cattle for the army's commissary."

Sounding half-serious, James adds, "You should." He struggles with the knotted hemp guy line, then takes out his knife and cuts it. This leaves him out of breath and he pauses to rest. "If we've learned anything, it's that no soldier deserves to dine on days-old rancid pork and wormy flour. Did you notice? Not one private, sergeant, or officer exclaimed their love of maggots."

Isaac's bitterness is evident in the face of James' sarcasm. "It all seems so poorly planned—our supplies and not knowing what will come next. Do you think there was ever really a plan?"

"No. No, I don't think there was ever a plan to raise and maintain an army. A contest of arms would have been unthinkable in the early days. Profit was the motive, and most men were thinking of themselves when it came to not wishing to pay ever-increasing taxes. Even when talk turned to organizing militias, it was to stop the regulars from coming into a town to seize the public stores of powder. Yet somehow this has become far more. Even yeomen—men such as you and I, of modest means and proud families—got caught up because our livelihoods were being limited. I also didn't expect to take up arms, did you?"

Isaac stacks the final tent pole and begins rolling up the guy lines. He sighs before answering. "Yes and no. There was a sense of a fight coming, but I don't think anyone imagined forming an army."

James pulls the tarp aside and shakes it out. "Yet here we are. Perhaps the colonels and generals were not so different in that they did not expect to be in a war or to be leading the prosecution of it"

Isaac sounds subdued and contemplative. "Even so, I find myself considering that I will take up my farm again and support the cause with what I can grow. Elizabeth would be happier. And nobody—sane or not—was happy with the maggots, no matter how much pork was around them."

James laughs, though it turns a little bitter. "Just watch out—Congress only pays in paper these days."

The two friends finish dismantling and tightly rolling their tent. They shoulder their gear and head towards the waiting bateaux.

15 CROWN POINT

Summary of the state of the Northern Army

14 May 1776: 5,040 of 7,006 fit for duty
12 Jun 1776: 3,591 of 6,261 fit for duty
24 Aug 1776: 4,899 of 9,157 fit for duty
12 Sep 1776: 4,490 of 11,124 fit for duty

From the rolls of Generals Sullivan and Gates

Just after midday on July 2, the officers of New Hampshire's regiments hold a meeting at Crown Point, a peninsula jutting northward from the west side of Lake Champlain, about thirteen miles north of Fort Ticonderoga. Crown Point commands a view of nearly fifteen miles, making it an ideal place to monitor activities on the southern third of the lake. Ruins of French and British fortifications dominate the tip of the peninsula. The stonework walls of a pair of long, two-story, French barracks stand lamenting the loss of their roofs, lost when the French burned and abandoned the fort in 1759. The British constructed a large series of earthworks, though the palisades burned three years earlier. There are no mature trees, the last of which were used fifteen years earlier when the British fortified the entire peninsula.

Repairs to the fort are underway, and new hospital buildings stand amidst a clearing where all the trees have been cleared. The area around the fort thrums with activity; soldiers shape logs into timbers and work to frame several new buildings. Most of the sixteen regiments that were in Canada are here now. Over a thousand tents, in clusters of fifty to as many as two hundred, occupy approximately seven acres of newly cleared land on the gentle slopes surrounding the fort.

From atop one of the many grass-covered earthwork berms, Colonel Stark addresses the assembled officers. Isaac is near the back of the semicircle of fifty who stand listening to Stark. They look hard-used, their uniforms dirty and baggy on their gaunt frames. They each have lost fifteen or more pounds since the campaign began.

"The other colonels and I have discussed it," announces Stark, "and feel our best course is to fortify this place. It is a better place to stage naval operations and to reconnoiter the lake country."

Isaac sees Major Scammell standing at the rear of the group, and makes his way over to him. In a low voice, Isaac greets the major, "Pleased to see you, sir." Scammell motions Isaac to back away a short distance so as not to distract the others.

Scammell's demeanor is somber. "The general asked for a roll call just prior to leaving the island. I did my best. Discipline and accountability were non-existent. Best I could tell, we lost nine hundred men. Fully a quarter of the six regiments who left New York only two months ago. A thousand are still sick."

Isaac, shocked by the news, takes a deep breath. "One in four dead? How could things have gone so bad?"

"I don't dwell on it, Quartermaster. Take heart. More than two thousand of our men are now inoculated and have nothing to fear from the pox."

The two rejoin the group as Stark finishes his speech with his usual fiery tone, "...I will write Generals Sullivan, Schuyler, and Arnold and make our recommendations in the strongest language. We will hold Crown Point! By God, we will contest every inch of this ground as General Washington ordered us to! No more of this tails-between-our-legs while we stumble backward!" The officers give

Stark a round of huzzahs.

Isaac remarks to Scammell, "If nothing else, Colonel Stark has got our morale turning around."

"He does, and I hope his own is high, as well, for I do not believe the generals will agree with his assessment of the importance of holding this ground. There are strategic considerations that preclude our fortifying this place, including being outnumbered by two to one, where half their force could keep us pinned here on this peninsula, while the other half carves a swath from here to Albany, or further."

Isaac raises an eyebrow. "I pray that will not come to pass. That's quite logical, now that I'm embarrassed not to have seen that possibility."

"I'm glad you see it that way. Well, let us be back to our work. Good day, Quartermaster."

"Yes, and good day to you, sir."

•••

Lieutenant Colonel Gilman leads a meeting of the officers of the 3rd New Hampshire Regiment. They gather outside the small marquee tent that he uses as the regiment's headquarters, near the center of the regiment's group of tents.

Six days have passed since Stark's rousing speech. The officers look better kempt now, though not yet in full health. The weather for the past few days has been warm, clear, and dry, which has helped greatly, both for bolstering the spirits of the men and for moving provisions from Fort Ticonderoga.

From the broad hillside along the shore the regiment's tents occupy, they can see the fort and hospitals. Now most of the buildings have their roofs. Gilman stands uphill of and facing the gathered officers. "Gentlemen, I'll begin by telling you Colonel Reed offers his sincere regrets. Just as he was feeling nearly recovered from the pox, he has taken ill with a new malignant fever and regrets he will be delayed in returning to us. Thus, the mantle of command continues to be my honor to wear." He pauses and looks around to gauge the concerned reactions of the men.

Captain Spaulding catches Gilman's attention, "Sir, has Colonel Reed regained his sight?"

"I am afraid not."

Seeing that many of the officers look downcast at this news, Gilman offers, "Dr. Beebe, who has attended him from the start, has not given up hope."

"Well, at least that's something," Isaac whispers to Lieutenant Hawkins, standing to his left.

Gilman clears his throat. "The reason I called you all here is," his tone becomes measured and a little peeved, as he continues, "a council was held between Generals Schuyler, Sullivan, and Arnold. We are ordered south to fortify the grounds southeast of Fort Ticonderoga. By southeast, I mean on the other side of the lake, at a place called Rattlesnake Hill. I've not heard much else. Thus, we are ordered to occupy yet another place where we must take great pains to safeguard our health against the land."

The officers look at each other in surprise. After Stark's speech a week earlier, they had spent their days building fortifications for a long-term stay.

Gilman continues, "Furthermore, the sick and wounded will be conveyed to Fort George where General Schuyler has had men working to construct hospitals. Have your companies begin preparations to remove to Rattlesnake Hill immediately. We will be leaving as early as tomorrow, and definitely by Wednesday. Dismissed."

The officers leave the meeting, moving into the rows of tents in ones and twos. Isaac and James walk together. James looks incredulous. "That was a bit of an about face."

Isaac nods. "It was. Though I suppose if the generals had been present for Colonel Stark's sermon last Sunday, they might have wondered how he'd been put in charge."

James laughs. "True enough. Well, at least Colonel Stark knows enough to be in charge, and to be seen. I swear, that General Schuyler..." James shakes his head in disgust. "I don't think I've seen the man twice since being reassigned to his command."

"Aye, the same goes for me. I agree with Colonel Stark's instincts for leading the men. We needed something to rally around after leaving Canada in a hungry and embarrassed state. When Major Scammell told me we'd lost nine hundred of the men who came north from New York City, it took the wind out of me."

"I swear that news chilled me to the bone when you told me."

"Aye, it's difficult to comprehend. For keeping the sick separate, and having so much work ourselves, I can scarcely admit to myself that it was hard to notice. Even at the end, when death was right under my nose, I made myself look at anything else." They reach their tent a moment later and Isaac is dismayed to find himself short of breath with his chest tight. He turns to James, whose downturned mouth and long expression cause him to swallow hard. Looking away, Isaac mumbles, "I need to get started on an inventory." Isaac fetches a satchel from the tent and heads back towards the headquarters tent.

Late that afternoon Isaac and James are returning from General Sullivan's headquarters by the French ruins and come upon Major Hale and Colonel Gilman, heading in the opposite direction. After exchanging salutes, Gilman comments, "Well, gentlemen. I expect the orders you heard this morning were a bit of a surprise."

James responds, "Yes, considering the past week of work here and why we began it."

Gilman tips his head back slightly, acknowledging that he's heard what he was expecting. "Major Hale and I are on our way to dine with the other field officers from the brigade to discuss the most recent news."

James asks, "Anything you can share?"

"Yes. Foremost, that General Sullivan was dismissed today; Major General Horatio Gates is now in command. Colonel Stark has sent a letter of protest to General Schuyler regarding the generals deciding not to fortify and invest this place fully. He sent a copy to General Washington, as well. He's definitely got his dander up. Myself and Colonel Reed, despite his condition, signed it, along with a dozen others. The gist of it is that we knew we had standing orders from his Excellency himself," his voice gains a quality of iron resolve, "to dispute every inch of the ground in Canada. Our retreat was many things, but disputing the ground was not one of them."

Isaac reacts with surprise to both pieces of news. "Sir, I hope it does some good. We've all agreed that Colonel Stark did right by us. Forgive my saying so, but General Schuyler seems less prone to action. Do you think the letter will change anything?"

Gilman grins without humor. "Frankly, no. The orders will not be changed. Delayed, perhaps. It deeply offend the pride of some, but if it gets a few of the colonels invited to the council next time, it will have been worth it, though I doubt Colonel Stark will be among them."

Hale reaches down and plucks a stem of wild rye. As he speaks, he strips it of seeds. "Colonel Stark does have a peculiar sense for which battles he picks."

Gilman, looking self-satisfied, says, "I've been watching Colonel Stark on just that count. Maybe I was hoping to learn something, but I discovered that he pursues the battles most obviously in front of him. He is fighter, not a schemer."

James agrees. "Well, he is the best we have in a battle."

"Where I would follow his lead," Gilman responds, "without question. But in politics—which is the province of generals and our Congress—the proponents of direct and straightforward tactics are too often easily tripped up by unseen details."

The lowering sun forces James to squint. "Sounds, sir, like you would put your money on the generals, given we are currently not in battle."

"Precisely. Well gentlemen," Gilman noticing the reason James was squinting. "Major Hale and I need to on our way. Good afternoon to you both."

The officers exchange salutes and go on their way.

•••

Five days later, on July 13, the sun is shining high overhead, causing tendrils of vapor to rise as the soggy ground dries. Isaac stands on a patch of matted grass above the mud-churned shore of Lake Champlain, watching the line of bateaux being rowed steadily south toward Fort Ticonderoga. The trip is expected to take six hours with today's heavy loads. Nearby, a line of soldiers waits beside a pile of neatly rolled and stacked tents and a stack of wooden boxes containing stakes, mallets, rope, and other supplies needed to set up an encampment. As the oarsmen guide the next bateaux into place, as Isaac instructs the soldiers what to load next.

Lieutenant Colonel Gilman approaches. "Quartermaster, how many more bateaux are needed for our regiment's supplies?"

"Just three, sir. After that, only some of the men remain. Yours and Colonel Reed's baggage is going on this next bateaux. I will be traveling on the third. Sergeant Blanchard has already gone."

"Very good. Colonel Reed and I will be on the next bateaux after that."

"I am glad he is able to make the trip. How is his condition?"

"Not much better, I'm afraid. The fever has not abated. Though he is at times in good spirits, he is also often annoyed for being unable to quickly make a full recovery. The last few days of rain have been particularly difficult."

"At least today," Isaac quips, "is a much better day than we've had recently to make this trip."

Gilman looks down in disgust to the ankle-deep muck a few feet in front of them. "All that rain two days ago made for a great deal of mud."

Isaac grins. "At least the enemy has as much mud as we do. You were quite right, sir, about Colonel Stark's letter not having much impact. It seems plans were already in place for the bateaux to arrive here."

Gilman raises an eyebrow. "Yes, that was part of a much larger plan. When Colonel Stark learned that Congress gave General Schuyler discretion to fortify either Crown Point or Ticonderoga, it was, shall we say, moot."

"We will control both sides of the lake at Fort Ti, just as well as here"

"And we will have an excellent view of the lake for six miles, which is all we will need to man the cannon and sink anything that Carlton or Burgoyne can send at us."

Isaac, with a calculating look, adds, "At least the work here will not go to waste. The orders to bring off as much of the lumber as possible was welcome news."

"Precisely. Our objective is to keep these bateaux moving steadily between here, Fort Ti, and Skenesboro, where they are constructing ships for the purpose of defending the lake. There will be two or three regiments kept here for that purpose, likely the militia that were called up a month ago."

Isaac squints down the length of the lake. "Do you have information as to whether any preparations have been made for our arrival?"

"Yes. A good well has been dug and a road has been started between the ground we are to occupy on Rattlesnake Hill and Skenesboro. A company of men has been working on it for the past week. So, a little work has been done, but we will need to take up that work, starting tomorrow."

"Well, sir, that is better than nothing."

•••

Five days later, on the shore opposite Fort Ticonderoga, up on the broad plateau known as Rattlesnake Hill, clearings and a road have appeared where the soldiers have cut down trees. It is the middle of the afternoon on a clear, hot, muggy day. Isaac is overseeing a group of soldiers filling one set of trenches, while another set digs a new trench alongside the old. The used trenches reek of the waste not yet covered, and draw large black flies by the thousands. Most of the men work without shirts, which they have hung on the branches of trees next to the clearing. The men, sweating heavily, have slowed their work to a pace they can sustain in the heat. Isaac's shirt sticks to much of his back and shoulders.

Isaac has a superb view from the clearing. The ground slopes down before dropping off over the bluffs of the plateau. A mile across the lake he can see the low marshes surrounding Fort Ticonderoga and to the left, the height of Sugarloaf Hill dominates. The sound of axes felling trees and the peens and tangs of sledgehammers on wedges and mauls shaping timbers rings from nearly every direction.

Ensign Hawkins approaches and salutes. "Quartermaster."

Isaac nods. "Ensign Hawkins, how do you fare today?"

"Well enough. Tired from making the round trip to Fort George yesterday."

"Aye, as am I. Who would have thought more than half the regiment would be sick, and there would barely be enough of us to take them to the hospital?"

"Well, it's a good thing the doctors refused those who were barely ill. We don't have enough men to do our work."

"I suppose that's why you are here?"

"Good guess. Captain Mann wants to know how much longer you'll need these men?"

"I expect it will be less than an hour now."

"Thank you, I'll let him know."

•••

Later that evening, Isaac is in his tent writing a letter by the light of a lantern.

July 17, 1776
Camp opposite Fort Ticonderoga

Dearest Wife, I realize I wrote to you only two days ago, but it seems I am in the luxury of having more time to write. There was much I neglected to write in those earlier lines. We are now camped just south of Fort Ticonderoga, and working on constructing a permanent camp here. Give my love to father and the boys as well.

Our regiment has suffered since early in June. 61 men died or deserted, tho now I have confirmed none of those are from Wilton. Our brigade lost nearly a quarter of its men, and we are slightly better than that. A full third o the men are sick with pox and camp fevers. We took them to the General Hospital at Fort George yesterday. So, just half of what we began with are present and fit today.

Our morale is low. If I am not to gain a captaincy, I doubt my role in pursuing liberty is with the army which has been a source of disappointment since we left Boston. But I will not burden you with a soldier's frustrations.

I continue to be well. My full health nearly recovered now that food is plentiful. Your Loving Husband, Isaac

P.S. it looks as though we shall be quartered here for some time as we must keep the redcoats from pushing south and severing New England from her sister colonies.

Isaac finishes writing, cleans his nib, and closes his inkwell. He puts the letter aside to dry overnight, hoping the humidity is not too high to keep the paper from drying enough to fold without transferring ink.

16 CAMP INDEPENDENCE

Fort Ticonderoga - 19 July 1776

"A Very Heavey Rain last night & continewd the chief of the Day. 2 men of Col. De Haas Regt. were found in there tents drownded in warter, many others lay half covered or Set up all night. such a heavey Rain is Sildom known..."

Revolutionary War Journal of Colonel Jeduthan Baldwin

Fort Ticonderoga - 29 July 1776

"...everything about this Army is infected with the Pestilence, The Cloaths, the Blankets, The Air, & the grounds they walk upon; To put this Evil from us, a General Hospital is Established at Fort George..."

Major General Horatio Gates to General Washington

A few days later, on Saturday, July 20, just past noon, Isaac picks his way through a very soggy clearing amidst a steady rain. At times, he has to make small leaps to thicker tufts of grass to avoid sinking into the soft ground and filling his boots with water, as he makes his way to where James is standing beneath the awning of an open wall tent. The rain is cascading off the back of the tent, and the awning still sags despite taller poles in front, and two extra poles added near the front corners to ensure the middle is higher than the back.

Isaac steps over the shallow ditch dug around the front of the tent to divert the water around and downhill. James, who despite being under the cover of the tent is exceedingly damp, takes a second look at Isaac. "Quartermaster, you look a bit put out."

"The men are back at their tents for their meal." Isaac's tone takes on a note of exasperation. "Yes, I am a bit put out. I just broke up the third fight of the morning. Our men and the Pennsylvania men cannot seem to focus on their assigned tasks. They'd rather give insults to one another's mothers and sisters. Is there any way you can get tasks assigned such that we are not working side by side with these southerners?"

James shrugs. "Me? No. But I've got good news on two counts: General Gates assigned new brigades for the regiments today. I think his intent was to provide the separation you observe to be needed. The new arrangement will take effect this afternoon."

"That's welcome news, and just in time. What will our place be in the new arrangement?"

"Colonels Reed and Stark have command of two of the three brigades, which will be quartered here on Rattlesnake Hill. We will be in the second brigade, which will be Reed's. Stark has the third. Just New Hampshire and Massachusetts regiments here on the east side of the lake." James raises a hand to hold Isaac a moment longer. "We will be moving our encampment to the southeastern part of the hill, and we'll be able to build proper quarters. Let the men know. That should raise their spirits a bit, especially with this confounded deluge."

"A proper barracks. That is good news. What was the other good news?"

James grins and fixes Isaac with a look that tells that he is curious to see what Isaac's reaction will be. "A dispatch arrived late the day before yesterday. The Continental Congress has declared independence from Great Britain. At least in writing we have won our own country. Though I'm afraid there were no additional details, aside from the expectation that this declaration will be published and circulated."

Isaac blows out a long exhale. "Well, that is..." Isaac pauses, his expression going blank as he considers the potential this news holds.

James smiles. "I know what you mean. Without the details, the possibilities are infinite."

Isaac nods. "Aye, true. More information would have helped. Still, I think it is good news. I'd better get back. I need my noon meal, and all the rain we've had makes going anywhere take three times longer."

...

A week later, on Sunday, July 28, the 3rd New Hampshire Regiment is paraded in the area they've cleared for their barracks. Isaac stands behind Lieutenant Colonel Gilman, who has just arrived and is holding several sheets of a newspaper. There is some anxiousness as the regiment has heard two outbursts of cheers in the past fifteen minutes. Most have whispered it must be news of a victory by General Washington.

With a strong voice, Gilman addresses the assembled regiment. "Gentlemen, I read this proclamation of the utmost importance and concern to the cause in which we are engaged. It is a copy of a Philadelphia newspaper having come here today." The men look around at each other, realizing that the details of Congress declaring independence have arrived, and they become very quiet.

Gilman continues,

"In Congress, July 4, 1776. The unanimous Declaration of the thirteen united States of America, When in the course of human events, it becomes necessary for one people to dissolve the political bands which have connected them with another, and to assume among the powers of the earth, the separate and equal station to which the Laws of Nature and of Nature's God entitle them, a decent respect to the opinions of mankind requires that they should declare the causes which impel them to the separation."

"We hold these truths to be self-evident, that all men are created

equal, that they are endowed by their Creator with certain unalienable Rights, that among these are Life, Liberty and the pursuit of Happiness.—That to secure these rights..."

Gilman goes on to read the entirety of the Declaration of Independence. As he speaks, Isaac notices the men in the regiment are now standing taller as though no longer collectively burdened by the weight of an unknown future.

Gilman finishes reading and looks at the assembled regiment. "Gentlemen, by order of General Gates and General Schuyler, the mount we now occupy will be known as Mount Independence, and the camp we are now constructing will be known henceforth as Camp Independence!"

Sergeant Major Gray responds, leading the regiment with, "Hip-hip—"

"HUZZAH!"

They repeat this cheer twice more, each louder than the previous.

Then Gilman holds his hand up to request quiet. "We will circulate copies of this momentous declaration to each company later this evening. We will need several men who can write with a clear, legible hand to expedite the production of those copies."

Several sergeants and lieutenants volunteer and Gilman dismisses the regiment. Isaac moves to intercept James.

"Adjutant, care to dine together tonight?"

James responds, "Why, I don't believe I am otherwise engaged. I'd be happy to, Quartermaster." The two lieutenants walk towards the wagons converted for serving food to the soldiers.

"That was the most unimaginably good news," says Isaac. "Every man stood straighter and taller the more Colonel Gilman read. Myself included."

"I was similarly moved. I had no idea that not being a British subject would feel so good. The dread of not knowing our fate, should we be victorious, was weighing heavily upon us all."

The weight of James's comment causes Isaac to stop and look at his friend. "Well put. It does put everything in a new light. I suppose liberty means a great deal more now. No king. No Parliament."

"These congresses and committees of safety become quite a bit more important now. I wonder how that will work?"

Isaac scratches the back of his head. "Well, we've governed ourselves for four generations now, even if by charter. Removing the king's approval of our governing decisions, and paying our taxes to our towns and counties instead of to a crown or to Parliament where we have no representation, seems possible. In fact, I think this change should not be much of an issue."

James shakes his head skeptically. "Perhaps, though just paying for an army will put pressure on each colony. Plus, it is not as though any of the others are like New Hampshire, where I think there are something like a total of four Tories in the whole province. The other colonies are rife with loyalists. You remember New York—men afraid to speak their minds in public."

"A fair point. Thus, I hope and expect this declaration will give them cause and courage take up arms against the redcoats."

"Aye, but for those who depend on the crown for their riches, I think this declaration will be just as strong in spurring them to supporting the redcoats."

"I suppose so." Isaac thinks a moment and his expression shifts to one of confidence. "I say, so be it. Independence sounds like a fine idea. Far better than the last dozen years of resisting the king and Parliament's efforts to make us second-class citizens."

James grins. "I can't argue. Now that I think about it, it was the only true way forward. I do wonder what will come of being independent."

"Aye. True. I feel optimistic now, and an hour ago the future offered few options."

James claps Isaac on the shoulder. "You're not the only one. See you tonight."

•••

More than three weeks later, nearing the end of August, Mount Independence has undergone a transformation from a mostly wooded plateau to most of the uplands now being denuded of trees. Two more brigades have been added, making for almost six thousand men on the mount. The barracks and a hospital are under construction. The stone walls of the main fort are in place.

It is early afternoon on another hot, humid day, and Isaac is out observing the companies as they practice a response drill wherein they run from their tents into company formations, then together quick march to the edge of the plateau, climb down the one-hundred-sixty-foot-high western scarp of the peninsula to a cache of bateaux hidden at the base. From there, it is a few dozen yards to launch the bateaux and paddle a mile across the narrow part of Lake Champlain to a landing just below Fort Ticonderoga. Then they form ranks and march quickly to the north side of the fort. From the top of the scarp, Isaac times the men's movements.

As the men reach the far shore, James Otis arrives to stand beside Isaac. "Good afternoon, Quartermaster. It looks as though the men have learned to make good time in crossing the lake."

"Yes, they're learning."

"I've got news: Colonel Reed's been promoted to brigadier."

Isaac, still intently tracking his men's progress, remarks, "That's excellent. How is his sight?"

"No better. He is still at the General Hospital at Fort George. Colonel Gilman told me Colonel Reed has already written back to Congress, declining the promotion. I think they will let him keep the rank, even if he cannot continue in the army."

Isaac waits, watching as the men disappear from sight over a rise to the left of Fort Ticonderoga, then he turns to James. "That's a shame. So, will he resign after December when our enlistments are out?"

"I believe so. There were quite a few other promotions announced—"

"One for you or me?"

"No, just for field officers and generals. Colonel St. Clair is now a brigadier. Major Scammell was reassigned to become General Sullivan's aide-de-camp. More telling though, is Colonel Stark was *not* promoted to brigadier. However, since Colonel Reed is declining, I imagine he will petition to be promoted."

"That makes sense. I hope he gets it. Where will Major Scammell be assigned?"

"New York. No surprise there. Sullivan was promoted to Major General and has been looking out for his former law clerk all along."

Isaac looks confused. "Clerk?"

"Scammell was a clerk in Sullivan's law office."

"Oh, I see. That's good about Scammell. Let's find him and offer congratulations. Always good to have friends in high places."

"No argument from me on that." Then James laughs. "Though I think I'd just prefer to be in the high places myself."

•••

Nearly two hours later, the two lieutenants make their way through the collection of tents that comprise their brigade's encampment. They arrive to find Major Scammell in the process of packing his tent and belongings.

Scammell's head snaps up when he sees them coming. He sets down a blanket he has just folded. He sounds alarmed and speaks rapidly when he asks, "Lieutenants. Am I needed?"

James holds his hands up. "No, sir—a social visit."

Isaac adds, "We've come to offer congratulations on your promotion. Looks like you'll be off to New York immediately."

"Thank you, and yes. I'm expected in New York as soon as I can arrive."

Isaac continues, "Best of luck, sir. I expect to hear you'll be given a regiment to command soon."

James laughs. "Easy, Quartermaster! He's only just been promoted to his new office."

Scammell chuckles. "It's okay, Lieutenant Otis. Lieutenant Frye knows well my impatient nature. I shall indeed be disappointed if I do not have a regiment of my own by year's end. Though for now my destiny has a quill in my hand rather than a sword or pistol, but that won't keep me out of the fray should a battle be nearby."

Isaac, sweat rolling into his eyebrows, wipes his brow on his sleeve. "You're assigned to General Sullivan, so I cannot imagine he will keep you at a desk, or task you with carrying correspondence."

"No, I don't imagine he will. I worked in his law office for some time, so I know he and I share a desire to act when faced with a conflict, instead of stewing about, hoping it will go away."

James ventures, "I've scarcely met the man, but it seems as though you find General Sullivan's character to your liking. What is his appeal?"

Scammell mops his brow with a handkerchief and for a moment is lost in thought, then comes to himself, laughing softly. "Now, you cannot repeat this to a soul, but—" He looks them both in the eye to see that they heard his warning. "I like him best when he's in his cups, or nearly so. He's an Irishman, you know. Fiery temper and fond of imparting wisdom on the human condition when in that blissful, blustery state. But—and this is most important—he's the sort you want on your side, if you know what I mean. He is loyal to a fault; and his chief fault is he expects loyalty from others. Thus, I have no qualms, as I give him mine without reservation. My eyes are open and my heart content, for I know he will keep my loyalty well."

Isaac nods. "Then I do not think General Sullivan is the sort to keep you chained to a desk and paperwork."

"No, he isn't. That said, he doesn't like to be kept waiting, and I've got to get going. I want to reach Fort George tonight, and Saratoga tomorrow night. You're both worthy officers and fine gentlemen. I'd welcome either of you into my service should I be given that regiment you've predicted for me to command."

Isaac shakes Scammell's hand. "Thank you, sir, and God speed."

"Yes, God speed to you, sir," James echoes as he shakes Scammell's hand.

.

17 THE MOST DEADLY ENEMY

Fort Ticonderoga
23d August [1776]

"We set of from our Lodging very Early and got up to Crown Point about ten o'clock in the forenoon and after taking some Refreshment there set off and landed at Putnam's Point (so called) and took our dinners; from there we set off with a fair wind and landed at Ticonderoga about two hours by sun and after I had delivered the Boats the Party was dismist and came to the Camp that Night, where I had the melancholy News of the Death of Caleb Putnam [of Wilton], who died the 22d and was buried a few hours before I came into Camp."

Ticonderoga Diary of Lieutenant Jonathan Burton of Wilton, NH

Burton and more than two dozen other men from Wilton marched with Colonel Wyman's regiment to reinforce Fort Ticonderoga on July 23, 1776

A month later, on September 17, just as twilight is settling in, Isaac and Sergeant Blanchard walk briskly to their quarters from the main fort at the center of Mount Independence, where they've just had their first look at the new gunpowder laboratory. Walking toward

221

them, having just left their brigade's encampment, is Lieutenant Butterfield. As they meet, they exchange salutes.

"It's good to see you Lieutenant Butterfield," Isaac begins. "Have you met Sergeant Blanchard? He is the Third's quartermaster sergeant."

Butterfield indicates he has not, and Isaac introduces the pair. After they've shaken hands, Isaac turns to Butterfield and asks, "Have you brought some news from home for me?"

"I have. I left three letters for you in your tent. Ensign Hawkins showed me where it was located, I did not see your wife this trip, though when I was in Wilton in June she was at the meetinghouse, and looked to be in good spirits

"Thank you, I'll have something written soon for you to carry back."

"You're welcome. I've got a few more letters to deliver tonight up to Colonel Wyman's regiment. I'll see you in the morning before I leave."

A few minutes later Isaac returns to his tent and can make out three letters on his small desk in the shadows. He lights two candles and settles in to read. The first is from Elizabeth.

Wilton
Sep 8, 1776

Dearest Husband, All is as well as can be expected here. Some good news from Brother Timothy who visited last week. He was surprised we were not somehow enriched through your position of quartermaster. I explained about your being prohibited from taking commissions on contracts. This was affecting him, and he sends his apologies for being so affected and not showing you his respect and affection.

I was glad as always to learn you are safe. Also I pray the enemy does not find a way this season to attack. The apple trees produced some small fruit this year which The boys enjoyed picking them. Maybe one or two more years before the trees, with proper weather, shall be profitable. I hope to have more lines by you soon. Your Loving Wife, Elizabeth

The second letter is from his brother Simon, who lives in Massachusetts Bay, to the east of New Hampshire.

Sep 2, 1776
Fryeburg

Dear Brother, My family and I are mostly well, though my youngest, Jonathan struggles to recover fully from the sickness that took his twin this past spring. Uncle Joseph is safely back here in Fryeburg. The Brigadier's commission meant a great deal to him. He was glad of being able to see you as well as his sons. He confided to me that he has realized war is a young man's vocation. We are still getting the harvest in, so I must get my rest. I will write more soon.

I have heard some of the news of the Canadian Department. I regret that you've had to suffer though the retreat and privations in that quarter. Fryeburg and other towns are sending supplies. The news from Congress was extraordinary. True freedom! That is worth fighting for. I hope your spirits have risen since getting that news. Stay the course. With greatest affection, Your Brother, Simon.

The third letter is from Elizabeth's brother, Timothy.

Andover
Sep 1, 1776

Dear Isaac, It has been far too long since I have written you. I apologize. I admit some jealousy was in my heart for thinking, as Elizabeth has undoubtedly conveyed to you by now, that you were profiting from your position as quartermaster. When I visited father and my sisters two days ago, I learned my thoughts could not have been further from the truth. Please accept my apology.

Sister Elizabeth misses you deeply. I hope for her sake your duty is almost done. With respect and affection, Yours, Timothy

Isaac sits back and lets loose a long sigh. A minute later, he gets out paper and ink, starting a letter to Elizabeth first.

17 Sep, 1776
Camp Independence

My Dearest Wife, I rec'd your lines this evening, and some from Simon, and Brother Timothy. I am glad he was able to visit and learn our situation first hand.

I am sending my pay again. Please endeavor to buy cyder soon. My thoughts are of a harvest I did not plant, and cannot taste, and of a wife and children I cannot see or hold.

We had news of General Washington's defeats. This has our camp in a somber state. This year has been all death and defeat. My earlier plans remain unchanged. I will do my duty til years end, but must have better prospects for committing another year.

I have seen some of the other men from Wilton who are in Colonel Wyman's regiment of 8-months men. They arrived some weeks ago, brother Richard and Josiah Parker among them. It was good to see Richard, please give sister Hannah my love and affection and the news that he is well, also give Father and sister Sarah my love and affection. Give the boys the same, and tell them I have missed seeing them these past seven months. Your Loving Husband, Isaac Frye

•••

Two mornings later, at a long workbench outside the gunpowder laboratory, Isaac supervises a squad of soldiers making cartridges by wrapping specially cut sheets of paper around a peg with a diameter a little larger than a musket ball. The privates wrap paper such that it produces a tube with one end closed. The ball and powder are added, then the open end of the tube is folded shut to finish the cartridge. Two men are responsible for measuring the powder, while eight produce the cartridges. Isaac keeps a tally of the completed cartridges.

Lieutenant Colonel Gilman and Captain Hinds, one of the regiment's company commanders, leave the main fort, which is about fifty yards north of the laboratory. They walk purposefully toward Isaac. Gilman clears his throat as they approach. The men working know better than to stand and salute given the delicate nature of their work. Isaac, however, turns and offers his commander a crisp salute.

Gilman returns the salute, and motions for Isaac to walk with him and Captain Hinds a short distance, out of hearing range from the men. "Quartermaster, I have a proposition for you."

"Sir, what do you propose?"

"Lieutenant Stone needed to resign his commission, and Captain Hinds' company requires a new subaltern. If you are willing, I would assign you as such. What do you say?"

Isaac eyes light up, recognizing the opportunity to not be a quartermaster for the rest of the war. "I will do it."

Captain Hinds grins and reaches his hand forward, which Isaac shakes vigorously. "I'm glad to have you with me," says Hinds. "We can get started introducing you to your duties once the colonel finishes with us."

Gilman remarks with obvious satisfaction, "Excellent. I think Sergeant Blanchard can handle the position of quartermaster, don't you, Lieutenant?"

Isaac laughs. "Even without my own incentive, I would recommend him."

"Good. Can you point me in his direction?"

Isaac points to a large cart where some troops are loading freshly cut timber. Gilman thanks him, reminds him to finish his current task with the cartridges before reporting to Captain Hinds, and moves off to see the sergeant.

•••

Later that evening, Isaac is in his tent writing a letter by the light of a lantern.

Sep 19, 1776
Camp Independence

Dearest Wife, The news today is I've had a change of assignment. I am no longer quartermaster of the regiment and am now Captain Hinds' subaltern. Lieutenant Isaac Stone, who is brother of Ephraim who you met last year, resigned. The unfortunate news is their father has died, which I expect is the reason for Isaac's resigning from the Army. I am now closer in line to be promoted to Captain. I don't have much hopes just yet, but by the end of the year it is possible, depending on which captains choose to continue in the Army.

I continue to be well, and am anxious to have more lines from you. Your Loving Husband, Isaac

Isaac, smiling to himself, sets aside the letter. He takes out a wooden trunk and prepares to pack his things as he hears footsteps approaching his tent.

Outside Isaac's tent, James flicks a finger into the canvas twice to knock. "You there, Isaac?"

"Yes. Come in, James."

"I figured you were, since I could see the glow of the lamp. I heard the good news from Colonel Gilman at dinner. Congratulations."

"Thank you. It sounds as though you see this as a good opportunity as well. Though I am afraid I won't be spending much time in headquarters."

"Don't worry, we will carry on. The Army cannot afford to depend on any one man, even yourself." James notes Isaac's open truck and nods to it. "That's right. You will be moving your tent tomorrow to Captain Hinds' company. I will look forward to hearing from you once you've had a few days to learn your new duties."

"Count on it."

James notes Isaac's smile. "I think this duty will agree with you. I'll let you get to your packing."

After saying good night, Isaac turns back to his trunk and begins packing his belongings.

•••

On the morning of October 7, Isaac's letters reach Elizabeth in Wilton. It is a fine, warm, early-fall day, with only a few trees changing to show autumn color, or dropping leaves. She thanks Lieutenant Butterfield, who continues on his mission of delivering the mail from the soldiers at Fort Ticonderoga.

Half an hour later, a letter from Corporal Josiah Parker reaches his wife. Phebe waves goodbye to Lieutenant Butterfield and opens the letter while on the front step of her home in the late morning sunshine. Within a few seconds, the color drains from her face and she runs toward the lane in front of her home. She turns up the lane, running as quickly as her skirts and shoes allow her, to the home of her neighbor, Hannah Whitney—Elizabeth's sister.

Not seeing Hannah outside, Phebe rushes through the gate at the Whitney's home and rushes to the door, where she commences to knock loudly. When no one answers, she bangs the knocker louder and louder. She calls out, "Hannah! Hannah! Are you home?"

It only takes Hannah about ten seconds to reach the door, but Phebe is in a panic by that time. Hannah opens the door to see Phebe, flushed and looking stricken—completely out of breath. "What on earth, Phebe? Are you okay?"

"No!" Phebe wails. "I've just had this letter from Josiah." Still clutched in her hand, she shakes the letter open with a hard snap of her wrist, as if trying to change the words by the sheer force. "He says he's very ill. Wilton's had three men die in the last month, and now I'm so worried!"

"Phebe, that's awful news. Does he write anything more?"

"Only that he fears he will not recover unless he gets a discharge so he can get home, away from the camp with all the diseases."

"Maybe Sister Elizabeth's husband Isaac can help. He's an officer. I'll watch your children. Go to Elizabeth, then to Josiah's parents."

"Yes. Yes." Phebe finally regains control of her breathing. "That's good thinking. Thank you so much." Phebe turns and starts running, though now pacing herself.

Just over twenty minutes later, and winded from climbing the path behind Isaac's farm, Phebe is now walking at a quick pace. She calls out for Elizabeth and her shout is answered from inside the barn, where her friend is cleaning out a stall. Phebe enters the barn and reaches out to a post to steady herself and catch her breath. Elizabeth leans the pitchfork against another post and waits for Phebe to explain.

Phebe's eyes are wide with the effort to master her composure. "Elizabeth," she gasps. "Your sister Hannah sent me. I've had a letter from Josiah with terrible news."

"Oh, no." Concern overtakes the look of focused exertion on her face. "What news? I had a letters from Isaac today, and he didn't write of any trouble."

Phebe bites her lower lip and shakes her head in distress. "It's Josiah." She wrings her hands as she continues. "He is sick—so sick he thinks only a discharge will save him."

Elizabeth's hands rise involuntarily to cover her mouth in horror. After a moment of shocked silence, practicality takes over. "What can I do to help?"

"Can you write Isaac and ask him help Josiah get a discharge?"

"Certainly. I'm almost done in here. I started a letter this morning; I'll add to it, and I should have it ready in an hour or so."

"Oh, thank you, Elizabeth! I must go next door now to Josiah's parents and see if they can help me find a way to get the letter carried right away."

"Yes, go. Come into the house straightway when you get back."

Phebe nods once. Elizabeth gives her a quick hug, then guides her out of the barn. Phebe looks around and asks, "I just noticed how quiet it is. Where are Sarah and your boys?"

"Sarah took them up the hill to gather chestnuts. You may see them on your way up. I expect they will be along soon."

"Thank you again. I will be back as soon as I can."

Once on the road, Phebe gathers her skirts and starts up the hill with long, determined strides.

•••

An hour past noon, Elizabeth sits at the table in the main room, writing. Also on the table are several chestnuts and two sacks, each half full of chestnuts still in their burrs. Phebe arrives at Isaac's home with Henry Parker and John Stevens in tow. They knock and enter without waiting for a response. Phebe is relieved to see that Elizabeth appears to be putting the finishing touches to the letter. "Thank you, Elizabeth."

Henry Parker removes his hat and dips his bald crown in humble gratitude. "We are in your debt, Elizabeth, you and Isaac. I'm paying John Stevens here to ride and deliver your letter as quickly as he can to Isaac; and then to assist Josiah back to Wilton."

Elizabeth smiles, though her eyes show she is worried. "I'm glad to help. Give me a moment and I'll add a line about John and why he's carrying this letter. John, thank you for agreeing. We will help look after your Sarah and the children while you're gone."

At that moment John, fifteen months old, and naked, emerges from the unlatched door to the bedroom, squealing with glee at successfully escaping from Sarah. John bolts to make a circuit around the table as Sarah, with a wide-eyed exasperated look, follows him into the main room. Isaac and Abiel poke their heads into view, giggling.

Elizabeth continues writing to exhaust the ink on her quill, then firmly and nuanced particularly for her youngest son, says, "John."

John stops and immediately shifts his expression to doe-eyed innocence.

With arched eyebrows and pursed lips, Sarah eyes John as she approaches him, then holds out her hand, which he immediately takes with his own.

"I am sorry to interrupt," Sarah begins. "I pray Josiah recovers quickly." She curtsies, inclining her head quickly toward the guests.

Phebe smiles appreciatively, though still tight with worry, and her father-in-law bobs his head once to Sarah. "Thank you."

John Stevens, not forgetting Elizabeth's promise, takes off his hat off. "My thanks to you all. My Sarah will appreciate your kindness. I'm glad to help. Plus, I may see my brothers. If I do, I'll ask them to help, as well."

Sarah leads the intrepid toddler to the bedroom. "I'll get his smock on and we will go outside while you finish."

Elizabeth finishes the letter half a minute after Sarah leads the boys outside, and waves it several times to hasten the ink's drying, and seals it. She rises and hands the letter to John, and adds a wooden box wrapped in oil cloth. "That's for Isaac, too. It might give him some cheer and a taste of home. It's butter and raisins, so take care to keep it out of the sun. It's sealed, so you can keep it in a stream at night."

"I'll make sure he gets it. The weather's turned cool enough, so I expect the butter will keep." John takes the package. "I'll leave now, and hope to be there in three or four days at the most."

Elizabeth smiles. "God speed to you, John." Then she clasps Phebe's hands in hers. "Keep your spirits up, Phebe. We'll get Josiah home and well again. That he was well enough to write bodes well."

Phebe, still looking pale and stricken, whispers, "I hope so, I really do. I hope that's true about his being well enough to write. Thank you, Elizabeth."

Elizabeth stands on the front step as her guests walk out of the front yard. She scoops up John who has tired of trying to keep up with his brothers, and balances him on her hip, and waves good-bye. Seeing his mother wave, John waves good-bye too.

•••

Eight days later it is Monday, October 16. Isaac is taking his noon meal with Captain Hinds and the rest of their company outside a nearly finished barracks. The men look fatigued from exertion, but there is plenty of food and they are eating with determination. Their uniforms are in various states of disrepair—muddy, covered with sawdust, some without hats—and none are wearing coats, as their work has kept them more than warm enough on this cool, autumn day. The trees on the shores of Lake Champlain are past their peak colors, and now exhibit a patchwork of browns and drab grays, with pockets of dark evergreens.

John Stevens rides down the lane from the main road that leads to the fortifications at the crown of Mount Independence. He dismounts in front of the group, and it is clear that he is searching for someone in particular amongst the faces before him. It is well over a year since he's seen Isaac, and he doesn't immediately recognize the mud-spattered, dusty, thinner Isaac until he gets to his feet and hails him.

"John? John Stevens!"

John, still looking uncertain, cocks his head and asks, "Isaac?"

Isaac nods, but is suddenly gripped with fear. His face shifts from being pleased at recognizing a familiar face from home—to worrying something has happened to Elizabeth.

John recognizes Isaac's concern and quickly starts speaking to put him at rest. "Your family is just fine. There is another urgent matter regarding Josiah Parker. I have a letter from your wife that explains everything."

Isaac directs John to walk with him until they are out of earshot of the soldiers. As they come to a stop, John hands him the letter and package from Elizabeth. Isaac, still a little uneasy but now curious, says, "Thank you, John."

John's solemn gaze remains fixed on Isaac, who cocks an eyebrow and asks, "I take it I should read this now?"

"Yes. It's got some lines about Josiah Parker that are vital."

Isaac unseals the letter and starts reading, sighing a few times as he reads.

"Wilton
Oct' 7, y. 1776

Loving Husband after my love to you I would inform you that through the Goodness of God we are all well at this time. Blessed be

God For it I have had a letter from you Dated Sept 18 which gave me Joy in hearing you was well. You also Signified your Desire that I Should purchase some cyder. I fear I shall not be able to purchase any but I will do the best I can. I also Rec'd a line by Lt Butterfield and was Glad to hear From you. I have nothing Strang to Write you at this Time but having an opportunity and not knowing whether I should have another opportunity to write to you or to send you anything comfortable. This same time, I Embrace this, and have sent to you by the bearer of this letter a # of butter and Sister Whitney has sent Brother 2 # and the Box is Brother Whitneys also I have Sent some Rasons & some ginger and hope that if you want anything further that I can help you too that you will Give me Notice and it will be my Care to Send it to You. I have not payed the Person that brings this to you for Mr. Parker Sayd if you would assist what you could do to git a Discharge for Mr. Josiah Parker he would not take anything for this transportation it is his Father that sends for him and has hired Mr. John Stevens to go. I have also Rec'd by Lt. Butterfield a note you signed to him for the sum of Ten Pound Sterling Dated January 21, 1775 which he Says he was ordered to Deliver me I Shall keep it safe til further orders. I hope you will Suffer me to remind you of my Uncomfortable Scituation whilst you are Absent not having your Company, Assistance or Advice, and the Care Revolving on me.

Perpluseing but I hope and Trust you will (if your life and mine is spared and our Health and Liberty continue) See me before you Engage another Season X. I have no desire you Should Heyht your Duty are not behind hand in the Cause of Liberty I shall wish for your Company, I have heard that you expect a Discharge before the Year is up, but I dare not Flatter myself with such Dear but hope to see you by that time and until then commit and commend you to the Preserved of Men and Subscribe myself your Loving Wife – Elizabeth Frye.

Father Remembers his Love to You.

If I buy any Cyder I should be good of a little Money

I Don't want any to Spend Otherwise and I will Acc't for all I have Rec'd"

(Author's note: the above letter has been transcribed from the original document found in Isaac's house late in the twentieth century.)

Once he finishes, Isaac tells John, "Just a moment. I should be able to help, presently."

Isaac turns and jogs over to Captain Hinds. "Captain Hinds, may I take leave for an hour? One of the men from Wilton is very sick. He is with Colonel Wyman's regiment, and his wife asked to see if I can get him discharged so he can go home and recuperate."

Captain Hinds thinks a moment before agreeing. "Yes. I'll assign Lieutenant Davis to oversee the men as they return to work."

"Thank you, sir." Isaac rejoins John Stevens, who is waiting with his horse, and points to the fortifications, indicating where they need to go. "I don't think it will be a problem to get Josiah a discharge. The major for Colonel Wyman's regiment is from Amherst. His name is Stephen Peabody, and I know him well."

"I am glad to finally hear some good news. Lead the way."

"Wyman's regiment is part of Colonel Stark's brigade. They're camped about a mile from here on the far side of the fort. So, what took so long? It's four days by horse, in good weather."

John sighs with some frustration. "They held me at Number Four for four days. The commander there swore there was an imminent attack, and stopped everyone from going through. Even after they let me through, I wasn't permitted to go alone for fear I would be an easy target."

"That makes sense. There was a battle up north on the lake, four days ago. We damaged some British ships at Valcour Island, and it looks as though we have curtailed the enemy's naval activities for the season. I suppose at Number Four they were worried that ground forces were coming, too. Damn, I hope Josiah can recover. I didn't know he was sick, but we don't learn anything from Wyman's regiment until it's the worst news. It is only a mile, but we don't see them too often. So, at least no news means he's likely still with the living."

"Oh, good. I was anxious for having to sit on my hands all those days. Phebe was beside herself with worry when I left."

Nearly twenty minutes later they arrive at Colonel Wyman's headquarters. Isaac asks John to wait outside and he will see what he can do. Isaac knocks on the door and enters. It takes a moment for his eyes to adjust and then Isaac recognizes Stephen and smiles. "Major Peabody, it's good to see you again."

"Isaac! What a pleasant surprise. Seeing you now reminds me just how long it has been since we've crossed paths."

"I know. Even with you on the same side of the lake, the work of building the fortifications and barracks has meant little opportunity. Plus your regiment has been out on commands quite frequently."

"Still, we should make a point of visiting at least once a week."

"We should. That said, I'm here on some business." Isaac fills Stephen in on Josiah Parker's situation.

A few minutes later, Isaac reemerges and fills John in. "Major Peabody agreed. He will ask Colonels Wyman and Stark, and then General Gates. Josiah is in the hospital at Fort George, which is a half day's boat trip to the south. We should have orders by this evening, and you can carry them to Fort George tomorrow. Be ready to travel by early morning. You can sleep with our company tonight. We have extra tents.

John nods. "Thank you, Isaac. I hope we're in time. I'm going to go find my brothers, Caleb and Theo, and see if I can get their help in getting Josiah home. They are in his company."

"I hope we're in time as well. You know where to find us when you get back later?"

"I do." John turns and leads his horse in the direction of the tents of Colonel Wyman's regiment.

•••

A little over a week later, in the early evening of October 24, Isaac finds his way to Captain Hinds' tent after being summoned. Isaac enters and salutes. "What is it, sir?"

Captain Hinds returns the salute, looking somber. "I'm afraid I've got some bad news. Mr. Stevens' brothers arrived back in camp tonight with the news that Josiah Parker died two days ago, at Castleton, in Vermont."

As he listens, Isaac sags under the weight of Hinds' words. "Thank you for giving me the news in person, sir. His father and mother live on the farm next to mine." Isaac runs a hand through his hair, distraught at the news. "I'll write them. It's a foul thing, all these diseases we brought back with us. Wyman's regiment seems to have gotten the worst of it. The pox, and God knows what else. John Stevens got held up at Number Four because of the naval battle. That may have cost Josiah his life."

"I know," agrees Hinds. "It's damned unfortunate. We thought we'd be fighting a war against men. This damnable sickness and filth we've found has become a worse enemy than those wearing red coats." Hinds sighs. "Still, we must keep our focus on the men who are fit. The redcoats must know we are in a bad way and so we must do our utmost to be ready for them." Hinds pauses, looking uncomfortable. "Unfortunately, I have more bad news. Do you know John Honey from Wilton?"

"No, not well, though I'd recognize him. Has he died, as well?"

"I'm afraid so."

"Shite!" Isaac's half-clenched fist shakes as he brings it to his temple, his head bowed and eyes tightly shut, barely able to control his outrage. "I'm beginning to doubt the wisdom of General Gates sending the men to Fort George. It's as if they are sentenced to death there. I am sure sending Colonel Reed there didn't do him any good either. Maybe it's me, but I've not seen many men return from there."

"Most don't. They're too ill by the time they leave here, though many of them are sent home to recuperate. I think that's better for their spirits, too. A hospital is the last place I'd want to be if I got sick. I'd be afraid of catching something even worse." Hinds shudders and with obvious effort banishes the dark thoughts. He looks Isaac squarely in the eye. "Get some sleep, if you can. We've got an early start tomorrow."

"Yessir."

Isaac leaves and heads back to his tent where he writes a sad, difficult letter to Henry and Sarah Parker. He writes Elizabeth afterward to explain what happened.

•••

Late on a chilly, late-October afternoon in Wilton, Elizabeth climbs the hill to the west of the farm. She turns to see Sarah Rideout walking toward her, arms clutching her thick shawl around her shoulders against the gusts of wind passing over the hill. The sky is more clouds than not, but does not completely obscure the sunset.

Elizabeth turns back to the sunset, waiting until Sarah stands beside her. "You heard?"

"Yes."

"Henry took his Sarah to stay with Phebe. Hannah is cooking for them, and Sarah Stevens is helping, too. Hannah says Phebe is distraught beyond anything she's ever seen—screaming for what seems like hours, and then just sitting there, rocking, not making a sound."

Sarah blows her nose. "It chokes me up just to think of it. I made it to Reverend Livermore's earlier. He and his wife will visit early tomorrow."

"It will be even harder. Today, Hannah learned that Phebe is with child. This much strain... I fear it will be too much. I sent my sister Sarah to stay with Hannah, just in case she needs more help."

"Oh, goodness. Phebe is a dear, sweet, Godly woman. She doesn't deserve such hardship."

Elizabeth purses her lips. "Nobody does. The men from Wilton who have died, died of sickness. Not fighting for anything; just sickness."

"I worry for Hannah, that she can keep her spirits up. She says Josiah and Richard's regiment was afflicted worse than all the Continental regiments."

Sarah reaches out and takes Elizabeth's elbow, and turns Elizabeth to face her. "Don't dwell on that. No good can come from it."

Elizabeth resists the urge to argue, then sighs. "I know what you say is true. The nature of hardships is we do not get to choose our hardships." After a few seconds, Elizabeth continues, "At least this year was proof that I can run this farm myself. It was hard work and I had help, but in the end, I did much of it."

Sarah smiles. "You and Isaac are a hard-working pair. Well matched, I think."

Elizabeth chuckles. "Yes, and I will be very happy to have him home so he can do every bit of the hard work next year."

They watch in silence for nearly a minute as the sun disappears. They turn, share a look of empathy, backed by the will to persevere, and then walk tiredly homeward.

18 DECISION

Mount Independence, opposite Ticonderoga
Sep. 27, 1776

Gentlemen—
"...Gentlemen, I wish you could transport yourselves to this place for a moment, to see the distressed situation of these troops; and no Medicines: near one half of this Regiment is entirely incapable of any service; some dying almost every day. Col. Wyman's Regiment in the same unhappy situation. There are no medicines of any avail in the Continental Chest... It would make a Heart of stone melt to hear the moans & see the distress of the sick & dying..."

Samuel Wigglesworth

Excerpt from a letter to the New Hampshire Committee of Safety

On the morning of October 28, at about eight o'clock, the alarm cannon at Fort Ticonderoga fires. Colonel Reed's brigade scrambles to equip themselves and respond. Within minutes, they come running from their tents to form ranks on the regiment's parade ground, then march on the double down to the bateaux along the western shore. Ten minutes later, they reach the far side, form ranks, and begin marching toward the northwest of the fort, along the recently reworked French redoubts—enclosed earthworks located two to three hundred yards to the west and north of the main fort. Reed's brigade are reinforcements to those already guarding the redoubts. Reed's regiment halts and awaits further orders.

The American lines are quiet...waiting. Out front of one of the works, Isaac hears the parole word issued, but frustratingly cannot hear the countersign, making him anxious as to whether a friend or enemy approached. Within a few seconds, two scouts come through the lines and confer with two of the colonels commanding the men inside the redoubts. Captain Hinds confers for a several seconds with Gilman and Stark and comes back within a minute with the report, "False alarm, men. A few Mohawks making mischief." At that moment, several more cannon are fired from the fort, at which the colonels order their men to continue the vigil. A few minutes later, word comes from the fort that they sighted several enemy ships and had fired the cannon to warn them to come no closer.

Isaac scans the soldiers of his company an appraising look. "We were fast today. Well done. When the order comes, let's march back in good order."

Twenty minutes later, the order comes to return to Camp Independence, and Captain Hinds' company begins marching back to the bateaux.

As they are marching, one of the men, Private Whiting from Wilton, speaks up. "The season is getting late for the redcoats to be paying us a visit. It's growing cold. What do you think, sirs?"

Isaac finds the question easy pickings. "It would be a lot easier for them to march on frozen ground and lakes. We must stay vigilant."

Captain Hinds joins in. "You heard the Lieutenant. Always vigilant. Never doubt the enemy's resolve."

Private Whiting, undeterred, "Vigilant I am, sir. Though I have noticed all the alarms have proved false. The fort has never been taken; at least not while occupied by such a large force as ours."

"Aye, and quite true," says Isaac, "but our enemy is well provisioned and believes themselves superior. We must not give them advantages. I believe we have not given any advantages, which is why the alarms turn out to be false. Always vigilant."

The next evening, Captain Hinds' company parades beside their area of the encampment, waiting to be dismissed for their evening meal. Captain Hinds hands Isaac a piece of paper and asks him to read it to the men.

Taking the paper, Isaac holds it up to the fading light from the setting sun.

"Headquarters, Oct 29, 1776

Parole, Dresden   *Countersign, Naples.*

The General returns his thanks to the officers and soldiers of the whole Army for the alert and spirited manner with which they prepared to face the enemy yesterday, and particularly to the regiments of Reed, Poor, and Greaton, for the dispatch they made in crossing the lake immediately upon their being ordered to reinforce the French lines and redoubts..."

General Orders - Major General Horatio Gates

Isaac looks to Captain Hinds, who nods; and Isaac dismisses the men.

James has been watching from a short distance and now approaches. "Well, it seems you are quite comfortable in your new role as commander of men."

Isaac corrects him. "Second-in-command. It was good of General Gates to recognize our efficiency yesterday. The men have worked hard."

James grins. "I have no doubt. You're not one to suffer anything but their best effort."

•••

Four days later, on November 2, Isaac and James sit outside the barracks for the 3rd Regiment's officers, eating their dinner. The sun has nearly set and the sky around Mount Defiance, the new name for

Sugarloaf Hill, is a mix of oranges and deep grays. Isaac's plate is stacked with turkey, cooked greens, and bread. After enjoying a bite from a drumstick, he remarks, "I'd forgotten how good turkey is. It's a shame we haven't had our hunters doing this more often."

"Yes, it's quite a delicacy," James quips, "compared to pickled or salted pork." We're lucky today. Over four thousand soldiers in this camp, and not all get the good meat every day."

They finish their meal, their enjoyment of the unusual fare outweighing the need to converse. As they walk to the newly completed officers barracks, Isaac asks, "Who were the group of riders that came up the Hubbardton road over an hour ago?"

"They're from Exeter and Boston. Delegations sent by our respective Congresses. They're here to secure enlistment for next year. They will meet with General Gates tomorrow."

Isaac inhales sharply and his eyes widen anxiously. "I s'pose I'll find out soon whether there's any captain's commissions open."

"So, you'll take a captain's commission if they've got one?"

Isaac lets the question hang for a moment. "Aye. Or not. Even as we are talking, my mind keeps going back to my farm. I'm thinking I don't want just any captain's commission; I want some hope of more active leadership and ambition to win this war quickly. We spent the best part of this year mired in this quarter, accomplishing nothing while squandering nearly half the army. I worry we'll be holed up in these fortifications next year, waiting to be attacked. We should be taking ground, or at least contesting every inch of it, like Colonel Stark kept saying."

"No arguments from me about that. Every man here felt ill used, and that's when they were not feeling just plain ill."

"That's well put. Do you think we could get this war over with by next year? I don't think General Washington would have lost New York had the army not been split up. They could've fortified this place with fewer men, and not lost so many by *not* sending them to Quebec in the first place."

"Well," James begins, " it's uncanny how we see what appear to be flaws now. There were two armies of redcoats, and they could very well have pinched us.

"I see."

"I've decided these delegations are not here for me."

"Do you plan to stay on?"

"Not for these wages, and definitely not for what usually passes for food and—until lately—quarters in this army. Today's food was passable, but given what we usually eat—no thanks."

"You add considerable weight to my thoughts that have me back on my farm next year, growing what I can to supply our army."

James throws up his hands to slow Isaac's thinking. "Whoa, Isaac. Please don't allow my reasons to make your decision. You threw yourself into transporting our provisions and baggage, then into training the men in Captain Hinds' company. I know you miss your wife, sons, and farm, but I had you figured to see this through to the end. You've got more fire in your belly than anyone I know."

"I know at one point, I did. I'm just not so sure, now. If there are captain's commissions, I likely will re-enlist. I've said and written as much to Elizabeth. All the time and work to fortify this place and all the sickness in the army, has me exceedingly impatient. I want to get on with winning this war."

"Aye, I know, and can see it. You'll make a fine captain. I can see that too, and I know that will help us win this war sooner. Let's go see if there's some rum. It's more satisfying than frustrations."

•••

Late the next morning, outside the main fort on Mount Independence, the New Hampshire officers have gathered to hear from the delegation from Exeter. Isaac stands with Captain Hinds as they listen to Colonel Stark introduce Colonel Jonathan Blanchard, who addresses the officers.

"Gentlemen. Myself, Mister Giles, Mister Evans, and Mister Gilman," he motions to the other three delegates standing with him, "represent the New Hampshire Assembly and have been sent here to secure the enlistment of officers and men for two regiments, for the next three years. There will also be a new Third Regiment, which we will have to recruit at home over the winter. General Gates and your colonels confirmed there are not enough men here to start—much less fill—that regiment."

There are several exclamations of surprise, and Isaac hears several officers muttering, "Three years," and shaking their heads.

Jonathan Blanchard holds his hands up to quiet the assembled men. "You heard right. General Washington asked Congress to secure the army for longer than a year. He fears the army may be gone at the end of December, when many of the enlistments will be up. We are authorized to give commissions to the field officers, captains, and lieutenants of these two regiments, here and now; and to commission captains for the new regiment, who will be immediately sent to New Hampshire to recruit."

This gets quite a few more officers talking, creating a general buzz. Isaac turns to Hinds, who gives him a skeptical look. "Don't hold your breath, Lieutenant. I believe the arrangements are mostly already made."

Isaac, inwardly disappointed, sets his expression to look serious, hoping to indicate he already knew this to be true, puts his hands on hips, and nods.

When the meeting breaks up, Isaac and Hinds turn away from the scene where the delegates are handing out commissions and enlistment papers to the officers who are part of the new arrangement.

Back at the 3rd Regiment's camp, they are greeted by James. One look is all it takes for James to realize that Isaac is not carrying any paperwork. "So, you decided not to take a commission?"

"No. Like we discussed, I was hoping for a captain's commission. Even though almost none of the captains from this year have reenlisted, most of the lieutenants did, and I was at the end of that list with respect to time in the rank."

James gives Isaac an optimistic look. "Well, in a couple months you'll be back on your farm with your family. That's not so bad."

Hinds clears his throat. "I'll put a word in for you, if you'd like. I think you are next in line. There are bound to be changes to the new arrangement, and the same is true for the new Third Regiment. So far, they've not found a colonel to command it."

"Thank you. I would appreciate your doing so. I couldn't bring myself to volunteer while not knowing who the commander for the Third Regiment would be."

Hinds and James nod in commiseration. James adds, "I think I will finish some letters with what's left of the afternoon. I'm guessing there is a good chance of the delegates leaving here in a day or so, and I figure someone in their party will carry some mail."

Hinds glances back at the delegates with an appraising look. "Yes, I think there will be a few more days yet. The captains and officers now have orders to recruit from among the men, and that will take longer." Hinds parts company with Isaac and James, and heads toward the captains' barracks.

Once Hinds is out of earshot, James offers tentatively, "Forgive me. I may be speaking out of place, but you don't sound fully enthusiastic. I mean about heading home."

Isaac, his voice thick with the emotions of his misgivings, admits, "I think my early zeal for this war was foolish; foolish to believe this war would be over soon; foolish to think we'd be done after a battle or two. When Colonel Blanchard said 'three years' today, it chilled my blood. Later it came out we could enlist for the entire war. What do you make of that?"

"I hope the war ends before those three years pass, but I think they want the same thing you do, which is to win as quickly as possible, and they want the army committed to winning, not just to a period of time. How many men do you think will enlist?"

Instead of answering, Isaac looks about, squinting and frowning with irritation. "Is there a lacrosse match today? I could use a distraction."

"I think Stark's regiment is up against Greaton's. They should be starting within the hour, so we should start walking now."

"I'm ready. You?"

"Yes, let's be on our way."

As they walk, James asks, "Who commands the new regiments for New Hampshire?"

"No surprises; Colonels Stark and Poor. Quite a few lieutenants are now captains in the new arrangement. I think my cousin Ebenezer is one of them. He is with Stark, I think. I should go congratulate him tonight."

"Just how many cousins do you have? Two... three hundred?"

Isaac laughs. "Ebenezer is a distant cousin—third, or so. It's closer to three hundred... I think."

James shakes his head. "Gads! You're serious. That many?"

"Aye, it's true. I'm glad I don't have to write letters to all of them. I'd never leave my desk."

•••

A little over a week later, on the afternoon of November 11, the 3rd New Hampshire Regiment is paraded south of the fort on Mount Independence. The regiment has undergone a transformation. The men who enlisted for the following years moved into their new regiments, and those who did not enlist were reassigned to the 3rd. Now, just over two companies of men—about half—are fit for duty, and stand in the ranks. The others are in the newly finished hospital to the west of their encampment.

Lieutenant Colonel Gilman is addressing the regiment. "Gentlemen! We have some good news today. It has been confirmed the enemy has gone into winter quarters."

One of the sergeants enthusiastically leads the men in three cheers. "Hip-hip, huzzah! Hip-hip, huzzah! Hip-hip, huzzah!" The men clearly sound happy at the news.

After Gilman dismisses the regiment, Isaac finds James. "That's good news."

James smiles. "Yes, it's quite a relief. Perhaps we will make it home to our families."

Isaac rubs his hands together in the chilly air. "We will. I think that's what got most of the men to raise the cheers with so much strength."

James winks. "Yes, perhaps the hope of returning to their homes and families, but I think the knowledge of never having to smell an army of sick men lined up to receive rancid meat for every meal might be a factor too. I know I won't forget the stench of rancid death."

Isaac shudders and then smiles. "You're right. We will never forget the fare we enjoyed while in Canada, will we?"

"No, never. My wife has no idea how good her cooking really is."

Isaac laughs. "Now that you mention it, I'm sure she doesn't know, and neither does my Elizabeth. She will wonder why I've got a smile on my face at every meal."

•••

Four days pass uneventfully, with no new orders—but that changes on Saturday, November 15. The 3rd New Hampshire Regiment is ordered to parade at ten in the morning on the south side of the fort on Mount Independence.

Gilman addresses the regiment. "We are ordered south, but not to Albany, as we heard earlier. We will begin by marching tomorrow to the landing at the north end of Lake George. We will board bateaux and continue south to Fort George. Most of the hospital space has been converted to barracks. We may stay there, or be ordered to Tryon County in New York, once an alarm there has been confirmed. Company commanders! The men are yours to address or dismiss." Gilman turns on his heal and heads towards the officer's quarters. Captain Hinds dismisses the company to begin preparations to move south.

Isaac finds James and they follow the men back to their encampment. "Adjutant. Do you have any other news?"

"Stark's and Poor's regiments will be marching with us, though I understand they are to continue south to Albany and then to join with General Washington. It looks as though the next few days will be quite busy."

"I expect so." Isaac adjusts his coat to keep the cold wind at bay. "It will be good to be moving and working hard. Without the threat of the enemy, we've not had so much to do of late. Inactivity breeds poor health."

•••

Ten days later, the 3rd New Hampshire Regiment is quartered at Fort George, on the southern end of Lake George. A blanket of snow covers the reconstituted fort, which is similar to the eight-pointed-star layout of the fort on Mount Independence. It is mid-afternoon as Isaac leads a scouting party of twenty men into the fort.

Gilman and James emerge from a long barracks built of recently hewn logs as Isaac dismisses his command. The two officers approach at a brisk pace, as the weather has turned cold. They exchange salutes. Gilman asks, "Any sign of the enemy?"

"None. No signs. The snow made it easy."

"Excellent. I will send word to Generals Gates and Schuyler. Go get yourself warmed up." Gilman leaves the lieutenants and heads to the fort's headquarters.

James accompanies Isaac back to the barracks. Isaac asks, "How are the preparations going for Stark's and Poor's regiments? They go to Albany next, right?"

"Well enough. They marched to Fort Edward today while your patrol was out, and will go on to Albany to get provisions."

"Do you know where they go after that?"

"No, just south. I presume to join General Washington."

"Any news concerning those staying here?"

"Just reiterating that the few troops fit for duty here will be kept busy constructing new fortifications, expanding the barracks 'til they can hold four hundred men, and going out on patrols to scout for the enemy."

They enter the barracks and Isaac heads to the fireplace to warm himself.

As Isaac unwraps the felted strips covering his shins, he laments," I wish I had a wig to keep my ears warm. The wind was bitterly cold today. Though, truth be told, being able to hear well while on patrol is more important."

"I'm curious," James says with a thoughtful look. "Given how cold your patrol was today, what do you think of General Gates' worry that the enemy, and the Indians they've allied with, will march around the lake and around Fort Ticonderoga, to attack here?"

"Well, it won't cut Ticonderoga off. We can still supply it from New Hampshire with staging at Number Four. The regulars have no interest in such out-of-season endeavors. I imagine they will encourage their Indian allies to harass us, but I doubt much effort will be put forth from that quarter."

"You'll be pleased to know Colonel Reed was feeling well enough to converse while you were out. I put the same question to him. You and he are of the same mind, and he believes it is more likely necessary to have troops close by, in case the New York Tories require a demonstration of who is in charge. Some of the Tories in Tryon County have been active of late."

"So, it looks," Isaac suggests, "as though we will finish our enlistments here."

"It does. My Sarah will be glad to have me home. The new baby kept her busy and the farm got ignored."

"Elizabeth will be happy to have me home, too. Her sister helped again a good deal this year." Isaac smiles and looks relaxed. "I haven't seen my home in nearly a year. It's odd, but I think in some ways it will be strange, at least at first, to be there." Isaac suddenly cocks his head, struck by an unsettling thought. "Any idea what will happen at the end of the month? Enlistments are up, and I've heard no plans for replacements for us."

"General Gates requested some from New Hampshire. I've not heard the response."

Isaac frowns with concern. "After the militia call-up this spring for Colonel Wyman's and Wingate's regiments, I'm not so sure there are any fighting-age men left in New Hampshire."

James laughs half-heartedly. "I guess it depends on what you call fighting age. Most of the men near our age are within thirty miles of here. Let's hope General Gates' request has been honored."

•••

A month passes by quickly at Fort George, with most of the time spent, as expected, on patrols ranging out to the west to ensure there are no signs of the enemy; and continuing to build up the fortifications and barracks. In the middle of the afternoon on December 26, Isaac and James are watching from the battlements of Fort George as two companies of militia march in the gates.

Ensign Hawkins joins them a minute later. Isaac greets him with a handshake. "Well, it looks as though the fort will be defended once our enlistments are up."

James also greets Hawkins cheerfully. "Yes it does. Seeing that our relief has arrived makes me feel much better. How about you, Ensign Hawkins?"

Hawkins agrees enthusiastically. "It certainly is. This time next week we'll be marching home." He turns to Isaac. "Speaking of which, I checked with the men from Wilton. They are all of a mind to march together with us, as you suggested."

"My thanks to you for doing that," says Isaac. "And you're right. In two weeks' time, at most, we will all be home. I'm hoping to bring in a deer on the last day of our trek, as that will feed us for much of the winter."

Hawkins rubs his hands together with anticipation. "I was thinking the same. I hope we see a herd, as I'm pretty sure every man marching with us has had the same thought."

They all laugh. After a few moments, James's teeth start to chatter. "I've had enough fresh air. I'm ready to get back inside where it is warm."

19 PREDICTION COME TRUE

Exeter,
Dec 10, 1776

"Voted, That Alexander Scammell Esqr.be Colonel of the third Continental Battalion to be raised in this State, during the War, and that Major Andrew Colborn, be Lieutenant Col. and Major John Hale, be Major of Said Battalion. Sent up by Mr. Lovewell [Concurred.]"

Journal of a new House of Representatives

The next afternoon four supply wagons trundle through the gates of Fort George followed by two companies of militia. Sergeant Blanchard pokes his head into the regiment's headquarters where Isaac, who has the day off from patrol, sits with James and Gilman not far from a warm fire. "Good sirs, more new arrivals and some supplies have arrived from Number Four." Then nodding to Gilman, adds, "Sir, their commander is with them."

Gilman gets up quickly, the dread of having to go out into the cold quickly replaced with happy anticipation. "Thank you, Sergeant Blanchard. We will be out to greet them shortly." Turning to Isaac and James, who have risen to get their coats, Gilman invites, "Come gentlemen, I would like to introduce you both to my brother, David."

A few moments later, Gilman leads them out of the headquarters and through the mix of frozen mud and snow that covers the interior yard of the fort.

Waving excitedly to his brother, Gilman exclaims, "David!"

His brother replies, "Israel! When I was told I would be relieving Reed's regiment, I couldn't believe my good luck." The brothers clasp arms warmly. "It's good to see you, brother."

Lieutenant Colonel Gilman holds his brother at arm's length. "It's good to see you wearing a uniform."

Colonel David Gilman shows off his new military coat and grins. "I suppose it was inevitable. Commander of a militia regiment. I suppose I deserve it, given all the recruiting I've done in the past weeks. It's good to see you again."

Israel Gilman turns to Isaac and James. "I am honored to present my brother, Colonel David Gilman. Brother, Lieutenant James Otis, the regiment's adjutant, and Lieutenant Isaac Frye."

They all shake hands and begin exchanging pleasantries when Israel Gilman turns his head aside and coughs violently, then composes himself. "As if I needed a reminder that it is cold out here. Brother, have your men take up quarters over there." He motions to one of the new barracks. "We've got room for better than two companies there." He points at another building. "The officers' quarters are over here. Once you've got your things in their place, meet me at headquarters, where it's warm, and we can discuss your regiment's needs, and then have some dinner."

An hour after dinner, the two Gilmans—Israel and David—are seated inside the headquarters building in what used to be General Schuyler's office. Isaac enters and the brothers stand to greet him. Isaac looks from his regiment's acting commander to the other, who he now recognizes as being one of the delegation at Mount Independence, tasked with reenlisting the men the previous month.

Isaac addresses his commander. "Colonel Gilman, I received word you wished to speak with me."

"Yes, please have a seat."

As the Gilmans and Isaac take seats, Isaac ventures to David Gilman, "Sir, if memory serves, you were a part of the delegation from Exeter visiting Fort Ticonderoga last month."

David Gilman answers, "Yes, Lieutenant Frye. I was, and it is in that capacity that I have some news you may be interested in. Colonel Alexander Scammell has been appointed as the commander of the Third New Hampshire Regiment that is now being recruited. I mention this because my brother recommended I discuss with you the possibility of accepting a captain's commission in the new arrangement for the new Third Regiment."

Israel Gilman picks up the thread of conversation. "Captain Hinds recommended you highly, Lieutenant. What do you think of the idea?"

David Gilman's offer was the last thing Isaac expected upon receiving the summons ten minutes earlier. Isaac looks at both men and thinks for a few seconds. "Well, sir, that is good news. I believe Major—I mean Colonel—Scammell would make an excellent commander. I had the chance to speak with him some while ago in Montreal. I'm surprised to hear of his appointment. Pleased, as well. With that said, I would like to accept, and—well, I do not wish to seem contrary." Isaac pauses, looking at both colonels before continuing, "I have one condition, which is that my commission be dated the same as the other captains who were appointed last month on Mount Independence. I learned a hard lesson, which is not to be last in line when promotions are at stake."

David Gilman considers the request. "The truth is, we have need of another captain to command a company. I tell you what. If you agree to serve for the duration of the war, I believe the committee will grant your request for equal seniority with those who gained rank on November eighth. What do you say?"

Isaac takes a deep breath, blowing it out slowly while his mind races, weighing his thoughts. Then he nods. "I will be pleased to accept this commission if the committee agrees to my terms."

David Gilman smiles. "Excellent! I'll write the necessary letters tonight and have them sent to Exeter. You can expect to hear about your commission in February or March, depending on when they next meet." Then he extends a hand to Isaac.

Taking the proffered hand, Isaac smiles with a deep sense of satisfaction. "Thank you. Thank you both."

Israel Gilman grins. "You're welcome, *Captain* Frye. In fact, we should be thanking you. I'm glad to see you are still fully committed to the cause of liberty, and now the cause of independence. Let us drink a toast to our commitment to liberty and independence." He rises to fetch three glasses and a bottle of rum. "Many who were on the campaign this summer had their fill of the Continental Service. I can't say as I blame them, with sickness being our chief enemy. Though if we let only that stop us, I do not think we deserve to succeed."

His brother pours the rum.

Isaac nods gravely. "I know. It was a trial for all of us. But I expect many who go home next week will serve in their town's militias, and may reenlist at a later date."

Israel Gilman nods in agreement. "We think so, as well—" A deep, racking cough interrupts his sentence. "As you can see, this campaign's left many of us feeling less than our whole selves. Still..." He pushes a glass to Isaac.

The three raise their glasses and toast in unison, "To liberty and independence!"

After emptying their glasses, David Gilman asks Isaac, "Do you have any recommendations for a subaltern?"

"Ensign William Adrian Hawkins. I know him to be a good man. He was promoted to Ensign for his valor at Bunker Hill on the rail fence, and I've found him to be consistently dependable and possessed of good judgment. Though I should inform you, it is his preference to be called William Adrian. He uses his full name."

Israel Gilman has another racking coughing spasm. "I would second Captain Frye's recommendation. Ensign Hawkins is as prudent as he is brave. I believe he will serve very well."

"Good," says his brother, sounding hopeful. "We will speak with him next, Thank you for your recommendation. Do you think he will accept?"

Isaac thinks for a moment, and not finding any reason to give to the contrary, concludes, "I think he may. It would be a promotion."

"Excellent. I am pleased to hear you think so."

Israel coughs strongly again and David's look changes to concern. "You do sound bad, Israel, with all that coughing. Perhaps more rum and some sleep will help. I can handle the business with Hawkins." He turns back to Isaac. "Captain Frye, you'll be on furlough until you get orders, which I expect will come with your commission. Expect to do some recruiting this winter."

Isaac nods happily. "Thank you, sirs, and a very good evening to you both."

The Gilman brothers raise their glasses in his direction as he sees himself out.

•••

Ten minutes later, Isaac pokes his head into the barracks he shares with the other lieutenants of the 3rd New Hampshire Regiment, and finds James. "I am of a mind to find our daily ration of rum. Have you had yours yet, James?"

James looks up from the letter he is reading. "Give me minute to find my coat and a scarf. I can feel the cold air you're letting in."

"Grab my cup, too," says Isaac, then he shuts the door to wait for James.

As the friends walk to the commissary building, James shivers and rubs his hands together, then sticks them beneath his armpits to keep them warm. "They should give us a double ration for the cold."

Isaac claps James on the back. "They should. I've just had some news worth drinking to, so perhaps they will agree and give us that double ration."

When they arrive at the commissary, James is still shivering, but Isaac appears not to notice the cold. The commissary sergeant give them both a generous ration, and once again they step outside and endure the frigid temperatures on their way back to their barracks.

Back beside the fire in their barracks, James holds his cup up. "To your health, Lieutenant Frye."

Isaac toasts James's cup. "Yours as well... and it's Captain Frye, now."

James, intent on getting warm, is mid-swallow when he hears

Isaac's new rank. The swallow goes down hard, causing his eyes to go wide as he gasps. After a moment, he breaks into a grin. "I knew it! I always figured you'd find a way to get that commission. Congratulations."

"Thank you."

"You handle the military life too well to leave it."

Isaac capitulates with a smile. "Perhaps, though I cannot say I felt anything particularly agreeable about our circumstances these past nine months."

"Ha! You know what I mean. You wanted a captaincy, but not just any captaincy. What lured your back from the precipice of a tranquil life on your farm?"

"Colonel Gilman summoned me to headquarters tonight, where I confirmed his brother David was one of the delegation from Exeter that came to Fort Ti last month."

James gives Isaac an appraising look. "I did not know about Mr. Gilman being Lieutenant Colonel Gilman's brother. Very interesting."

Isaac continues, "Colonel Gilman, the brother, had news from Exeter. The new commander of the Third Regiment is Colonel Scammell."

"I'll be damned if you aren't prescient. You told then Major Scammell he'd have a regiment to command by the end of the year, and you all but foretold you'd have a commission to be a captain."

"Well, now that you mention it, maybe I am. No, in all honesty, I was just being half serious in a friendly way with Major Scammell, when I did that. Besides, if you aim high, you hit high, and if you don't aim, nothing good happens. Anyway, I'm on furlough until the Committee of Safety confirms my commission, and then Colonel Gilman said I'd likely be ordered to recruit a company."

James raises his cup again. "Congratulations, Captain Frye, and give Colonel Scammell my regards when you see him."

•••

On the evening of January 8, 1777, Isaac trudges over the bridge on the Souhegan River and begins the climb up the hill to his farm. Six inches of snow blanket the open ground. A few more flurries continue to blow. As he comes to the crest of the hill, he sees the light from the farmhouse window and gazes across the field he was plowing over twenty months earlier. The waning crescent of the moon barely illuminates a trail of smoke rising from the chimney before the wind chases it into the night sky. Isaac hears the wind in these trees and knows it; recognizes its familiar courses, brushing branches and sweeping the curves and faces of the hills, welcoming him home.

He turns off the path and crosses the field by the shortest route to the house. A dozen paces from the door he begins brushing the snow off his coat and hat, and pounds his gloved fists against his thighs to knock the caked snow loose. As he climbs onto the back steps, he sets his mind to make the best of the news of his promotion. Through the window, he catches sight of Sarah moving across the kitchen, then his hand is on the door latch.

Elizabeth's eyes go wide. "Isaac!" Her scream wakes John, who was asleep, head on her shoulder. She launches herself out of the rocking chair. Sarah whips around at Elizabeth's shocked exclamation and before she knows it, Elizabeth has pushed John into her arms. Isaac closes the door and sets his firelock and pack down. He begins knocking the ice off the buttons as Elizabeth springs towards him. Isaac recovers and catches his wife in a fierce hug.

"I am so glad to see you, my darling wife. Let me get out of this coat and get out of these frozen boots and leggings, and I'll be able to greet you properly." Not taking his eyes off Elizabeth's for a second. Isaac pushes his numb fingers to the work of unbuttoning the coat. He slips out of it and pulls the still-frozen, felt leg wraps away from his boots. "Now I'm ready—"

Smiling with joy, Elizabeth doesn't wait, wrapping her husband in a warm embrace.

For more than a minute they cling to each other. "Is it really you?" She pulls back to gaze at him, her face beaming, her warm hands cradling his cold face. "Back to stay? For good?"

"Yes, my dear, it is really me. I've missed you so." He pulls her close again for half a minute, without saying anything; then releases her. He surveys the room, taking in the details. "Sarah, it's good to see you, too."

Sarah smiles. "I'm glad you've made it home."

"And John! I can't believe it—he looks so much like Abiel did at that age." Isaac takes a step and reaches to take John from Sarah.

Elizabeth shivers. "You're cold. Warm up a bit before you hold him."

"I am. You're right." Isaac changes direction and walks to the stove. "It was a long walk, these past eight days. Though I will be here some weeks on furlough."

Elizabeth frowns and her shoulders sag a little. "Weeks? Your enlistment was up. You didn't get a captain's commission in November. That was it, right?"

Isaac turns, putting his back to the stove. "It was—at least 'til this past twenty-sixth of December. The Committee offered me a captain's commission in the new arrangement for the Third Regiment."

Elizabeth takes a couple of assessing breaths, realizing there is no way to change what he has done, so she decides to bury her expectations and put on a positive and happy face for him. She smiles and warmly says, "Well... Captain Frye, I suppose we should make the most of these next weeks."

Isaac's relief is plain on his face. "If there's some food, I'm more than a little hungry, and have a lot more to tell you. Though first, I wouldn't mind setting my eyes on our boys."

Elizabeth shakes her head to Sarah. "Not John—Isaac's too cold yet to hold him. Bring him here. The other boys are sleeping." She turns to look at the bedroom door, which is now open a crack. "At least they were." She winks and nods with approval at the door.

The door swings into the bedroom, revealing Isaac Jr. and Abiel, who stand perfectly still for moment before rushing at their father.

Isaac kneels, catching the pair in a big hug, then stands, wearing a boy on each hip. "My, these boys have grown. They've gotten heavy." He bounces them for emphasis. He notices each boy holds a button. Abiel starts to look for where it came off Isaac's waistcoat. "I am so pleased you got those buttons. I am afraid I no longer have the coat they came from. It didn't last though the campaign this summer."

Sarah gets a couple pieces of wood to feed the stove. "I'll get some food and cider warmed."

"Thank you, Sarah," says a grateful Isaac. "And not just for warming some food and cider, but for everything."

Sarah's face flushes. "I'm just doing my part. Everyone has had to."

"I know. Your part was to help me, and I know it wasn't easy."

Sarah dips in a quick curtsy, causing her dark braid to sway across her shoulder. Elizabeth bustles about. "Let's roast some of the chestnuts Sarah and the boys gathered this fall." She pulls plates off the shelf for everyone, and soon she and Sarah have the table laden with a late evening homecoming feast.

•••

An hour later Isaac is still eating, though now relaxed, slowly finishing the last of what was laid out. The older boys have gone back to bed. Elizabeth pours more cider for herself and Sarah, who is sitting in the quilt-covered rocking chair, holding John, who is asleep.

"It has been a month since we last heard from one another," says Elizabeth with a sigh. "It worries me when so much time goes by. When I didn't hear from you for almost two months in the summer, I was anxious, though when it was so close to your enlistment ending, I suppose I took comfort in knowing you were almost done and the enemy was no longer active. I suppose we've been preoccupied with what's been happening here."

Sarah's eyes go wide. "You're right! Isaac will not have heard about Reverend Livermore's summons."

Isaac looks at Sarah and then Elizabeth. "Summons?"

"Yes," says Elizabeth, her mouth set in disapproval. "In the middle of December, word came from the Committee or Assembly, or whatever they call themselves now, in Exeter. They summoned Reverend Livermore to present himself to them two Wednesdays hence, in Exeter. That was the first of this month. Someone charged him with being inimical to the cause, to liberty."

Sarah, looking insulted, says, "On various and sundry occasions, they said."

"Who brought such charges?" asks Isaac. "Surely nobody from

Wilton."

Elizabeth taps her index finger on the table accusingly. "It was Frances Epes."

"From Lyndeborough?"

"Yes."

"What was he doing at the meeting? Surely Christopher Martin represents Wilton and Lyndeborough."

Elizabeth shakes her head. "No, I don't think Mr. Martin went at all this year. Jacob Abbot replaced Mr. Martin at the two meetings prior to the one in December. Mr. Epes replaced him at the December meeting and made his accusations"

Isaac looks deeply concerned. "Well, do you know what happened?"

Elizabeth nods. "Happily, he was acquitted. He defended himself vigorously, as he put it. Lord knows it was an awful year, with so many dying. I can only imagine how embittered those families must have felt upon receiving the news, and other than Josiah Parker, no one from Wilton was brought home to be buried. It is enough to shake one's faith in our Lord, and certainly enough to blame and decry the cause of liberty as the cause of the deaths. I am sure that some, in their grief, spoke against the cause, and the reverend rightly chose to see to their comfort, and not rebuke them. I suspect someone took the way he consoled any of those families who lost a man this season, out of context. Yet I still have no exact idea what caused Mr. Epes to speak such an accusation. The news that he had done so came as a surprise."

Isaac's concerned look softens. "How is Reverend Livermore?"

Elizabeth's expression clouds. "I hope our reverend's pride recovers quickly. I still cannot believe he was summoned in such a way. It's not right for anyone's good name to be challenged over giving comfort to a grieving family by listening to them rail against the army, the cause, Providence, or whatever their righteous anger drove them to blame for their loss."

"It was a coward's way to press a grievance," Sarah adds, her expression showing emotion she managed to keep from her voice. "I heard the Reverend say no one had confronted him, much less given a gentle warning."

"Not only that," declaims Elizabeth, "but it was wrong to use the Committee to prosecute such nonsense when their time is s'posed to be put towards securing our liberties and matters of governance."

"I can only imagine," Isaac offers, "the sentiments you might level at General Washington, or the Congress, if any harm comes to me." Isaac turns as Sarah laughs, and then looks back to see Elizabeth's face color a little. "Luckily for them, I came through this year with only my pride wounded, though I did endure some physical discomforts."

Sarah rises. "It is getting late, I'll take John and put him to bed on my way to mine."

As Sarah leaves, Isaac helps Elizabeth clear the plates off the table. "Being home has my mind going, despite my body being ready for a long sleep. Have we got any rum on hand?"

Elizabeth pulls out a bottle and two glasses.

Nearly two hours later, Isaac and Elizabeth are still talking quietly, sitting across the table from one another, holding hands, the empty glasses in front of them. The talk has turned to the prospects of winning the war.

Isaac speaks with conviction. "The generals think the war could last at least two more years. They asked men to sign on for three, or for the duration of the war. I had to take the latter to get the date of my rank set back to November with the others... to have equal seniority.

"That was good thinking." Elizabeth pauses, with a new thought clearly forming behind her eyes. She takes a deep breath and holds it, as her thoughts ripen and become clear. Her next words are slow and deliberate. "Everything is at stake for us now... Everything." She draws another deep breath, this time holding it because she despises the fact that her next words are the truth. "This war... Winning it is our only future."

Isaac eyes burn, mirroring the intensity and sincerity of Elizabeth's words. He draws his response directly from his heart. "We will win. I know it in my bones. Our enemy cannot comprehend such resolve as we now possess."

The War Has Begun

SOURCES

Chapter 1: The Alarm

Bailey, Sarah Loring 1880. "Historical Sketches of Andover, Massachusetts (Comprising the Present Town of North Andover and Andover)"Houghton, Mifflin and Company, The Riverside Press, Boston, MA, reprinted in 1974 by the Andover Historical Society and the North Andover Historical Society, Edward Brothers, Inc., Ann Arbor, MI.

- p. 277: Shows Isaac's father, Abiel Frye, as a militia Captain in Andover

Bouton, Nathaniel D.D. 1873. "Provincial Papers. Documents and Records Relating to the Province of New-Hampshire, from 1764 to 1776; Including the whole Administration of Gov. John Wentworth; the Events immediately preceding the Revolutionary War; the Losses at the Battle of Bunker Hill, and the Record of all Proceedings till the end of our Provincial History." Published by the Authority of the Legislature of New-Hampshire. Volume VII. Orren C. Moore, State Printer, Nashua, NH.

- pp. 777-778: 1775 Census for Wilton:

Boylston, Edward D. 1884. "Historical Sketch of the Hillsborough County Congresses held at Amherst, (N.H.) 1774 & 1775: with other Revolutionary Records" Farmers' Cabinet Press, Amherst, N.H.

- pp. 14-17: Resolution of the 2nd Congress with instructions for militias to meet at least once per week.

Clark, Charles E. 1998. "The Meetinghouse Tragedy: An Episode in the Life of a New England Town" University Press of New England, Hanover, NH.

- p. 107: Showing Isaac among the injured on Sep 7, 1773. The injury occurred during the raising of Wilton's new meetinghouse when a major support beam burst, causing fifty-three men to fall from the upper story of the building's frame. Five were killed, and many of the survivors sustained serious injuries.

Livermore, Abiel Abbot and Putnam, Sewall 1888. "History of the Town of Wilton, Hillsborough County, New Hampshire with a Genealogical Register" Marden & Rowell, Printers, Lowell, MA.

- pp. 31-34: Describes the layout of the town of Wilton and the original lots. This information was used to locate the population of Wilton in 1775 from the genealogical information in the latter portion of this book, which included the lots and ranges people where lived or settled.
- pp. 85: April 4, 1775 town meeting with vote to raise militia.
- pp. 88: Names of militia.

Neimeyer, Charles Patrick. 1996. "America Goes to War, A Social History of the Continental Amy", New York University Press, New York.

- pp. 9: Describes days of carrying arms to Sunday services to be followed by militia drill.

New Hampshire, Province of, 1774. Judgment against Isaac Frye by Plaintiff Samuel Eames on Apr 1, 1774. From original document at the New Hampshire Archives, Concord, NH.

- Samuel Eames is married to Isaac's sister, Abigail, who is eight years older than Isaac. The reason for the debt was not specified.

Sargent, Winthrop 1920 "Colonel Paul Dudley Sargent" Printed for Private Circulation by Winthrop Sargent in 1921.

- p. 9: Describes Paul Dudley Sergeant as organizing the militia as early as 1773 in Amherst and Hillsborough County.

Temple, Josiah H. 1887 "History of Framingham, Massachusetts, Early Known as Danforth's Farms, 1640-1880 with a Genealogical Register." The Town of Framingham.

- pp. 271-272: Narrative written by Ensign D'Bernicre detailing his mission with Captain Brown to find the route to Worcester, MA from Boston in March of 1775.

Wilton, Town of, 1769. Transfer of Deed from Dorothy Thompson to Isaac Frye of lands in lots 7 and 8 in ranges 3 and 4 for the sum of 120 pounds on 8 Jun, 1769. pp. 89-91 of Wilton Deed book.

Wilton, Town of, 1770. Transfer of Deed from Isaac Frye to James Holt and John Abbot of eleven acres of land for seven Pounds on Oct 24, 1770. pp. 22-23 of Wilton Deed book.

Chapter 2: The Road to Boston

Boyleston, Edward D. 1884. "Historical Sketch of the Hillsborough County Congresses, held at Amherst, (N.H.) 1774 & 1775 Revolutionary Records" Farmers' Cabinet Press, Amherst, NH

- p. 16: In the minutes of the Apr 5, 1775 Hillsborough County Congress in Amherst, the call for towns to organize militias is given.

Clark, Charles E. 1998. "The Meetinghouse Tragedy: An Episode in the Life of a New England Town" University Press of New England, Hanover, NH. Page 107.

- p. 25: Illustration of the Wilton Meetinghouse and it's rows of large mullioned windows.

Colburn, Frank W. 1912 "The Battle of Apr 19, 1775, in Lexington, Concord, Lincoln, Arlington, Cambridge, Somerville and Charlestown, Massachusetts" Published by the author, Lexington, MA.

- Used to produce the summary provided by Captain Spaulding.

Farmer, John 1837 "Historical Sketch of Amherst in the County of Hillsborough, in New-Hampshire, From its First Settlement to the Year MDCCCXXXXVII" Second Edition Enlarged. Printed by Asa McFarland, Concord, New Hampshire. Reprinted by the New Hampshire Publishing Company, Somersworth, New Hampshire in 1972.

- p. 17: Describes Amherst's response to the Apr 19, 1775 alarm as a company of men under Captain Josiah Crosby.
- p. 46: lists Nahum Baldwin as a deacon of Amherst's Congregational Church, beginning in 1774.

Hammond, Isaac, W. 1885. "Rolls of the Soldiers in the Revolutionary War 1775, to May, 1777 with an appendix, embracing diaries of Lieut. Jonathan Burton " Volume I of War Rolls. Volume XIV of the Series. Parsons B. Cogswell, State Printer, Concord, NH

- p. 38: Lists the captains and staff officers of what would become the 3rd New Hampshire Regiment, including the captains who marched from Amherst and Lieutenant Stephen Peabody.

Livermore, Abiel Abbot and Putnam, Sewall 1888. "History of the Town of Wilton, Hillsborough County, New Hampshire with a Genealogical Register" Marden & Rowell, Printers, Lowell, MA. Pages 31-34 and 85-88

- p. 88: Lists the men and ranks of Wilton men who responded to the Apr 19, 1775 alarm.

Sargent, Winthrop 1920 "Colonel Paul Dudley Sargent" Printed for Private Circulation by Winthrop Sargent in 1921.

- p. 9: Describes Sargent arriving in Concord on Apr 19, 1775 alarm with a column of three hundred men. These are presumed to be those from southern Hillsborough County, and Sargent was in command of, though not by order of a duly authorized body.

Chapter 3: A Siege

Bouton, Nathaniel D.D. 1878. "Provincial Papers. Documents and Records Relating to the Province of New-Hampshire, From 1764 to 1776; Including the whole Administration of Gov. John Wentworth; the Events immediately preceding the Revolutionary War; the Losses at the Battle of Bunker Hill, and the Record of all Proceedings till the end of our Provincial History." Volume VII. Orren C. Moore, State Printer. Nashua, NH.

- p. 453: Lists Paul Dudley Sargent in attendance at the Apr 21, 1775 meeting of the Provincial Congress.
- p. 455: A letter from Governor Wentworth dated 25 Apr, 1775 claiming to be too ill to attend the meetings of the New Hampshire Congress.
- p. 458 A letter from the Massachusetts Committee of Safety indicating their action to enlist the men of New Hampshire so as to give them reason to continue besieging Boston.
- p. 460: Letter from Andrew McClary to the provincial congress characterizing the false pronouncement that the New Hampshire Militia was no longer needed.

- p. 477: Shows on May 20, the New Hampshire Congress voted to raise 2,000 men
- p. 480: Shows on May 23, the 2,000 men be divided into three regiments.
- p. 483: May 24, 1775 the New Hampshire Congress appointed Enoch Poor as commander of the second New Hampshire regiment.
- p. 487: On May 26, the New Hampshire Congress voted to back up the borrowing of up to ten thousand pounds for the use of military supplies by the commissary and the members of the Congress would act as bondsmen for those sums.
- p. 496: Jun 1, 1775, the New Hampshire Congress appointed James Reed as commander of the third New Hampshire regiment.
- p. 503: Jun 3, 1775, the New Hampshire Congress appointed John Stark as the commander of the first New Hampshire regiment.
- p. 505: The oath of allegiance for the New Hampshire troops.
- p. 510: Jun 9, 1775, The New Hampshire Congress approves the sum of ten thousand and fifty pounds to be given as notes guaranteed by the province. This is the source of funds Colonel Reed exclaims in surprise about to Isaac.

Boyleston, Edward D. 1884. "Historical Sketch of the Hillsborough County Congresses, held at Amherst, (N.H.) 1774 & 1775 Revolutionary Records" Farmers' Cabinet Press, Amherst, NH

- p. 16: Item 5 contains the entire text for the quoted excerpt at the beginning of the chapter.

Force, Peter, 1837, "American Archives: Fourth Series Containing a Documentary History of the English Colonies in North America, from the King's message to Parliament, of Mar 7, 1774 to the Declaration of Independence by the United States " Series 4, Volume 2. M. St. Clair Clark and Peter Force Under Authority of an Act of Congress, Passed on the Second of March, 1833. Washington D.C.

- p. 520: Shows Paul Dudley Sargent in attendance at the May 4, 1775 meeting of the Provincial Congress

Frothingham, Richard, 1873, "History of the Siege of Boston, and of the Battles of Lexington, Concord, and Bunker Hill. Also, an Account of the Bunker Hill Monument. With Illustrative Documents. Fourth Edition, Little, Brown, and Company, Boston, MA.

- p. 94: A letter from Joseph Warren on behalf of the Massachusetts Committee of Safety to the inhabitants of the town of Boston describing the treaty proposed by General Gage on their behalf.

Hurd,D. Hamilton 1885. "History of Hillsborough County, New Hampshire" J.W. Lewis & Co., Philadelphia, PA

- p. 225: Shows Col. Shepard's delivery of 57.5 pounds of pork, one half bushel of beans, etc.

New Hampshire Historical Society 1888. "Proceedings of the New Hampshire Historical Society." Vol. 1 Part 4 1884-1888.

- pp. 109-115: Biographical Sketch of Gen. James Reed. Includes his whereabouts in early Jun 1775, including Exeter on the 1st, to western New Hampshire, back in Fitzwilliam on the 8th, and then Cambridge by the 12th.

Page, T. H. 1775 "Boston, Its Environs and Harbour, With the Rebels Works Raised Against That Town in 1775." [Map] Retrieved from the Library of Congress, https://www.loc.gov/item/gm71000623/.

- Shows the footprint of New Hampshire's fortifications on Winter Hill just after the Battle of Breeds Hill.

Sargent, Winthrop 1920 "Colonel Paul Dudley Sargent" Printed for Private Circulation by Winthrop Sargent in 1921.

- p. 9: Describes Paul Dudley Sargent as being urged to move to New Hampshire shortly after the fall of 1772.
- p. 9: Describes Paul Dudley Sargent as not receiving a commission to command a New Hampshire regiment, and General Ward of Massachusetts taking him into his command.

Wright, Robert K. Jr. 1989. "The Continental Army" Center of Military History United States Army, Washington, DC.

- pp. 197-199: shows three New Hampshire regiments were authorized on May 22, 1775.

Chapter 4: New Orders

Beaurain, Chevalier de, fils., and Choisey, P. 1776 "Carte du port et havre de Boston avec les côtes adjacentes, dans laquel on a tracée les camps et les retranchemens occupé, tant par les Anglois que par les Américains." Paris. [Map] Retrieved from the Library of Congress, https://www.loc.gov/item/gm71005483/.

- Shows the soundings taken by the British Navy, and that these do not extend past the northeastern tip of the Charlestown Peninsula, indicating no soundings taken in the Mystic River.

Force, Peter, 1837, "American Archives: Fourth Series Containing a Documentary History of the English Colonies in North America, from the King's message to Parliament, of Mar 7, 1774 to the Declaration of Independence by the United States " Series 4, Volume 2. M. St. Clair Clark and Peter Force Under Authority of an Act of Congress, Passed on the Second of March, 1833. Washington D.C.

- p. 1013: Full text of Israel Gilman's letter to the New Hampshire Committee of Safety.

Frothingham, Richard, 1873, "History of the Siege of Boston, and of the Battles of Lexington, Concord, and Bunker Hill. Also, an Account of the Bunker Hill Monument. With Illustrative Documents. Fourth Edition, Little, Brown, and Company, Boston, MA.

- pp. 108-110: Describes the actions during the earlier weeks of the siege, including at Grape Island and Chelsea Creek.

Hammond, Isaac, W. 1885. "Rolls of the Soldiers in the Revolutionary War 1775, to May, 1777 with an appendix, embracing diaries of Lieut. Jonathan Burton " Volume I of War Rolls. Volume XIV of the Series. Parsons B. Cogswell, State Printer, Concord, NH

- pp. 95-97: Aug 1775 muster roll of Captain Walker's company showing some of the Wilton Men
- pp. 100-101: Aug 1775 muster roll of Captain Mann's company showing some of the Wilton Men
- pp. 102-103: Aug 1775 muster roll of Captain Crosby's company showing some of the Wilton Men

Livermore, Abiel Abbot and Putnam, Sewall 1888. "History of the Town of Wilton, Hillsborough County, New Hampshire with a Genealogical Register" Marden & Rowell, Printers, Lowell, MA. Pages 31-34 and 85-88

- p. 238: In his ammunition account for Jun 13, 1775 for one hundred fifty weight of powder, and 300 weight ball, and 650 flints.
- p. 238: May 29, 1775, the receipt of 1600 rounds of cartridges for Colonel Sargent's regiment. The size of which is unknown at this time due to the new arrangements being formed. It was most likely three or four large companies, meaning anywhere from 4-6 rounds per man. Thus, may have been why Colonel Reed requested

additional ammunition for guard duty on Jun 12th for feeling his new arrangement with nine companies had been shorted.
- p. 238: Jun 14, 1775 entry shows twenty balls per man on guard duty.
- p. 88: Lists the men from Wilton militia.

Page, T. H. 1775 "Boston, Its Environs and Harbour, With the Rebels Works Raised Against That Town in 1775." [Map] Retrieved from the Library of Congress, https://www.loc.gov/item/gm71000623/.

- Shows the soundings taken by the British Navy, and that these do not extend past the northeastern tip of the Charlestown Peninsula, indicating no soundings taken in the Mystic River.

Pelham, H, and Jukes, F. 1777 "Plan of Boston in New England with its Environs. Including Milton, Dorchester, Roxbury, Brooklin, Cambridge, Medford, Charlestown, parts of Malden and Chelsea. With the Military Works Constructed in those Places in the Years 1775 and 1776." London. [Map] Retrieved from the Library of Congress, https://www.loc.gov/item/gm71000619/.

- Shows the soundings taken by the British Navy, and that these do not extend past the northeastern tip of the Charlestown Peninsula, indicating no soundings taken in the Mystic River.

Chapter 5: Battle of Breeds Hill

Bailey, Sarah Loring 1880. "Historical Sketches of Andover, Massachusetts (Comprising the Present Town of North Andover and Andover)"Houghton, Mifflin and Company, The Riverside Press, Boston, MA, reprinted in 1974 by the Andover Historical Society and the North Andover Historical Society, Edward Brothers, Inc., Ann Arbor, MI.

- p. 323: Tells of James Frye on the battlefield during the Battle of Breeds Hill.

Bouton, Nathaniel D.D. 1878. "Provincial Papers. Documents and Records Relating to the Province of New-Hampshire, From 1764 to 1776; Including the whole Administration of Gov. John Wentworth; the Events immediately preceding the Revolutionary War; the Losses at the Battle of Bunker Hill, and the Record of all Proceedings till the end of our Provincial History." Volume VII. Orren C. Moore, State Printer. Nashua, NH.

- p. 596: lists Isaac Frye as having lost his coat and hat at the battle on Bunkers Hill.

Frothingham, Richard, 1873, "History of the Siege of Boston, and of the Battles of Lexington, Concord, and Bunker Hill. Also, an Account of the Bunker Hill Monument. With Illustrative Documents. Fourth Edition, Little, Brown, and Company, Boston, MA.

- p. 136: lists the three companies, including Crosby's from Reed's regiment, sent to the American right, in Charlestown, initially on Main Street.
- General information about the Battle of Breeds Hill.

Frothingham, Richard, 1875, "The Centennial: Battle of Bunker Hill, with a View of Charlestown in 1775, Pages's Plan of the Action, Romane's Exact View of the Battle, and Other Illustrations" Little, Brown, and Company. Boston

- p. 99: Mentions that General Sullivan described Stephen Peabody acted with "great courage and intrepidity" during the Battle of Breed's Hill. This was the basis for what I imagined Stephen Peabody's actions may have been.

Greele, George Hiram, 1903, "Genealogy of the Greely—Greeley Family" Boston MA

- Describes the relationships between John, Jonathan, and Nathaniel, as having the same grand father, Samuel Greele.

The Greeles in the Wilton Militia had another cousin who was a captain in the Nottingham, NH militia, Samuel Greele, who later moved to Wilton, and died there when a tree fell on him. There is a monument to him at the location of his death on Russell Hill road about a mile from the lot Richard Whitney owned.

Hammond, Isaac, W. 1885. "Rolls of the Soldiers in the Revolutionary War 1775, to May, 1777 with an appendix, embracing diaries of Lieut. Jonathan Burton " Volume I of War Rolls. Volume XIV of the Series. Parsons B. Cogswell, State Printer, Concord, NH

- p. 102-103: Aug Pay Roll of Captain Crosby's company showing John Cole as killed and James Hutchinson as wounded. Note that Hutchinson died of his wounds a week later.

Livermore, Abiel Abbot and Putnam, Sewall 1888. "History of the Town of Wilton, Hillsborough County, New Hampshire with a Genealogical Register" Marden & Rowell, Printers, Lowell, MA.

- p. 388: Describes the relationships between John and Jonathan Greele.
- p. 432: Describes Archelaus Kenney as the son of Blacksmith David Kenney
- p. 464: Listing Jonas Perry, however lacked specific information about a vocation and so he is inferred to be a farmer.
- p. 495: Lists Nathaniel Sawyer as a storekeeper.

Lossing, Benson J. 1860. "Pictorial Field-Book of The Revolution" vol 1 Harper & Brothers, Publishers, Franklin Square, New York NY

- General information about the Battle of Breeds Hill.

Secomb, Daniel F. 1883. "History of the Town of Amherst, Hillsborough County, New Hampshire, (First known as Narraganset Township Number Three, and subsequently as Souhegan West) From the Grant of the Township by the Great and General Court of the Province of Massachusetts Bay, in Jun, 1728 to March, 1882. With Genealogies of Amherst Families, Biographical Sketches of Natives and Citizens of the Town, and a Sketch of the Narraganset Fort Fight, 19 Apr, 1675." Evans, Sleeper, & Woodbury, Concord, NH.

- p. 371: Full account of Andrew Leavitt regarding General George Washington taking command of the Army around Boston.

Unknown, 1854. "Pedigree of Frye, Compiled by a member of the New England Historic-Genealogical Society" The New England Historical and Genealogical Register, Vol. VIII No 3.

- p. 226-227: Includes information regarding James Frye, particularly during the Battle of Bunker Hill.

Ward, Christopher. 1952. "The War of the Revolution" vol. 1 Macmillan, New York, NY.

- General information about the Battle of Breeds Hill.

Chapter 6: A Lesson on Patience

Bouton, Nathaniel D.D. 1878. "Provincial Papers. Documents and Records Relating to the Province of New-Hampshire, From 1764 to 1776; Including the whole Administration of Gov. John Wentworth; the Events immediately preceding the Revolutionary War; the Losses at the Battle of Bunker Hill, and the Record of all Proceedings till the end of our Provincial History." Volume VII. Orren C. Moore, State Printer. Nashua, NH.

- p. 522: Letter form James McGregore to the New Hampshire Committee of Safety dated Jun 19, 1775 from Medford in which he indicates arriving in Medford that same day.
- p. 530: Letter from James McGregor writing to the New Hampshire Committee of Safety Written from Medford on Jun 24, 1775.
- pp. 538-543: Rules and Articles of War for the Province of New Hampshire, where article 1 requires the attendance of Divine service and sermon.
- p. 557: Committee of Safety's letter dated Jul 1, 1775 to Colonel Reed notifying him of the commissioning of James McGregore as the Adjutant of the 3rd Regiment.
- p. 565: Letter to the Committee of Safety from Colonel Reed dated Jul 19, 1775, which politely refuses the appointment of James McGregor, for various reasons.

Fitzpatrick, John C. 1970. "The Writings of George Washington from the Original Manuscript Sources, 1745-1799" in "The George Washington Papers at the Library of Congress, 1741-1799" 39 vols. Washington, D.C.: Government Printing Office, 1931-1944; reprint, Greenwood Press New York. Accessed online at: https://memory.loc.gov/ammem/gwhtml/gwhome.html

- General Orders, Jul 16, 1775:Contains the orders for a day of prayer on Jul 20, 1775.

Chapter 7: At Home

Becker, Ann M., 2004. "Smallpox in Washington's Army: Strategic Implications of the Disease during the American Revolutionary War" The Journal of Military History, Vol. 68, No. 2

- p. 393: Describes the various levels of concern about small pox during the Siege of Boston, before and after George Washington arrived.

Bouton, Nathaniel D.D. 1878. "Provincial Papers. Documents and Records

Relating to the Province of New-Hampshire, From 1764 to 1776; Including the whole Administration of Gov. John Wentworth; the Events immediately preceding the Revolutionary War; the Losses at the Battle of Bunker Hill, and the Record of all Proceedings till the end of our Provincial History." Volume VII. Orren C. Moore, State Printer. Nashua, NH.

- pp. 482-483: Letter to the Continental Congress from the Convention of the Colony of New Hampshire apprising the Continental Congress, among other things, of New Hampshire's commitment to raise 2,000 men, including officers and pay them until the last day of Dec.
- p. 511: On Jun 10th New Hampshire's Committee of Safety voted to pay the officers an men one month's wages as soon as possible.
- p. 530: James McGregore's letter to New Hampshire Committee of Safety of Jun 24, 1775 indicating the one month's pay promised on Jun 10th had yet to be given out.
- p. 537: On Jun 29, 1775 the New Hampshire Committee of Safety appoints Joseph Welch and Samuel Hobert as paymasters with directions to go to pay one month's wages contingent on receiving an accurate muster roll from the commanders.
- p. 538: Rules and Articles of War for the Army Raised by the Province of New Hampshire - Article 1 requiring all men, including officers to attend services, under punishment, including forfeiture of pay.
- p. 585: New Hampshire Committee of Safety on Sep 4, 1775 votes to pay all outstanding officer's accounts and one month's pay.
- p. 612: General Sullivan's Sep 23, 1775 letter to the Committee of Safety carrying the complaint that all other colonies, except New Hampshire have complied with General Washington's orders to pay the troops up through Aug 4.
- pp. 612 - 613: Committee of Safety's response dated 28 Sep, 1775 which states the committee paid one month at the end of Jul as promised, and that the balance of pay would be given when the militia is disbanded. The committee's understanding was that once a Commissary General was appointed for the Army, General Washington would take over the payments, etc., leaving it possible to know the remaining amounts owed to the troops.

Congress, 1780. "Plan for Conducting the Quartermaster General's Department Agreed to In Congress Jul 15th, 1780" Printed by David C. Claypool, Printer , Philadelphia

- General Reference for the types of activities managed by the quarter masters of the American Army.

Fitzpatrick, John C. 1970. "The Writings of George Washington from the Original Manuscript Sources, 1745-1799" in "The George Washington Papers at the Library of Congress, 1741-1799" 39 vols. Washington, D.C.: Government Printing Office, 1931-1944; reprint, Greenwood Press New York. Accessed online at: https://memory.loc.gov/ammem/gwhtml/gwhome.html

- General Orders, Jul 4, 1775: Troops "are now the Troops of the UNITED PROVINCES of North America; and it is hoped that all Distinctions of Colonies will be laid aside"
- General Orders, Jul 14, 1775: Includes order for commanders to ensure their quartermasters to see the pikes greas'd twice a week.
- General Orders: Jul 22, 1775: Appointment of Brigadier General John Sullivan as commander of a brigade consisting of the three New Hampshire regiments and three Massachusetts regiments.
- General Orders, Aug 14, 1775: Appointment of Thomas Mifflin as Quartermaster General.
- General Orders, Aug 17, 1775: Appointment of Brigade Major who is responsible for parading the
- Letter, George Washington to Continental Congress, Aug 31, 1775 commenting on Congress appointing Joseph Frye a Brigadier.
- Letter, George Washington to Continental Congress, Oct 12, 1775, note 30 references the meeting of congressional delegates and governors, whose purpose was to discuss the issues for organizing the Continental Army, particularly for the year 1776.
- General Orders, Nov 18, 1775: General Washington command that all troops observe the day of thanksgiving declared by the Massachusetts Provincial Congress, which will be Thursday, Nov 23, 1775. The day is to be observed with solemnly with prayers to Almighty God that their endeavors are a success.

Force, Peter, 1848, "American Archives: Fifth Series. Containing a Documentary History of The United States of America, from the Declaration of Independence, Jul 4, 1776, to the Definitive Treaty of Peace with Great Britain, Sep 3, 1783." Series 5, Volume 3. M. St. Clair Clark and Peter Force Under Authority of Acts of Congress, Passed on the Second of March, 1833, and on the third day of March, 1843. Washington D.C.

- pp. 1035-1036: General Return of the Officers in Sullivan's Brigade for 1776. Lt. Brown is not listed.
- p. 1099: in the "Return of Vacancies in Reed's Regiment' dated Oct 18, 1775, Reed specifically mentions the valor of Sergeant William Adrian Hawkins during the Battle of Breed's Hill as the basis for promotion to the rank of ensign.

Frye, Isaac 1775 Letter to his Wife Elizabeth dated Oct 25, 1775.

- Manuscript in the library of Scott Mason.

Hammond, Isaac, W. 1885. "Rolls of the Soldiers in the Revolutionary War 1775, to May, 1777 with an appendix, embracing diaries of Lieut. Jonathan Burton " Volume I of War Rolls. Volume XIV of the Series. Parsons B. Cogswell, State Printer, Concord, NH

- p. 48: Lists David Osgood as Chaplain of Stark's regiment, that his travel distance was zero, indicating he is the Reverend David Osgood, the minister of Medford's First Congregational Parish. As the New Hampshire troops chiefly occupied Medford, it stands to reason that Osgood served as their chaplain while they were in Medford.
- p. 49: Lists Samuel MacClintock as a chaplain, though only serving one month.
- p. 80: Isaac Frye's Aug, 1775 Pay
- p. 86: Lists Ephriam Stone as quartermaster sergeant for Colonel Reeds Regiment.
- Does not list Lieutenant James Brown of Wilton past 1775 references.

Livermore, Abiel Abbot and Putnam, Sewall 1888. "History of the Town of Wilton, Hillsborough County, New Hampshire with a Genealogical Register" Marden & Rowell, Printers, Lowell, MA

- p. 129: Describes Wilton's first church and form of religion to be Congregationalist.
- p. 329: James Brown's family history.

Orcutt, Samuel, W. 1886. "A History of the Old Town of Stratford and the City of Bridgeport, Connecticut."Part II Fairfield County Historical Society, Press of Tuttle, Morehouse & Taylor, New Haven, Connecticut.

- p. 886: Describes Colonel James Frye's son, Frederick, as being in the Battle of Bunker Hill. Noting there is a discrepancy about Frederick's age, which is shown as 18 here. However, according the the Andover Vital records, Frederick was born Jun 9, 1760, making him just barely fifteen on the day of the battle.

Risch, Erna 1962. "Quartermaster Support of the Army A History of the Corps 1775 - 1939" Quartermaster Historian's Office, Office of the Quartermaster General, Washington, D.C.

- General Reference and background regarding the types of items the quartermasters of the army were responsible for and the notion that extensive networks of contracts were set in place to supply the army. Specifically for Isaac, the idea that regimental quartermasters initially had to manage via relationships with colony and town public stores, then later when funds were approved to purchase via contract what the army needed, and later as the Quartermaster General's office was established, this gradually became the province of that office, and the regimental quartermasters became more responsible for the internal logistics for their regiments.

Chapter 8: Spirit of '76

Bouton, Nathaniel D.D. 1878. "Provincial Papers. Documents and Records Relating to the Province of New-Hampshire, From 1764 to 1776; Including the whole Administration of Gov. John Wentworth; the Events immediately preceding the Revolutionary War; the Losses at the Battle of Bunker Hill, and the Record of all Proceedings till the end of our Provincial History." Volume VII. Orren C. Moore, State Printer. Nashua, NH.

- p. 662: Nov 15, 1775, Voted to pay up the officers and soldiers through August 4, and assigned two paymasters.
- pp. 663-674: Various entries regarding the payment of the troops. Particularly the the Committee of Safety voted on Nov 15 to pay the troops up through Aug 4, 1775. This means the Continental Congress was to pay Aug-Dec, and it is quite possible the New Hampshire troops received no pay for Aug and Sep. On Pp 674, is a note indicating the Continental Congress would pay Oct-Dec 1775.
- p. 678: Showing orders for the paymasters in early (presume 1 or 2) Dec to pay the troops up through Aug 4, 1775.
- pp. 697-698: Dec 27, 1775 Committee ordered paymasters to pay Stark's, Reed's, and Poor's regiments - presumably the balance owed.
- p. 699: Dec 28, 1775 letter from Paymaster Samuel Hobert to the Committee, indicating he how he was paying the troops, thus 12/28/1775 was when New Hampshire finally paid the balance owed her soldiers.

Fitzpatrick, John C. 1970. "The Writings of George Washington from the Original Manuscript Sources, 1745-1799" in "The George Washington Papers at the Library of Congress, 1741-1799" 39 vols. Washington, D.C.: Government Printing Office, 1931-1944; reprint, Greenwood Press New York. Accessed online at: https://memory.loc.gov/ammem/gwhtml/gwhome.html

- General Orders, Oct 31, 1775, Nov 12, 1775 noting pay would be monthly with allowances taken out for clothing, etc. These orders also included remonstrations for the officers regarding their obligation to reinlist: "Commissions in the new Army are not intended merely for those, who can inlist the most men; but for such Gentlemen as are most likely to deserve them. The General would therefore, not have it even supposed, nor our Enemies encouraged to believe, that there is a Man in this army (except a few under particular circumstances) who will require to be twice asked to do what his Honour, his personal Liberty, the Welfare of his country, and the Safety of his Family so loudly demand of him: When motives powerful as these, conspire to call Men into service, and when that service is rewarded with higher pay, "
- General Orders, Dec 18, 1775 - promise of three months (Oct - Dec 1775 Pay, plus one extra for Jan 1776)
- General Orders, Dec 29, 1775 - Washington expresses disappointment that only having enough money for one month of pay, instead of three, though it looks as though the troops were paid by the end of Feb.

Chapter 9: Winter on Winter Hill

Bailey, Sarah Loring 1880. "Historical Sketches of Andover, Massachusetts (Comprising the Present Town of North Andover and Andover)"Houghton, Mifflin and Company, The Riverside Press, Boston, MA, reprinted in 1974 by the Andover Historical Society and the North Andover Historical Society, Edward Brothers, Inc., Ann Arbor, MI.

- p. 342: Mentions death of James Frye and the inscription on his gravestone.
- p. 406: Mentions James Frye as owner of one of several public houses (inns) in Andover. That Isaac may have worked there is only a supposition.

Fox, Charles J. 1846 "History of the Old Township of Dunstable, including Nashua, Nashville, Hollis, Hudson, Litchfield, and Merrimac, NH; Dunstable and Tyngsborough, Mass" Charles T. Gill, Nashua, NH.

- pp. 178-179: Describes James Blanchard as starting service in early 1776 in Captain Walker's company of Colonel Reed's regiment. Given a year later he is the quartermaster for the 3rd Regiment, I inserted him as quartermaster sergeant, though I've not found any corroborating documents.

Frothingham, Richard, 1873, "History of the Siege of Boston, and of the Battles of Lexington, Concord, and Bunker Hill. Also, an Account of the Bunker Hill Monument. With Illustrative Documents. Fourth Edition, Little, Brown, and Company, Boston, MA.

- General information about the fortification of Dorchester Heights.

Frye, Joseph 1770, Manuscript: Letter from Joseph Frye to Simon Frye, Apr 26, 1770, Fryeburg Hist. Soc.

- "...Lt. Col. James Frye, always pregnant with ill nature, watched for your Brother Isaac's coming to Town and a few days ago catched him before Carlton knew he was in Town and Bargained for his part in this land and yesterday I wrote a Deed of it to James so he has got it and I am sorry. And now, he seems to undervalue your part (as I am told) which I suppose he thinks he may do safely, since he has got Isaac's part and thereby pleases himself with the thoughts that no body will buy of you besides himself, so he shall get it very cheap."
- Simon is one of Isaac's two older brothers.

Hammond, Isaac, W. 1885. "Rolls of the Soldiers in the Revolutionary War 1775, to May, 1777 with an appendix, embracing diaries of Lieut. Jonathan Burton " Volume I of War Rolls. Volume XIV of the Series. Parsons B. Cogswell, State Printer, Concord, NH

- p. 86: Lists Ephriam Stone as quartermaster sergeant for Colonel Reeds Regiment.
- p. 263: Lists Ephriam Stone as a lieutenant in Bedel's regiment in Feb of 1776.

Lossing, Benson J. 1860. "Pictorial Field-Book of The Revolution" vol 1 Harper & Brothers, Publishers, Franklin Square, New York NY

- General information about the fortification of Dorchester Heights.

Unknown, 1854. "Pedigree of Frye, Compiled by a member of the New England Historic-Genealogical Society" The New England Historical and Genealogical Register, Vol. VIII No 3.

- pp. 226-227: Includes information regarding James Frye, particularly during the Battle of Bunker Hill and the date of his death.

Ward, Christopher. 1952. "The War of the Revolution" vol. 1 Macmillan, New York, NY.

- General information about the fortification of Dorchester Heights.

Washington, George, 1776. "Letter from General George Washington to Brigadier General John Sullivan dated Jan 20, 1776" Available online at http://founders.archives.gov/documents/Washington/03-03-02-0108, accessed in 2015 and 2016.

- General Washington permits Stephen Peabody to be discharged and names his replacement to be James Otis, son of Massachusetts Colonel Joseph Otis, commander of the Barnstable regiment of militia.

Chapter 10: The Sickness

Fitzpatrick, John C. "The Writings of George Washington from the Original Manuscript Sources, 1745-1799" in "The George Washington Papers at the Library of Congress, 1741-1799" accessed throughout 2015 and 2016 at https://memory.loc.gov/ammem/mgwquery.html

- Mar 23, 1776: General Orders. Sullivan's brigade, including Reed's regiment are put on alert to march at a moment's notice.

Livermore, Abiel Abbot and Putnam, Sewall 1888. "History of the Town of Wilton, Hillsborough County, New Hampshire with a Genealogical Register" Marden & Rowell, Printers, Lowell, MA. Pages 31-34 and 85-88

- pp. 403-404: Lists Amos Holt and lineage showing he is the first cousin of Isaac's wife Elizabeth. He was born in 1740 and more of an age with Isaac's older brothers, and would have known them and Isaac in Andover.
- pp. 252-253: 436: Describes Jonathan Livermore as the first pastor of the Congregational Church in Wilton.
- p. 376: Shows Timothy, son of Isaac and Elizabeth Frye, died on Mar 17, 1776.

Chapter 11: Moving South to Go North

Baldwin, Thomas W. 1906. "The Revolutionary War Journal of Col. Jeduthan Baldwin 1775-1778" The De Burians, Bangor, ME.

- p. 33: Indicates Sullivan's brigade arrived in New York City on Apr 9, 1776.

Barker, Ellen Frye, 1920. "Frye Genealogy" Tobias A. Wright, New York.

- p. 64: Simon Frye's family. This indicates two sets of twins. The first were John and Jonathon born Jul 21, 1775. The second were born Dec 19, 1777 and were named John Hancock and George Washington. The older John is shown as dying 22 Mar, 1796, however, I believe this is a typo, and should have been 1776. Having two sons named John would have been peculiar, and more likely was a 7 was drawn to look like.

Fitzpatrick, John C. "The Writings of George Washington from the Original Manuscript Sources, 1745-1799" in "The George Washington Papers at the Library of Congress, 1741-1799" accessed throughout 2015 and 2016 at https://memory.loc.gov/ammem/mgwquery.html

- Apr 1, 1776 Letter to B.G. Sullivan explaining that once he reaches Providence he will be informed as to whether the alarm from Governor Cook was " well founded".
- Aril 1, 1776, a second letter to B.G. Sullivan with a copy of Governor Cook's letter enclosed and instructions relative to General Greene being on his way to Providence.
- Apr 22, 1776: General Orders include that Poor's regiment is being sent north with three Massachusetts regiments under Colonels Greaton, Bond, and Patterson. They left on Apr 21. Only Poor's was from Sullivan's brigade.
- Apr 27, 1776: Washington's general orders convey an order from Congress to send a Brigadier General to Canada, in the person of John Sullivan and his brigade of six regiments, including Reeds.
- Apr 28, 1776: "Horatio Gates, Apr 28, 1776, Report on Brigade Going to Canada under John Sullivan." This shows 3,496 enlisted and musicians, plus 182 officers. Earlier orders alloted nine wagons per regiment, which meant civilian wagoners, and other followers, which is where the figure of nearly four thousand in Sullivan's column is derived.
- Apr 29, 1776: The proceedings of a Courts Martial Respecting Lt. Grover.

Force, Peter, 1837, "American Archives: Fourth Series Containing a Documentary History of the English Colonies in North America, from the King's message to Parliament, of Mar 7, 1774 to the Declaration of Independence by the United States " Series 4, Volume 5. M. St. Clair Clark and Peter Force Under Authority of an Act of Congress, Passed on the Second of March, 1833. Washington D.C.

- Mar 31, 1776: Letter from Nicholas Cook to B.G. John Sullivan.

Livermore, Abiel Abbot and Putnam, Sewall 1888. "History of the Town of Wilton, Hillsborough County, New Hampshire with a Genealogical Register" Marden & Rowell, Printers, Lowell, MA. Pages 31-34 and 85-88

- p. 488: Shows the genealogy of Benjamin Rideout's family, including their youngest son Joshua dying on Apr 17, 1776, aged 8 1/2 months.

Chapter 12: To Fort Ticonderoga

Bailey, Sarah L. 1880 "Historical Sketches of Andover Massachusetts" The Riverside Press, Cambridge, MA.

- p. 251: Shows Abiel Frye as a captain under Colonel Williams.
- p. 277: List Abiel Frye, Isaac's father, as a captain in the Andover militia.

Beebe, Lewis, 1935 "Journal of a Physician on the Expedition Against Canada in 1776" The Pennsylvania Magazine Vol LIX, Number Four.

- p. 328: May 19, 1776 entry shows General Thomas countermanded General Arnold's order for the men to be inoculated.
- p. 330: May 24, 1776 entry shows the past week of weather to have been "severe".

Congress's Commission in Montreal, 1776 "The Commissioners to Canada to Philip Schuyler, 10 May 1776," Founders Online, National Archives, last modified Dec 28, 2016, http://founders.archives.gov/documents/Franklin/01-22-02-0254. [Original source: The Papers of Benjamin Franklin, vol. 22, Mar 23, 1775, through Oct 27, 1776, ed. William B. Willcox. New Haven and London: Yale University Press, 1982.

- pp. 427-429: Notifying General Schuyler of the situation regarding the lack of provisions

Dodge, Edward J. 1998. "Relief is Greatly Wanted: the Battle of Fort William Henry" Heritage Books, Bowie, MD

- General Reference for Joseph Frye's story.

Fitzpatrick, John C. "The Writings of George Washington from the Original Manuscript Sources, 1745-1799" in "The George Washington Papers at the Library of Congress, 1741-1799" accessed throughout 2015 and 2016 at https://memory.loc.gov/ammem/mgwquery.html

- Apr 28, 1776: General Orders, which detail that Sullivan's brigade is to depart for Albany the following morning.
- May 5, 1776: Notes that Sullivan has not yet arrived at Albany.
- Philip J. Schuyler to James Price, May 7, 1776 - Letter written from Fort George, which puts General Schuyler there and not at Albany.
- Philip J. Schuyler to George Washington, May 14, 1776 - Letter written from Saratoga, placing him there, near Fort Miller.
- Philip J. Schuyler to George Washington, May 16, 1776 - Letter written from Fort George. General Schuyler describes meeting Colonel Reed's regiment twenty three miles below Fort George, which is roughly at Fort Miller on May 14, when they were five days out of Albany. He gave orders to pick 300 men, to remove their heavy baggage from their bateaux, and take 109 barrels of pork to Fort Ti. Provisions had become the army's priority given the needs of the troops already in Canada. Schuyler goes on to say he had to leave, and heard that Reed's men decided to toss the food and reload their baggage, so 48 barrels did not make it on the 16th. Schuyler said he would take it with a wink lest circumstances become more retarded.
- May 18, 1776, Letter from John Sullivan to George Washington detailing the issue of wagon teams tapping and drawing off the pickle from the barrels of pork to lighten their loads, but at the cost of preserving pork.
- May 24, 1776 Philip J. Schuyler to George Washington, Estimate of the number of men to transport 10,000 weight of pork from Albany to St. John's in Canada. This details the route taken by Reed's regiment, and travel times from Albany to St. John's
- May 28, 1776 Philip J. Schuyler to George Washington, with request for troops and engineers to repair and make Fort Ticonderoga defensible.
- May 31, 1776: Philip J. Schuyler to George Washington, includes learning General Thomas has small pox, which means Reed could not have known of it until arriving.

Force, Peter, 1837, "American Archives: Fourth Series Containing a Documentary History of the English Colonies in North America, from the King's message to Parliament, of Mar 7, 1774 to the Declaration of Independence by the United States " Series 4, Volume 6. M. St. Clair Clark and Peter Force Under Authority of an Act of Congress, Passed on the Second of March, 1833. Washington D.C.

- p. 412: May 10, 1776 letter from General Sullivan to General Washington, written from Albany, noting that Reed's and Starks regiments were there for want of boats.
- p. 482: Shows Benjamin Franklin, with the other commissions still in Montreal as late as May 11, 1776.
- Franklin's letters to Congress details the lack of provisions/food for the troops in Canada, and advises Sullivan not proceed until they get some food to carry up.

Hammond, Isaac, W. 1885. "Rolls of the Soldiers in the Revolutionary War 1775, to May, 1777 with an appendix, embracing diaries of Lieut. Jonathan Burton " Volume I of War Rolls. Volume XIV of the Series. Parsons B. Cogswell, State Printer, Concord, NH.

- pp. 335-336: Roll of Captain William Barron's company in Colonel Isaac Wyman's regiment, showing several men from Wilton, particularly Richard Whitney as a Sergeant, and Josiah Parker as a Corporal.
- p. 311: Provides that Wyman's regiment was authorized on Jun 14 and mustered to march to Ticonderoga on Jun 22, 1776.

Livermore, Abiel Abbot and Putnam, Sewall 1888. "History of the Town of Wilton, Hillsborough County, New Hampshire with a Genealogical Register" Marden & Rowell, Printers, Lowell, MA. Pages 31-34 and 85-88

- p. 455: In Josiah Parker's genealogy, Livermore includes that he mustered to leave for Fort Ticonderoga on Jun 16, 1776.

Roberts, Kenneth, 1938 "March to Quebec - Journals of the Members of Arnold's Expedition" Doubleday, Doran, & Company, New York.

- pp. 449 and 498: Journals with weather for May 19-21, with rain and raw hard winds, respectively. The 20th was the worst.

Souther, Samuel, 1864. "The Centennial Celebration of the Settlement of Fryeburg, ME., with the Historical Address by Rev. Samuel Souther, of Worcester, Mass." Tyler & Seagrave, Worcester, MA.

- p. 22: Lists Simon Frye as one of the earliest settlers of Fryeburg.
- General information on Joseph Frye.

Steele, Ian K. 1990 'Betrayals, Fort William Henry & the "Massacre'" Oxford University Press, New York, NY.

- General Reference for Joseph Frye's story.

Chapter 13: Welcome to Quebec

Beebe, Lewis, 1935 "Journal of a Physician on the Expedition Against Canada in 1776" The Pennsylvania Magazine Vol LIX, Number Four.

- pp. 328-332: May 19 through Jun 2 entries at intervals describe General Thomas' condition with the small pox worsening and him eventually dying.
- p. 332: on Jun 3rd, describes the regiments under Sullivan who Marched to Chambly as 1,200 men, well equipped , smartly officered, and warlike.
- p. 332: for Jun 5th Entry, tells of Colonel Reed having small pox very lightly. Noting Beebe was at St. Johns, and he described Reed as being on the other side of the river, establishing he was not at Chambly with his regiment.

Department of Interior, c1925. "Guide to Fort Chambly, Chambly, Quebec" The Government Printing Bureau, Ottawa, Canada

- Describes the fort and it's layout.

Fitzpatrick, John C. "The Writings of George Washington from the Original Manuscript Sources, 1745-1799" in "The George Washington Papers at the Library of Congress, 1741-1799" accessed throughout 2015 and 2016 at https://memory.loc.gov/ammem/mgwquery.html

- May 8, 1776: Letter from General John Thomas to George Washington describing the loss of the powder and field pieces, as well as the state of small pox in the army.
- May 30, 1776: Continental Army War Council, May 30, 1776, Proceedings at De Chambault, Canada. Lieutenant Colonel Gilman is there representing the 3rd Regiment, Stark with the first. Showing some of the officers arrived at least two days sooner than the bulk of the regiment on the following day.
- Jun 5, 1776: Letter from Benedict Arnold to John Sullivan telling he is in the process of seizing the goods in town for the use of the

Army, but the day before had sent DeHaas to Sorel to assist him.

- Jun 10, 1776: Letter from Benedict Arnold to Philip Schuyler, writing from Montreal, saying he had sent the supplies he had seized to St. Johns—this is the one day after Reed's regiment arrives under Gilman's command.
- Jun 8, 1776: Letter from General Sullivan to George Washington, where he tells that Reed's regiment is described as having only forty effective men for most being under inoculation; this is likely a strong exaggeration.
- Alexander Scammell, Jun 12, 1776, Report on Troops in Canada: Shows about two thirds of Reed's regiment, at Montreal, now fit for duty. For the 6,261 total men under Sullivan, 1,550 were sick at this date.
- Jun 13, 1776: Letter from Benedict Arnold to Philip Schuyler, writing from St. Johns, detailing the fate of the goods seized at Montreal as having been sent to Chambly, not yet documented, though each parcel was labeled with the owner's name, piled carelessly on the river bank, poorly guarded and as a result pillaged and ultimately a mess.
- Jun 13, 1776: Letter from Benedict Arnold to John Sullivan, written from Chambly, where he says there are nearly three thousand sick men, and at St. Johns things were a mess.
- Jun 25, 1776: Letter from Benedict Arnold to George Washington, written from Albany. He says he left Montreal the night of the 15th when the enemy were twelve miles away, with his little garrison of three hundred men. Suspect these were Patterson's as that regiment had been inoculated much ealier than Reed's, which would have gone back to Chambly on the 11th.

Force, Peter, 1837, "American Archives: Fourth Series Containing a Documentary History of the English Colonies in North America, from the King's message to Parliament, of Mar 7, 1774 to the Declaration of Independence by the United States " Series 4, Volume 6. M. St. Clair Clark and Peter Force Under Authority of an Act of Congress, Passed on the Second of March, 1833. Washington D.C.

- pp. 922-923: Letter from John Sullivan to George Washington begun on Jun 5 and finished on Jun 6. Sullivan describes artillery being sent to Chambly and St. Johns on the 5th.

Salsig, Doyen. 1980. "Parole: Quebec; Countersign: Ticonderoga; Second New Jersey Regimental Orderly Book 1776" Fairleigh Dickinson University Press, Toronto

- p. 135: Lists Reed's and Patterson's regiments at Montreal under Arnold.

Chapter14: Isle of Death

Beebe, Lewis, 1935 "Journal of a Physician on the Expedition Against Canada in 1776" The Pennsylvania Magazine Vol LIX, Number Four.

- p. 336: Jun 20: Notes that Sullivan ordered the sick to be removed to Crown Point.

Fitzpatrick, John C. "The Writings of George Washington from the Original Manuscript Sources, 1745-1799" in "The George Washington Papers at the Library of Congress, 1741-1799" accessed throughout 2015 and 2016 at https://memory.loc.gov/ammem/mgwquery.html

- Jun 24, 1776 Letter from John Sullivan to George Washington, written from Isle Aux Noix, where he details having recently begun sending the sick to Isle La Motte
- Jun 24, 1776 Letter from John Sullivan to Philip Schuyler, written from Isle Aux Noix. He describes ordering the sick to Crown Point.

Salsig, Doyen. 1980. "Parole: Quebec; Countersign: Ticonderoga; Second New Jersey Regimental Orderly Book 1776" Fairleigh Dickinson University Press, Toronto.

- pp. 136-140: Describes the journey of Arnold's detachment from Montreal to Isle Aux Noix. Note it mistakenly references the supplies Arnold had seized at Montreal nearly two weeks earlier.
- p. 141: Orders on Jun 19 to dig vaults (latrines) at a proper distance from each regiment's encampment.
- p. 142: Orders on Jun 20 for Adjutant of Reed's regiment to attend at Headquarters tomorrow.

Chapter15: Crown Point

Baldwin, Thomas W. 1906. "The Revolutionary War Journal of Col. Jeduthan Baldwin 1775-1778" The De Burians, Bangor, ME.

- pp. 58-59: Entries starting Jul 8, 1776 when he reviews Rattlesnake Hill, which he calls, "the grounds on the east", and for next days describes them, builds a road, and Jul 11, being very rainy.

Fitzpatrick, John C. "The Writings of George Washington from the Original Manuscript Sources, 1745-1799" in "The George Washington Papers at the Library of Congress, 1741-1799" accessed throughout 2015 and 2016 at https://memory.loc.gov/ammem/mgwquery.html

- The Rolls of the troops in Canada in the spring and summer of 1776 produced by John Sullivan, Alexander Scammell, and last two by Horatio Gates. The first two do not include Canadian regiments under Colonels Hazen and Livingston, and last two include militia called up who were at Fort Ticonderoga, but did not go to Canada. No accurate accounting of the losses exists, most historians put the number of dead from battle or sickness between 1,000 and 1,500 men.
- Jul 7, 1776 Council of War: Generals Schuyler, De Wodke, Sullivan, Arnold, and Gates, indicating the reasoning for not fortifying Crown Point.
- Jul 9, 1776 Letter from Colonel John Stark to General Philip Schuyler listing the reasons for fortifying and basing the army at Crown Point.

New Hampshire Historical Society 1888. "Proceedings of the New Hampshire Historical Society." Vol. 1 Part 4 1884-1888.

- pp. 109-115: Biographical Sketch of Gen. James Reed. Includes contacting a malignant virus while at Crown Point.

Salsig, Doyen. 1980. "Parole: Quebec; Countersign: Ticonderoga; Second New Jersey Regimental Orderly Book 1776" Fairleigh Dickinson University Press, Toronto

- pp. 169-170: Time line for the Army leaving Crown Point on Jul 13, 1776.

Chapter16: Camp Independence

Baldwin, Thomas W. 1906. "The Revolutionary War Journal of Col. Jeduthan Baldwin 1775-1778" The De Burians, Bangor, ME.

- p. 61: Jul 19th Entry used at the beginning of the chapter.

Batchellor, Albert Stillman, 1910. "Miscellaneous Revolutionary Documents of New Hampshire, Including the Association Test, the Pension Rolls, and other Important Papers" Vol. 30 State Papers Series, Printed for the State by The John B. Clarke Co., Manchester, NH.

- p. 460: Lists Reed's regiment as having seven Captains: Spaulding, Place, Oliver, Wilkinson, Mann, Jones, and Towne. Note, Wilkinson left in Jun of 1776 to become Arnold's aide, and then Gates' aide in Aug of 1776.

Crockett, Walter Hill, 1909. "A History of Lake Champlain - The Record of Three Centuries 1609 - 1909" Hobart J. Shanley & Co., Burlington VT.

- p. 181-182: Contains the account of St. Clair reading the Declaration of Independence on Jul 28, and that a currier arrived in camp on Jul 18th, with the news that independence had been declared.

Fitzpatrick, John C. "The Writings of George Washington from the Original Manuscript Sources, 1745-1799" in "The George Washington Papers at the Library of Congress, 1741-1799" accessed throughout 2015 and 2016 at https://memory.loc.gov/ammem/mgwquery.html

- Jul 16, 1776: Horatio Gates to Congress, where near the end he writes, "Colonel Reed's New Hampshire Regiment is now at the carrying place going to the General Hospital, They have upwards of Three Hundred Sick, and only just well men enough to row those over the Lakes."
- Jul 29, 1776: Horatio Gates to George Washington.
- Aug 14, 1776: General Orders, where Alexander Scammell is appointed aide-de-camp to General Sullivan. Weeks later he is still referred to as a major.

Force, Peter, 1848, "American Archives: Fifth Series. Containing a Documentary History of The United States of America, from the Declaration of Independence, Jul 4, 1776, to the Definitive Treaty of Peace with Great Britain, Sep 3, 1783." Series 5, Volume 1. M. St. Clair Clark and Peter Force Under Authority of Acts of Congress, Passed on the Second of March, 1833, and on the third day of March 1843. Washington D.C.

- Pp 655: Jul 20, 1776 General orders establishing the new brigades under Reed, Stark, and St. Clair.
- Pp 857: Jul 26, 1776, Dr. Potts' return of the Sick at Fort George shows Reed's regiment had 127 men there (not three hundred as Gates reported), though the Hospital was likely full and the less sick were likely sent back. The report also shows 40 were sent back by the 26th.
- Pp 1125: Aug 11, 1776, shows Colonel Patterson put in command of Reed's Brigade in the absence of Colonel Reed.
- Pp 1199-1200: Aug 24, 1776 General Return of the Forces in the Northern Department under the command of Major General Horatio

Gates. For Reed, this shows 348 effect Rank and File, 34 Non-commissioned, 6 Captains, 8 Lieutenants, and 5 Ensigns. Compared to:

- o Apr 28 roll with 460 Rank and file, 42 Non-commissioned, 5 Captains, 14 Lieutenants, and 5 Ensigns,
- o May 14 roll with 441 Rank and file, 44 Non-commissioned, 6 Captains, 10 Lieutenants, and 5 ensigns.
- o Jun 12 roll with 439 Rank and file, 44 Non-commissioned, 6 Captains, 10 Lieutenants, and 5 ensigns
- o The result is an estimate of losses due to death, desertion, or discharge are 103 Rank and file, 10 Non-commissioned, and between 2 and 6 Lieutenants.

- Pp 1201: Aug 12 and 13, shows Reed's regiment at 279 effectives who drew provisions.
- Pp 1202: Aug 24, show Reed's at 307 effectives who drew provisions.
- Pp 1267-1268: Sep 2, 1776, a letter from General Gates to Congress mentioning Brigadier General James Reed is still very ill at Fort George, and he imagines Reed will not be fit for duty for the remainder of the campaign.
- Pp 1269-1270: Aug 25, news of Congress promoting Colonels Reed and St.Clair to Brigadier General.

Trumbull, John. 1776 "Fortifications and Disposition of Troops at Ticonderoga, New York" Fordham University Libraries Digital Collections, http://digital.library.fordham.edu/cdm/ref/collection/trumbull/id/0, Accessed Sep 2016.

- This is a sketch map showing the layout of Camp Independence, including the locations of each brigade's encampments.

Wintersmith, Charles 1780 "Plan of Ticonderoga and Mount Independence, including Mount Hope, and shewing the rebel works & batteries, as they were when His Majesty's troops took possession of them on 6th July 1777, expressing also the encampment of the British on the 5th instant, with the extensive communication which was made in one day, for the transport of the heavy artillery from the 3 Miles Point to the proposed batteries, including likewise Sugar Hill, where a battery of 4 12 pounders would have been ready to open on the 6th at noon" John Carter Brown Library, http://jcb.lunaimaging.com/luna/servlet/detail/JCBMAPS~1~1~2703~101233 :Plan-of-Ticonderoga-and-Mount-Indep, Accessed March 2017.

- This map shows depicts, in detail, the terrain and fortifications of Camp Independence after the British captured it in 1777.

Chapter17: The Most Deadly Enemy

Batchellor, Albert Stillman, 1910. "Miscellaneous Revolutionary Documents of New Hampshire, Including the Association Test, the Pension Rolls, and other Important Papers" Vol. 30 State Papers Series, Printed for the State by The John B. Clarke Co., Manchester, NH.

- p. 460: Lists the officers of Reed's regiment in 1776.

Force, Peter, 1848, "American Archives: Fifth Series. Containing a Documentary History of The United States of America, from the Declaration of Independence, Jul 4, 1776, to the Definitive Treaty of Peace with Great Britain, Sep 3, 1783." Series 5, Volume 1. M. St. Clair Clark and Peter Force Under Authority of Acts of Congress, Passed on the Second of March, 1833, and on the third day of March, 1843. Washington D.C.

- p. 1125: General Orders from Fort Ticonderoga placing the regiments of Colonels Wingate and Wyman under the command of Colonel Stark.

Force, Peter, 1848, "American Archives: Fifth Series. Containing a Documentary History of The United States of America, from the Declaration of Independence, Jul 4, 1776, to the Definitive Treaty of Peace with Great Britain, Sep 3, 1783." Series 5, Volume 3. M. St. Clair Clark and Peter Force Under Authority of Acts of Congress, Passed on the Second of March, 1833, and on the third day of March, 1843. Washington D.C.

- pp 1035-1036: General Return of the Officers in Sullivan's Brigade. Lists Lieutenant Davis as the remaining officer in Captain Hinds company. This is undated, and is likely early in the year, before going to New York, as James Wilkinson is not listed as the captain of the company Lieutenant Grover is in.

Frye, Elizabeth 1776 Letter to her husband Isaac dated Oct 7, 1776. Manuscript in the library of Scott Mason.

- The letter is addressed to Lieutenant Isaac Frye, The Army att [sic] Mount Independence. Hinds Company, Reed's Regiment. This was peculiar because it was not to Quartermaster Frye, Reed's regiment, which would have been appropriate for a staff officer, rather than a line officer. This is the basis for reassigning Isaac to be Captain Hinds' subaltern. Isaac would have replaced Lieutenant Isaac Stone, who possibly resigned. Isaac Stone is brother to Ephraim Stone, formerly the regiment's quartermaster sergeant. Their father was ill and passes away in September of 1776. The letter provides the information about Josiah Parker being dangerously ill.

Hammond, Isaac, W. 1885. "Rolls of the Soldiers in the Revolutionary War 1775, to May, 1777 with an appendix, embracing diaries of Lieut. Jonathan Burton " Volume I of War Rolls. Volume XIV of the Series. Parsons B. Cogswell, State Printer, Concord, NH

- pp.: 335-336: Roll of Captain William Barron's company, which includes Sergeant Richard Whitney and Corporal Josiah Parker.

Livermore, Abiel Abbot and Putnam, Sewall 1888. "History of the Town of Wilton, Hillsborough County, New Hampshire with a Genealogical Register" Marden & Rowell, Printers, Lowell, MA

- p. 245: Oct 22, 1776 entry in Jonathan Burton's diary notes the passing of Josiah Parker.
- pp. 453-455: Information about the Park Families
- pp. 510-511: Information about John Stevens and his family.
- pp. 522-523: Information about Richard Whitney and Hannah Holt Whitney.

Chapter 18: Decision

Beebe, Lewis, 1935 "Journal of a Physician on the Expedition Against Canada in 1776" The Pennsylvania Magazine Vol LIX, Number Four.

- p. 357: Oct 28, 1776: Records the alarm given at 8AM and the enemy boats arriving at three-mile point, to be fired up on by the batteries at the fort.

Bouton, Nathaniel. 1874. "State Papers. Documents and Records Relating to the State of New Hampshire During the Period of the American Revolution, from 1776 to 1783; Including the Constitution of New-Hampshire, 1776; New-Hampshire Declaration for Independence; the "Association Test," with names of Signers, &c.; Declaration of American Independence, Jul 4, 1776; the Articles of Confederation, 1778." Published by the Authority of the Legislature of New-Hampshire. Volume VIII. Edward A. Jenks, State Printer, Concord, NH.

- pp. 386-387: Instructions for the committee sent to Ticonderoga.
- p. 387: Letter dated Oct 21, 1776 from the Provincial Congress to General Washington notifying him of their appointment of a committee of Jonathan Blanchard, Benjamin Giles, Stephen Evans, and David Gilman, Esq. To repair to the camp & there use ther utmost endeavors to promote the raising our Quota of men for the new army.

- p. 390: Nov 9, 1776 Letter from Colonel Jonathan Blanchard to the Provincial Congress written from Camp Independence, indicating he and the rest of the committee of men sent to recruit arrived at Fort Ticonderoga late the previous day.
- p. 391: Report from Colonel Blanchard on raising two regiments at Fort Ticonderoga. This included the appointments of Stark and Poor as Colonels and a number of the officers under them. This report also included a number of officers also appointed in New York by Benjamin Giles and David Gilman who left on Nov 10th for that purpose. The narrative is that the committee arrived on Nov 2, 1776, met with General Gates then the New Hampshire Field Officers and Captains on Nov 3. Giles and Gilman left for Albany after that. The commissions of the officers were dated Nov 8, 1776.
- p. 502: Representation of Isaac Frye's Commission to rank as a captain in the Continental Army, signed by John Jay, President of the Continental Congress.

Force, Peter, 1848, "American Archives: Fifth Series. Containing a Documentary History of The United States of America, from the Declaration of Independence, Jul 4, 1776, to the Definitive Treaty of Peace with Great Britain, Sep 3, 1783." Series 5, Volume 3. M. St. Clair Clark and Peter Force Under Authority of Acts of Congress, Passed on the Second of March, 1833, and on the third day of March, 1843. Washington D.C.

- p 533: Oct 29, 1776 Letter from Major General Horatio Gates to thank the officers and solders of Reed's Poor's and Greaton's regiments for their rapid response the previous day in crossing the lake. Also on this page are after orders for Oct 30, which direct the commissary to allow all fit men and non commissioned officers a half gill of rum each evening. This to be distributed to the quartermasters of the regiments for them to give to the men, and those on guard duty will receive theirs in the morning.
- p. 575: Oct 26, 1776 Letter from Major General Philip Schuyler to the New York Committee of Convention at Albany, advising them of the unlikelihood of the enemy bypassing Fort Ticonderoga to disrupt the Mohawk and Hudson confluence.
- pp. 620-622: Oct 31, 1776 Letter from General Horatio Gates to General Philip Schuyler where he describes a potential Tory and Indian threat under the leadership of John Johnson, he discounts it due the likelihood of the Mohawk River being soon frozen.
- p. 624: Nov 9, 1776 Letter from Horatio Gates to General Ward recommending that Starks, Reed's and Poor's regiments be removed to Portsmouth to be closer to home as they had suffered greatly during the campaign.
- p. 640: Letter from Major General Philip Schuyler to the President

of Congress dated Nov 11, 1776, written from Albany. He writes that as of 4 Nov the enemy has not been seen below Crown Point and it is supposed they have gone into winter quarters.

- p. 641: Nov 11, 1776 Letter from Philip Schuyler to George Washington
- p. 744: Nov 17, 1776, Muster Roll for Gates, which Shows Reed's regiment to have 251 men—which is the number of men not enlisting.
- p. 877: Nov 15, 1776 General Gates' orders for Stark, Reed's, and Poor's regiments to be at the landing of Lake George the next morning.

Chapter 19: New Commitment

Bouton, Nathaniel D.D. 1874. "State Papers. Documents and Records Relating to the State of New Hampshire During the Period of the American Revolution, from 1776 to 1783; Including the Constitution of New-Hampshire, 1776; New-Hampshire Declaration for Independence; the "Association Test," with names of Signers, &c.; Declaration of American Independence, Jul 4, 1776; the Articles of Confederation, 1778." Published by the Authority of the Legislature of New-Hampshire. Volume VIII. Edward A. Jenks, State Printer, Concord, NH

- p. 413: On the afternoon of Dec 10, 1776, the New Hampshire Provincial Congress appointed Alexander Scammell Esq. to be Colonel of the 3rd Continental Battalion to be raised in New Hampshire. Andrew Colburn was appointed as the Lieutenant Colonel.
- p. 404: On Dec 5, 1776, Appointed David Gilman to be Colonel of a regiment of militia to be sent to New York.
- p. 409: On Friday, Dec 6, 1776 in the Provincial Congress it was represented "That Rev'd Mr. Jonathan Livermore of Wilton has in Sundry instances been Enimical to the Liberties of America— Therefore Voted, That the said Mr. Jonathan Livermore be cited to appear before the general Assembly of this State on the Second Wednesday of the sitting of said Assembly after the twentieth day of Dec instant to answer what may be objected against him in that behalf..."
- p. 414: Notes Colonel David Gilman's regiment of militia is being raised for reinforcing the Army at New York.
- p. 449: On Jan 1, 1777, "Rev'd Jonathan Livermore of Wilton appeared before the Provincial Congress and defended himself against the charges of being Enimical to the Liberties of America, and the Congress voted that the complaint be dismissed.".

ABOUT THE AUTHOR

Charles E. Frye is a geographer, cartographer, information scientist, and U.S. Army veteran. His interests include genealogy, history of the American Revolutionary War, and major league baseball. As he learned of Isaac Frye's story, he applied his skills to design an approach to use geographic information systems to organize and document historical research projects. Applying this approach to Isaac Frye's story yielded a wealth of information that could be organized many ways. This supplied the skeleton for *The War has Begun*, the first of four books in the *Duty in the Call of Liberty* series. Today he lives and works in southern California.

The War Has Begun

The War Has Begun

Made in the USA
San Bernardino, CA
04 April 2017